Representations of Nature of Science in School Science Textbooks

Bringing together international research on nature of science (NOS) representations in science textbooks, the unique analyses presented in this volume provide a global perspective on NOS from elementary to college level and discuss the practical implications in various regions across the globe. Contributing authors highlight the similarities and differences in NOS representations and provide recommendations for future science textbooks. This comprehensive analysis is a definitive reference work for the field of science education.

Christine V. McDonald is Senior Lecturer in Science Education, School of Education and Professional Studies, Griffith University, Australia.

Fouad Abd-El-Khalick is Dean and Professor, School of Education, The University of North Carolina at Chapel Hill, U.S.

Teaching and Learning in Science
Norman G. Lederman, Series Editor

Visit www.routledge.com/education for additional information on titles in the Teaching and Learning in Science Series

Representations of Nature of Science in School Science Textbooks

A Global Perspective

Edited by
Christine V. McDonald
and Fouad Abd-El-Khalick

 Routledge
Taylor & Francis Group

NEW YORK AND LONDON

First published 2017
by Routledge
711 Third Avenue, New York, NY 10017

and by Routledge
2 Park Square, Milton Park, Abingdon, Oxon, OX14 4RN

Routledge is an imprint of the Taylor & Francis Group, an informa business

© 2017 Taylor & Francis

The right of Christine V. McDonald and Fouad Abd-El-Khalick to be
identified as the authors of the editorial material, and of the authors
for their individual chapters, has been asserted in accordance with
sections 77 and 78 of the Copyright, Designs and Patents Act 1988.

Library of Congress Cataloging-in-Publication Data
A catalog record for this book has been requested

ISBN: 978-1-138-12240-6 (hbk)
ISBN: 978-1-315-65052-4 (ebk)

Typeset in Bembo
by Apex CoVantage, LLC

"To my father, Leslie Allan Hunter, who passed away during the writing of this book—thank you for always believing in me"

Christine V. McDonald

"To Lama, Kareem, and Farrah"

Fouad Abd-El-Khalick

Contents

Preface

This volume brings together the work of 22 science teachers, teacher educators, and education researchers, as well as scientists from around the globe, who examined the content of science textbooks in eight nations, both large and small, across all six inhabited continents. Together, the studies reported here analyze textbooks across precollege school science curricula, levels, and content areas, as well as college science textbooks and elementary science trade books. We found that the textbooks overlooked certain crucial science concepts altogether (e.g., mitosis and cell division), perpetrated erroneous and inaccurate scientific information (e.g., in explaining oxidation numbers), and/or misinformed readers about crucial scientific processes (e.g., grossly inaccurate accounts of how scientists control for variables when performing laboratory experiments). Textbooks either did not address at all, or in some cases conveyed inaccuracies about, what scientific and education authorities around the globe agree to be the most relevant, current, and accepted knowledge and processes for the purpose of educating the public about science. Textbooks got their science wrong: They likely will hamper rather than facilitate the development of scientific literacy among the greater majority of learners, except those who end up specializing in science. These findings should cause serious alarm among all of us who care about science and scientific literacy, and serve as a call for urgent action.

While we hope to have caused you some alarm, we should note that the above account is only partially true. We did *not* examine all those textbooks across all those disciplines, school levels, nations, and continents for their accuracy in depicting scientific content and processes. Instead, we focused on how textbooks depicted another, equally central dimension of science, namely, nature of science (NOS). Our findings, nonetheless, are essentially *similar* in their character: Science textbooks mostly overlooked several crucial domains of NOS (e.g., codified and widely used social processes that are essential to validating claims to scientific knowledge, such as blind peer review), conveyed explicit and grossly inaccurate information about the nature of scientific knowledge (e.g., that scientific laws were certain or proven true beyond doubt, that scientific facts do not lend themselves to interpretation, or that scientific concepts are devoid of human creativity), misinformed students and their teachers about how scientists carry out their practice (e.g., asserting that all scientists follow a single or some variant of a well-defined, step-wise method that would unerringly lead them to valid scientific claims), and simply were not true to the history and philosophy of science. We knew since the early 1990s, thanks to Gene Chiappetta and colleagues, that science textbooks paid little attention to NOS as a theme. This volume shows, beyond doubt and in painstakingly great depth and detail, that the status quo is much worse than previously imagined: Science textbooks not only failed to address many crucial NOS aspects; they mostly conveyed, both implicitly and explicitly, naive and inaccurate messages about NOS. Science textbooks mostly got their NOS wrong: They likely will hamper rather than facilitate the development of scientific literacy among the greater majority of learners across the globe. This true account about our volume, we still hope, will be as alarming as our opening account, which focused on getting science content wrong!

At this point some might object: Irrespective of their 'truth,' the two accounts, they would claim, are not totally commensurate. In particular, they would continue, the claim about wide-ranging consensus regarding scientific content and processes that are crucial to scientific literacy, simply does not carry to assertions about NOS in science education. There is lack of consensus that applies, they would assert, *both* to NOS as a domain and to the specific content invoked under the NOS rubric. They are simply wrong or their objections do not apply to this work. First, over the course of the past six decades, without fail, science educators across the globe have repeatedly and consistently affirmed NOS as a crucial component of scientific literacy. The latter emphasis has survived several pendulum swings, which have oscillated from precollege science curricula that are devoted to preparing citizens for making informed decisions regarding science-related personal and societal issues, all the way to curricula primarily aimed at preparing students for college studies in science, mathematics, engineering, and technology (STEM) fields. The exception is the most recent reform document, the 2012 *Framework for K-12 Science Education* produced by the U.S. National Research Council and its affiliated 2013 *Next Generation Science Standards* (NGSS), which are primarily focused on preparing school students for STEM careers. Early NGSS drafts were virtually devoid of NOS content. Public feedback from science educators, which decried this omission, resulted in the reintroduction of NOS, albeit the time frame for producing the NGSS did not allow for more than a *sprinkling* of NOS content across NGSS concepts, core ideas, and practices. We surely hope that the world will take notice of this omission, make sure to address it, and continue to pay NOS the regard and attention it deserves toward achieving the much coveted scientific literacy for all learners.

Second, it is true that science education researchers disagree about perspective-taking when it comes to NOS, about the specific aspects that fall under the rubric of NOS and the specific content of these aspects, and/or about the best approaches for teaching about NOS. However, these disagreements are irrelevant to the main thrust of this volume because various perspectives on NOS are represented. Contributors to this volume range in their views from those who strongly endorse a domain-general, consensus approach to NOS to those committed to domain-specific and family resemblance approaches, with various shades of perspective in-between; from those who view these various perspectives on NOS to be mutually exclusive, to those who deem them complementary and synergetic. The crucial point is that, irrespective of their lens on NOS or its content, and their analytic approach to textbook analysis, all our authors shared the view that textbooks have an unavoidable and substantial impact on school science teaching and learning; and they reached the same conclusion, namely, that the science textbooks they examined did a very poor job in representing NOS to science students and teachers. This convergence is a powerful message and its implications should be taken seriously.

This has been a journey for us: What started as an exploratory examination of the implicit and explicit representations of a few aspects of NOS in four science trade books that Abd-El-Khalick prepared for the editor of the *New Advocate* in 2001, has taken a life of its own over the past 15 years, elevated by wonderful colleagues around the world who share our passion for NOS and its centrality to school science education, into a full-blown research domain in science education. This volume will hopefully make clear the few successes and many failures of science textbooks in addressing NOS, raise serious concerns about the lack of progress evident over the past several decades, and—most importantly, help chart a pathway forward through a focus on crucial NOS aspects that we show to have received little attention, or are thoroughly misrepresented in science textbooks, and by ascertaining the relatively more substantial impact of textbook authors over their publishers in influencing the treatment of NOS and the need to work with our author colleagues.

Above all, we hope this volume will serve to convince those who care deeply about NOS that scientific literacy and science teaching and learning are not well served by solely focusing on endless debates about shades of NOS modalities, or the minute particulars of what and how many NOS aspects would deserve a place in the curriculum. This volume shows we all agree that current NOS representations in science textbooks and, likely, associated NOS teaching in most science classrooms stand at odds with the various current NOS modalities. Instead, we would better serve learners of science by ensuring a continued and expanded emphasis on NOS as a central component of scientific literacy, and by focusing on improving the *current* status of NOS curricular content and instructional practices.

Fouad Abd-El-Khalick
Chapel Hill, North Carolina, USA

Christine V. McDonald
Mt Gravatt, Queensland, Australia
October 2, 2016

1 Representations of Nature of Science in School Science Textbooks

Christine V. McDonald and Fouad Abd-El-Khalick

The development of informed nature of science (NOS) views is considered an integral component of scientific literacy, and a central focus of the majority of national science education reform documents worldwide (e.g., American Association for the Advancement of Science [AAAS], 1993; Australian Curriculum and Reporting Authority [ACARA], 2015; National Research Council [NRC], 2012; Next Generation Science Standards [NGSS], NGSS Lead States, 2013). Reform documents in the United States and elsewhere have articulated a range of NOS concepts students need to know to become scientifically literate. More broadly, to be scientifically literate demands acquiring the ability to 1) apply and reason scientifically, 2) command the discourse of science, and 3) understand the historical and epistemological significance of the learned concepts. Numerous studies have explored the views held by teachers and students about NOS, and many of these studies have indicated that students and teachers hold deep-seated, uninformed views about NOS that are resistant to change. They have also indicated that NOS ideas need to be taught more deliberately and explicitly for positive change to occur (e.g., Abd-El-Khalick & Lederman, 2000). Importantly, it is an undeniable reality that in the larger majority of science classrooms across the world, textbooks become the curriculum and determine, to a much larger extent than envisioned by science educators, what is taught and learned about science in these classrooms (Kahveci, 2010; Roseman, Stern, & Koppal, 2010). Such an impact gains significance in light of the fact that very few, if any, commercially viable science textbooks have been recently designed specifically to help K-12 students develop informed conceptions of NOS, as emphasized in current science education reform documents.

Previous research exploring how NOS is represented in school science textbooks is limited (e.g., Abd-El-Khalick, Waters, & Le, 2008; Irez, 2009; Vesterinen, Akesla, & Lavonen, 2013), with findings generally indicating NOS does not receive much attention and is not represented in an informed manner. This raises a number of important questions, for example, are these findings typical for different countries with diverse education systems? Are there differences in NOS representations in science textbooks across the years of schooling (from elementary grades through college level), and between science textbook disciplines (biology, chemistry, physics)? What are the possible reasons for the inadequate representations of NOS in school science textbooks? How can representations of NOS be improved in school science textbooks? Thus, there is a need for further scholarship in this vitally important area. This book attempts to fill this void by presenting the findings of the latest research currently being conducted across the globe.

This chapter provides a rationale for the need for research exploring representations of NOS in school science textbooks. The first section will discuss the role of textbooks in school science education, with a consideration of the current usage of textbooks, and the limitations and affordances of textbooks. A review of previous research on representations of NOS in school science textbooks will follow, categorized into three lines of research. The chapter concludes with a discussion of the contribution of this book to the field, and an overview of the individual chapters reporting on empirical studies examining NOS representations in school science textbooks in a variety of science disciplines, year levels, and countries across the world.

The Role of Textbooks in School Science Education

Textbooks play a central role in school science education in both developing (Irez, 2009; Kahveci, 2010; Ogan-Bekiroglu, 2007), and developed countries (Chambliss & Calfee, 1998; Roseman et al., 2010). Bensaude-Vincent (2006) noted that textbooks surfaced as a literary genre early in the eighteenth century, and a typical textbook in this era was part of a tradition that "focused on commentary rather than to a scientific tradition based on the observation of nature" (p. 668). A shift occurred in the nineteenth century with the mandatory inclusion of science education from primary school to university level in many Western countries, resulting in the emergence of the 'science textbook' as an independent genre. Since that time, the science textbook has carved out a niche as a key instructional resource, and in the twenty-first century is considered to be a dominant influence in school science classrooms, often 'becoming' the curriculum (Chiappetta & Koballa, 2002).

International studies have indicated that both classroom instruction and homework activities are heavily organized around the textbook (Chiappetta, Ganesh, Lee, & Phillips, 2006; Lumpe & Beck, 1996). Textbooks have been shown to strongly influence the sequence of learning and teaching strategies employed by teachers, and having a significant influence on the learning experiences of students (Kesidou & Roseman, 2002; Penney, Norris, Phillips, & Clark, 2003). A recent, large-scale National Science Foundation (NSF) study conducted with 7752 science and mathematics teachers in the United States found that approximately three-quarters of middle school and high school science classes use textbooks, and just under 70 percent of elementary classes use textbooks (Banilower et al., 2013). Similar findings have been reported in the United Kingdom and Australia with over 80 percent of junior secondary, and high school teachers currently using science textbooks in their classrooms (King, 2010; McDonald, 2016).

Interestingly, approximately 75 percent of middle and high school teachers in the recent NSF study considered their textbooks to be of relatively high quality (Banilower et al., 2013), with results from other countries, such as Australia, showing similar trends (McDonald, 2016). These findings are somewhat surprising, given the large body of research highlighting the limitations of science textbooks. Previous studies report textbooks often present vast amounts of information in a superficial manner (Chiappetta, Sethna, & Fillman, 1993), contain high quantities of technical terms (Groves, 1995; Kesidou & Roseman, 2002), and place specialized language demands on students (e.g., Carnine & Carnine, 2004; Unsworth, 1997). Textbooks have been shown to emphasize lower cognitive-level questioning (Overman, Vermunt, Meijer, Bulte, & Brekelmans, 2013; Shepardson & Pizzini, 1991) and fail to take into account students' prior knowledge (Stern & Roseman, 2004). They have been found to contain scientific misconceptions, inaccuracies, and generalizations (Holliday, 1991; Hubisz, 2003), and promote gender biases (Bazler & Simonis, 1991; Elgar, 2004). Other studies report limited attention to science-technology-society (STS) topics (Chiang-Soong & Yager, 1993; Rosenthal, 1984), and the absence of a multidisciplinary emphasis when integrating socio-scientific issues (SSIs) into school science textbooks (Morris, 2014). Recent studies focused on scientific practices have reported science textbooks provide limited opportunities to engage students in reasoning with data (Morris, Masnick, Baker, & Junglen, 2015), and continue to implicitly emphasize a narrow and traditional view of scientific methodology (Binns & Bell, 2015).

However, it is also imperative to recognize the body of research reporting on the affordances of science textbooks, as studies have shown that science textbooks can help to organize information, guide inquiry, present important scientific facts, improve problem solving skills, consolidate learning, illustrate abstractions, and develop reading skills (e.g., Chiappetta et al., 2006; Dunne, Mahdi, & O'Reilly, 2013; Lee, Eichinger, Anderson, Berkheimer, & Blakeslee, 1993; Ogan-Bekiroglu, 2007; Penney et al., 2003; Schmidt, McKnight, & Raizen, 1997). Previous research suggests that teachers have an increased reliance on textbooks when they are inexperienced or teaching outside of their subject area (Ball & Feiman-Nemser, 1988; Reddy, 2005; Stern & Roseman, 2004). In developed countries, such as the United States and Australia, many teachers in the middle school/junior secondary years tend not to hold a university major in science, or lack adequate tertiary preparation to teach science, thus limiting their ability to plan and teach science classes effectively (McKenzie, Kos, Walker, & Hong, 2008; Weis, 2013). Thus, it is imperative these teachers have access to high quality textbooks to support their classroom instruction.

Consequently, calls to remove textbooks from science classrooms might be overzealous and surely impractical for a number of reasons. Kloser (2013) reminds us that textbooks play an integral role in science education, as the practices of reading and writing are core components of the scientific enterprise. For example, scientists are required to develop and communicate their knowledge via grant applications, journal articles, and conference presentations, amongst other practices. To successfully engage in these practices, scientists require highly developed literacy skills, thus, it is important to ensure these skills are developed in students to promote scientific literacy. In recent times, science education scholars have extended their conceptualization of scientific literacy to focus on the 'literacy' component of the construct (Fang & Wei, 2010; Johnson & Zabrucky, 2011; Norris & Phillips, 2003). These scholars claim that student conceptualizations of science are developed via oral and written communication, thus highlighting the central role of literacy practices in science education. Furthermore, these practices need to be explicitly integrated into science classrooms, as reading and writing are often de-emphasized in favor of practical, hands-on activities.

Unfortunately, research suggests that students' motivation to read deteriorates in early adolescence (Guthrie & Wigfield, 2000), with research from the United States indicating that up to three-quarters of students in some middle and high school classes are unable to read textbooks effectively (Carnine & Carnine, 2004). Fang and Wei (2010) argue that limited reading skills hamper the development of deep understanding of science concepts. In addition, the manner in which textbooks are written influences the development of students' scientific literacy, as students are required to negotiate meaning from the written text, which requires an understanding of the structure and organization of expository texts (Penney et al., 2003). Recent recommendations in the United States now require students to use expository or informational texts from the first grade of primary school, with the goal of ensuring students are 'college literate' by the time they finish high school (Bryce, 2013).

Finally, it is important to be mindful that textbook development and production are highly influential processes impacting the content and structure of textbooks. The multi-billion-dollar industry of commercial textbook production is influenced by a myriad of factors, as textbooks are commodities produced by publishers who are under economic, political, social, and cultural constraints to design books with marketability to a range of stakeholders. A recent study conducted by DiGiuseppe (2014) examined the role of the author, publisher, editor and reviewers of a Canadian twelfth grade high school chemistry textbook with respect to how representations of NOS were developed and incorporated in two chapters of the textbook. A number of factors were found to significantly influence the development and incorporation of NOS representations in the textbook; however, two factors—marketability and workplace resources—appeared to have an overarching influence.

Sharma and Buxton (2015) contend that decisions regarding the scope and level of simplification of content in textbooks are not only influenced by concerns about comprehensibility, but also policy and societal discourses in both science and education. As a result, there are strong incentives to maintain a conservative tone in science textbooks, and in many cases this results in superficial coverage of a broad range of non-controversial, established knowledge that fails to illustrate the processes of science, and the manner in which scientific knowledge is justified (Bensaude-Vincent, 2006). As such, students are provided with a false impression of the scientific community, which fails to acknowledge many aspects of the nature of the scientific enterprise.

Previous Research on Representations of NOS in Textbooks

Science textbooks are influential teaching resources that play a dominant role in the classroom. Thus, it is imperative to examine these resources to ascertain how they represent NOS to students, as it is highly likely that the values and assumptions embedded or explicated in the language of the textbook, and its associated images, will influence students' views about the nature of the scientific enterprise. So, what is NOS? How do we define it? There currently is not, and most likely will never be, a single or straightforward answer to this question as historians, philosophers, sociologists, and psychologists of science actively continue to examine the workings of the sciences, trying to explain the incredible success of this complex and multifaceted human endeavor. Thus, it is inevitable for science educators to transform and translate scholarship about NOS into frameworks that lend themselves to curriculum and instruction in precollege science classrooms. One possible way to group current NOS frameworks are the domain-general (e.g., Abd-El-Khalick, Lederman, Osborne, Niaz) versus domain-specific (e.g., Allchin, Duschl, Hodson, van Dijk) perspectives. The domain-general view of NOS can be considered to be the dominant framework utilized in science education with substantial theoretical and empirical support, but has been the subject of criticism by domain-specific scholars (e.g., Duschl & Grandy, 2013; Wong & Hodson, 2010). A domain-general view of NOS asserts that there are a set of largely agreed upon, non-controversial aspects of science that are able to be effectively taught in school science education; whereas a domain-specific view of NOS proposes that different science disciplines have their own distinct natures of science (Kampourakis, 2016). The latter view itself has been the subject of criticism, albeit we believe that, unlike domain-specific scholars, that the two approaches could be synergistic (for details see Abd-El-Khalick, 2012; also see Chapter 3 in this volume for examples).

Importantly, the focus of this book is to explore *how* NOS is represented in school science textbooks, not to engage in debates about definitions or conceptualizations of NOS. The studies reviewed in this chapter, and the empirical studies presented in the proceeding chapters adopt a variety of theoretical perspectives to guide the development of their analytical frameworks and to inform scholarship in the field. In the final chapter we synthesize findings from these diverse perspectives to provide a set of recommendations for future research and practice. However, prior to this, it is important to review previous studies that have examined NOS in school science textbooks. A literature review of research published in mainstream science education journals over the past 30 years was undertaken, and the reviewed studies were categorized into three lines of research. These included studies that examined science textbooks for the: 1) emphasis given to NOS as a single theme, 2) historical and philosophical accuracy of representations of science content and its development, and 3) accuracy and/or extent of representation of specific aspects or domains of NOS drawn from reform documents.

Emphasis Given to NOS as a Single Theme

The first empirical study published in the mainstream science education literature was conducted 25 years ago by Chiappetta, Sethna, and Fillman (1991), who carried out a quantitative analysis of scientific literacy themes in seven high school chemistry textbooks. This research followed a series of previous studies carried out by Chiappetta's research group in the late 1980s that addressed themes of scientific literacy in physical science and biology textbooks (e.g., Fillman, 1989). Curriculum balance was the theoretical perspective guiding the content analysis, and the researchers sought to examine the textbooks for their emphasis on the following aspects of scientific literacy: 1) science as a body of knowledge, 2) science as a way of investigating, 3) science as a way of thinking, and 4) the interaction among science, technology, and society. The third examined aspect—science as a way of thinking—encompasses aspects that are most aligned with NOS as it focuses on thinking, reasoning, and reflection about how the scientific enterprise works. Using a five-percent random sample of pages from each textbook, results indicated that the majority of the seven textbooks emphasized science as a body of knowledge, placed some emphasis on science as a way of investigating, and very little emphasis on the interaction among science, technology, and society. The examined textbooks, importantly, were found to de-emphasize science as a way of thinking.

Shortly after, Chiappetta et al. (1993) examined five middle school life science textbooks for their presentation of four themes of scientific literacy. In addition, the researchers sought to examine how well the textbooks presented NOS at the beginning of the text. In addition to a five-percent random sampling of textbook pages for each textbook, the entire first section of each textbook was examined for evidence of the scientific literacy themes and NOS. Results indicated the textbooks emphasized science as a body of knowledge, and science as a way of investigating, but placed little emphasis on the interaction of science, technology, and society. Practically no text addressed science as a way of thinking, although all textbooks included at least one introductory chapter that included references to NOS. However, most of the latter chapters presented a stereotypical view of the 'Scientific Method.'

Other scholars have utilized Chiappetta and colleagues' scientific literacy framework to examine textbooks. Lumpe and Beck (1996) analyzed seven biology textbooks for the four examined themes and found that science as a body of knowledge was heavily emphasized, with little attention to science as a way of thinking, or the interaction among science, technology, and society. Similar findings were reported in Australia, with Wilkinson (1999) examining 20 high school physics textbooks for scientific literacy themes. Results indicated that the majority of texts stressed science as a body of knowledge, with little emphasis on science as a way of thinking.

Two additional studies identified in the literature explored broad NOS themes utilizing different theoretical and analytical frameworks. Knain (2001) examined the images of science portrayed in four Norwegian lower secondary science textbooks. A sample of 30 pages from three topics was selected from each textbook for analysis. Using discourse analysis, results indicated the books presented an individualistic image of science, whereby experimentation leads to the discovery of truths about the world, instead of a social constructivist image of science. The textbooks prioritized the end products of science over the processes of science, and tended to portray the scientific method as a universal procedure. Shortly after, Ford (2006) examined 44 trade books published in the United States for explicit and implicit representations of science, using a heuristic developed by Helms and Carlone (1999). Results indicated the majority of trade books represented scientific knowledge as disconnected from the community who produce it. Although some books were found to be effective in outlining the processes of scientific activity, others promoted a view of science as following a step-wise scientific method. The authors concluded that the selected trade books were unlikely to convey sophisticated views of NOS to their readers.

Sixteen years after the publication of their first work, Chiappetta and Fillman (2007) re-developed their original framework to examine five high school biology textbooks for emphasis on themes of NOS. The theoretical framework utilized the four categories of science literacy originally used and added a NOS framework informed by recent research. Instead of using a five-percent random sample of pages for analysis, the authors chose to utilize a larger sample of pages from six topic areas including ecology, cells, methods of science, DNA, heredity, and evolution. Results indicated the biology textbooks included a more balanced presentation of scientific literacy themes compared to earlier studies. A considerable portion of textbooks was still devoted to science as a body of knowledge; however, an increased emphasis on science as a way of investigating was noted. Little change was noted for the theme of interaction among science, technology, and society. However, science as a way of thinking was found to have an increased emphasis, with a significant improvement in the representation of this theme reported, in contrast with earlier research.

In summary, the contribution of Chiappetta and his colleagues' seminal research set the scene for much of the work that is now taking place in examining representations of NOS in school science textbooks. Findings from studies that utilized his original, and later reconceptualized, scientific literacy framework found that textbooks pay little attention to NOS-related themes (e.g., Chiappetta et al., 1991, 1993; Lumpe & Beck, 1996; Wilkinson, 1999), with small improvements noted in more recent studies (e.g., Chiappetta & Fillman, 2007). Other studies assessing broad NOS themes (e.g., Ford, 2006; Knain, 2001) reported textbooks generally portrayed naïve views of NOS.

Historical and Philosophical Accuracy of Textbook Representations of Science Content and its Development

Another line of research utilized a history and philosophy of science perspective to examine textbook content, with many early studies in this area conducted by Mansoor Niaz and his colleagues. The majority of these studies examined U.S. college-level textbooks and focused on discipline-specific topics drawn from the chemical and physical sciences, including atomic structure (Niaz, 1998; Rodríguez & Niaz, 2002), the oil drop experiment (Niaz, 2000a), kinetic molecular theory (Niaz, 2000b), laws of definite and multiple proportions (Niaz, 2001a), covalent bonds (Niaz, 2001b), and the periodic table (Brito, Rodríguez, & Niaz, 2005). More recent discipline-specific studies have examined quantum mechanics (Niaz & Fernández, 2008) and the photoelectric effect (Niaz, Klassen, McMillan, & Metz, 2010). Overall, these studies generally found that science textbooks either ignored or lacked coherent history and philosophy frameworks to address the development of theories and constructs, or help students appreciate the role of competing frameworks in scientific progress.

Other scholars have utilized a history and philosophy of science perspective to examine textbook content. For example, Leite (2002) developed an analytical framework to examine the historical content of Portuguese high school physics textbooks. Five textbooks with differing amounts of historical content were selected, and results indicated that the textbooks failed to provide an adequate image of NOS. None of the textbooks included historically organized chapters, nor did any of the chapters explicitly refer to the dynamic NOS. Comparable findings were also reported in a specific physics context focused on theories of magnetic field. Guisasola, Almudí, and Furió (2005) examined 30 college-level physics textbooks and found the majority of these textbooks failed to adequately represent NOS.

A recent study conducted by Gericke and Hagberg (2010) examined the use of multiple historical models for gene function in upper secondary biology and chemistry textbooks. A total of 13 Swedish biology and chemistry textbooks, and seven international textbooks (from Australia, Canada, United Kingdom and United States) were analyzed holistically, with results indicating that many different historical models were utilized in parallel when discussing gene function, and discussions of the role of models and theories were absent from the majority of examined textbooks. Implications of these findings highlight the limitations of textbooks in presenting ideas about the tentative NOS.

More recent research by Niaz and his colleagues focused on analyzing the introductory chapter, instead of the discipline-specific chapters, of textbooks to gain an overall sense of the NOS perspective of the author(s). Niaz and Maza (2011) evaluated 75 college-level general chemistry textbooks published in the United States for their representations of NOS in the introductory chapters. Results indicated the majority of textbooks did not adequately address NOS in these chapters; however, they provided effective examples from the history and philosophy of science to provide a context for considering relevant NOS aspects. Niaz and Maza developed an analytical framework of nine NOS-related criteria drawn from aspects of NOS emphasized in recent reform documents, and science education research (Abd-El-Khalick, Waters, & Le, 2008; Lederman, Abd-El-Khalick, Bell, & Schwartz, 2002; McComas, 2008; Smith & Scharmann, 2008). A central component of the framework was drawn from a study conducted by Abd-El-Khalick and colleagues (2008), which spurred a new wave of research focused on assessing the accuracy and/or extent of representations of NOS aspects drawn from reform documents. This line of research will be discussed in the following section.

Accuracy and/or Extent of Representation of NOS Aspects Drawn From Reform Documents

This line of research focuses on assessing the quality of NOS representations in school science textbooks, and the extent to which textbook authors and publishers have been responsive to the consistent emphasis by reform documents on accurately depicting NOS for K-12 students. The latter NOS frameworks squarely fall under the domain-general perspective on NOS (e.g., AAAS, 1990; NGSS Lead States, 2013; NRC, 1996).

Abd-El-Khalick (2002) initiated this line of research in a small, exploratory study that examined images of NOS in four award-winning, middle level science trade books published in the United States. Drawing on the AAAS (1993) and NRC (1996) frameworks, Abd-El-Khalick coded the books for "NOS ideas that were either explicitly presented or implicitly conveyed in the text" (p. 122). The target domains included, among other things, the empirical, tentative, creative, and theory-laden NOS, as well as myth of the 'Scientific Method.' The books were virtually devoid of explicit references to NOS, and the implicit messages therein conveyed naïve representations of NOS.

Abd-El-Khalick et al. (2008) followed up with the first systemic study in this area and examined representations of NOS in 14 secondary chemistry textbook series published in the United States. Drawing on aspects of NOS included in national and international science education reform documents (e.g., AAAS, 1990; NRC, 1996), the authors developed a rubric to score the textbooks. Ten NOS aspects were examined, including the tentative, inferential, creative, empirical, social, and theory-driven NOS; the nature of scientific theories and laws; the social and cultural embeddedness of science; and the myth of 'The Scientific Method.' Criteria for assessment of each NOS aspect included the accuracy, completeness, and manner (explicit or implicit) of each NOS representation. Results indicated the examined textbooks failed to provide informed representations of NOS, and scores for textbook series remained the same, or decreased, over the four-decade period of analysis. Other findings highlighted the significant influence of the textbook author on the observed trends in NOS representations, with Abd-El-Khalick et al. calling for further research to explore this influence.

More recently, Abd-El-Khalick and colleagues (2017) extended their original study to conduct a longitudinal analysis of the extent and manner of representation of NOS in U.S. high school biology and physics textbooks. A total of 34 textbooks spanning one–five decades were analyzed using the scoring rubric developed in the earlier study. Results indicated that very little attention—now estimated in textbook pages—was afforded to NOS in the examined textbooks, and when NOS was included in the textbooks, it was predominantly conveyed in a naïve manner. The Abd-El-Khalick et al. (2017) study presented more conclusive evidence to show that textbook authors had a relatively more substantial impact on representations of NOS in the science textbooks they analyzed than textbook publishers. These two studies will be examined in detail in Chapter 2, and the reader is referred to this chapter for full details of this research.

Since the publication of the Abd-El-Khalick et al. (2008) seminal study, other researchers have sought to utilize and/or adapt the analytical framework for use in their studies. As discussed in the previous section, Niaz and Maza (2011) adapted the framework and integrated it within a history and philosophy of science-based study in the United States. Wei, Li, and Chen (2013) sought to assess representations of NOS in three series of junior secondary science textbooks in China. Specifically, the authors focused on how aspects of NOS were represented within selected histories of science contained in the textbooks. Abd-El-Khalick et al.'s (2008) analytical framework was utilized to assess the NOS representations, and results indicated NOS was poorly addressed within the histories of science in the examined textbooks. Similar to Abd-El-Khalick et al.'s study, the empirical and inferential NOS were treated in the most informed manner, with the myth of the scientific method showing the most naïve representation in the examined textbooks. Other findings indicated disparities with the manner in which aspects of NOS were represented within the individual histories of science.

In addition, results indicated differences in how NOS was represented for the same selected history of science across different textbooks, with the authors highlighting the possibility of an 'author effect' in the examined textbooks, similar to findings reported by Abd-El-Khalick et al. (2008). In the present study, the textbook with the highest overall score was written by a philosopher of science, whereas the lowest scoring textbook was authored by an academic scientist.

Irez (2009) assessed the nature and quality of representations of NOS in five secondary school (Grade 10) biology textbooks in Turkey. A qualitative research approach was used in the study, and the methodological framework employed was ethnographic content analysis. Eleven themes of NOS were used to analyze the selected textbooks, many of which were the same as the NOS aspects used by Abd-El-Khalick et al. (2008), with some emerging as part of the data analysis process (e.g., characteristics of scientists). Cognitive maps were generated in the study, with results indicating numerous issues with the manner in which NOS was represented in the textbooks. Many important aspects of NOS were disregarded in the textbooks, including the inferential and social NOS, and science was represented as a collection of facts. The tentative NOS and the myth of the scientific method were the most frequently misrepresented themes, and when NOS was addressed, it only occupied a very small space in the textbook content and was not well integrated with the other textbook chapters.

A recent study informed by a domain-specific perspective on NOS from the philosophy of chemistry was reported by Vesterinen et al. (2013) who examined representations of NOS in Finnish and Swedish upper second-ary chemistry textbooks. The sample included two Finnish textbook series with a 70 percent combined market share, and three widely used Swedish series. The study proceeded in two phases. First, following Chiappetta et al.'s (1991) framework, the authors analyzed the textbooks for their treatment of the four themes of scientific literacy. They reported that all textbooks had little emphasis on science as a way of knowing. In the second phase, Vester-inen et al. used a quantitative approach to examine the theme of 'science as a way of knowing' from a framework that comprised seven dimensions of NOS. While dubbed as domain-specific by the authors, five of these aspects were identical to the domain-general NOS dimensions emphasized in reform efforts and addressed in Abd-El-Khalick et al. (2008) and Irez (2009): the tentative, empirical, inferential, and model-based NOS; and the social and societal dimensions of science. The remaining two dimensions were 'techno-logical products' and 'instrumentation,' which the authors deemed specific to disciplinary practice in chemistry. The first is related to the focus in chemical research on the production and manipulation of substances at the molecu-lar level. These products, in turn, become objects for further chemical study. The second dimension speaks to the intimate and reciprocal relationship between chemical research and technological developments in instrumenta-tion. The authors contend that instruments play "a huge role in the process of creating chemical knowledge" (p. 1845); however, they nonetheless eventually noted that even the latter two dimensions "need not be limited to chemistry" (p. 1851). They reported that when parsed out in accordance to the target NOS aspects, explicit and implicit references in the analyzed textbooks to science as a way of knowing mostly were focused on the tentative NOS (23 percent to 52 percent of the documented instances), while the remaining NOS dimensions received much less attention, mostly ranging from 2 percent to 14 percent of instances. Close examination of these instances revealed they were mostly implicit, particularly in addressing the creative and social aspects of science, and naïve in terms of emphasizing a universal scientific method.

Finally, a recent study conducted by Campanile, Lederman, and Kampourakis (2015) assessed representations of NOS and scientific inquiry in seven high school biology textbooks. Four of the textbooks were selected as they are commonly utilized in introductory high school biology courses in the United States, one textbook was selected as it is commonly utilized in advanced placement high school biology courses in the United States, and the remaining two textbooks were included as they are commonly utilized in the International Baccalaureate Diploma Program in many countries across the world. Focusing on the Mendelian genetics sections and utilizing an analytical framework including many aspects of NOS and scientific inquiry emphasized in reform documents, results indicated that numerous implicit representations of NOS and scientific inquiry were identified in the Mendelian genetics sections of the textbooks; however, no explicit representations of NOS were included. Three of the introductory textbooks and the advanced placement textbook included more instances of both NOS and scientific inquiry in the examined sections.

In summary, similar to findings reported in the previous lines of research, the emerging body of recent research focused on assessing the accuracy and/ or extent of representation of specific aspects or domains of NOS drawn from reform documents, has continued to highlight the poor or inaccurate representation of NOS in school science textbooks. Many new studies utilizing analytical frameworks adapted from Abd-El-Khalick and colleagues' (2008) original scoring rubric are reported in the chapters of this book.

Overview of Book Chapters

This book will explore new research examining representations of NOS in school science textbooks across the globe. Working across the full span of schooling years—elementary, middle, secondary, and college level—this book will provide a holistic analysis and synthesis of the state of the field. Each of the chapter authors will provide insights from their empirical studies to help inform the field, and the final chapter will provide a set of empirically justified recommendations for future research and practice with the broad aim of improving how NOS is represented in our most heavily utilized curricular resource—the school science textbook.

In Chapter 2, Fouad Abd-El-Khalick and colleagues synthesize results from two published studies to examine the manner, extent, and changes of representations of NOS in high school chemistry, biology, and physics textbooks in the United States, as well as examining the relative impact on representations of discipline, and textbook publishers versus authors. This major contribution to the field sets the scene for many studies reported in the proceeding chapters of the book, and provides a comprehensive picture of how the various aspects of NOS promoted in recent reform documents are represented over several decades, and across 48 textbooks.

Drawing on his extensive scholarship in the history and philosophy of science, seminal researcher Mansoor Niaz explores the relationship between the domain-general NOS aspects, and historical episodes (domain-specific) found in science textbooks. In Chapter 3, Niaz provides numerous examples highlighting how domain-general and domain-specific aspects of NOS can work together to facilitate a better understanding of the scientific enterprise, based on a history and philosophy of science framework.

The following two chapters utilize a new analytical approach to explore NOS representations that draws on domain-general and domain-specific aspects of NOS using Erduran and Dagher's (2014) reconceptualized Family Resemblance Approach (FRA). In this approach, science is viewed as a cognitive-epistemic system and a social-institutional system, encompassing 11 interacting components. In Chapter 4, Saouma BouJaoude, Zoubeida Dagher, and Sara Refai explore Lebanese middle school chemistry, life and earth science, and physics textbooks for their representations of NOS, and propose a set of recommendations to guide future textbook development. Chapter 5 takes a slightly different approach, where Christine McDonald explores Australian junior secondary textbooks representations of NOS in a specific topic—genetics. In her case-based analysis of representations of NOS using the reconceptualized FRA, a sample of relevant NOS aspects in this context are highlighted, in addition to identifying the location of NOS representations.

Kostas Kampourakis explores representations of NOS in Greek secondary school biology textbooks in Chapter 6. In addition to identifying explicit and implicit representations of NOS in the introductory and main text chapters, Kampourakis highlights the historical inaccuracies presented throughout the examined textbooks, and discusses obstacles to effectively teaching NOS in Greek schools. A shift from the secondary school level to the elementary school level occurs in Chapter 7, where Jeanne Brunner and Fouad Abd-El-Khalick examine representations of NOS in U.S. elementary science trade books. This study extends the limited empirical research conducted in the elementary area and provides a set of specific recommendations for more effectively using trade books to teach NOS in elementary grades.

Improving representations of NOS in textbooks has been a goal of science education in Canada for many years. Several factors seem to have contributed to limited progress in this area, including lack of a NOS focus in provincial curricula; market forces promoting the status quo; inadequate NOS learning among teachers, authors, editors, and publishers; and lack of a pan-Canadian K-12 science curriculum framework. In Chapter 8, Maurice DiGiuseppe provides details of an empirical study of science textbook development using an action research framework.

In Chapter 9, Nizar El-Mehtar and Sahar Alameh examine NOS representations in a chemistry textbook following the curricular mandate of the International Baccalaureate Diploma Program (IBDP), a curriculum that is becoming commonplace in a network of schools around the globe. Using an analytical framework involving 17 NOS aspects and aligning with the essentials of NOS integration in IBDP, and a rubric that conforms to the method employed by Abd-El-Khalick et al. (2008), the authors examine the consistency of NOS treatment and distribution of NOS occurrences in the textbook.

The following two chapters both utilize Abd-El-Khalick et al.'s (2008) scoring rubric to explore NOS representations in their countries' textbooks. In Chapter 10, Umesh Ramnarain synthesizes research conducted in South Africa on middle and high school science textbooks on their portrayal of NOS. Following a discussion of the place of NOS in current curriculum documents, research findings on the analysis of textbooks used in Grade 10 Life Sciences and Physical Science, and Grade 9 Natural Science, are presented. In Chapter 11, Karl Marniok and Christiane Reiners provide an analysis of German high school chemistry textbooks' representations of NOS. In addition to providing a contextual overview of the German school system, and the findings of their research, Marniok and Reiners discuss the various constraints present in the German system limiting the development of students' understandings of NOS.

The book concludes with a synthesis chapter bringing together the contributions from a range of science textbook disciplines, years of schooling, and diverse countries; to propose a set of evidence-based recommendations to move the field forward. This will help inform future empirical studies, and the development and refinement of analytical frameworks to assess NOS representations, in addition to providing a set of evidence-based recommendations to improve the NOS content of school science textbooks across the globe.

References

Abd-El-Khalick, F. (2002). Images of nature of science in middle grade science trade books. *New Advocate, 15*(2), 121–127.

Abd-El-Khalick, F. (2012). Examining the sources for our understandings about science: Enduring conflations and critical issues in research on nature of science in science education. *International Journal of Science Education, 34*(3), 353–374.

Abd-El-Khalick, F., & Lederman, N. G. (2000). The influence of history of science courses on students' views of nature of science. *Journal of Research in Science Teaching, 37*(10), 1057–1095.

Abd-El-Khalick, F., Myers, J. Y., Summers, R., Brunner, J., Waight, N., Wahbeh, N., . . . Belarmino, J. (2017). A longitudinal analysis of the extent and manner of representations of nature of science in U.S. high school biology and physics textbooks. *Journal of Research in Science Teaching*, *54*(1), 82–120.

Abd-El-Khalick, F., Waters, M., & Le, A-P. (2008). Representations of nature of science in high school chemistry textbooks over the past four decades. *Journal of Research in Science Teaching*, *45*(7), 835–855.

American Association for the Advancement of Science (AAAS). (1990). *Science for all Americans*. New York: Oxford University Press.

American Association for the Advancement of Science (AAAS). (1993). *Benchmarks for scientific literacy: A project 2061 report*. New York: Oxford University Press.

Australian Curriculum and Reporting Authority (ACARA). (2015). *Australian curriculum: Science F-10*. Sydney: Commonwealth of Australia.

Ball, D. L., & Feiman-Nemser, S. (1988). Using textbooks and teachers' guides: A dilemma for beginning teachers and teacher educators. *Curriculum Inquiry*, *18*, 401–423.

Banilower, E. R., Smith, P. S., Weiss, I. R., Malzahn, K. A., Campbell, K. M., & Weis, A. M. (2013). *Report of the 2012 national survey of science and mathematics education*. Chapel Hill, NC: Horizon Research.

Bazler, J. A., & Simonis, D. A. (1991). Are high school chemistry textbooks gender fair? *Journal of Research in Science Teaching*, *28*, 353–362.

Bensaude-Vincent, B. (2006). Textbooks on the map of science studies. *Science & Education*, *15*, 667–670.

Binns, I., & Bell, R. L. (2015). Representation of scientific methodology in secondary science textbooks. *Science & Education*, *24*, 913–936.

Brito, A., Rodríguez, M. A., & Niaz, M. (2005). A reconstruction of development of the periodic table based on history and philosophy of science and its implications for general chemistry textbooks. *Journal of Research in Science Teaching*, *42*, 84–111.

Bryce, N. (2013). Textual features and language demands of primary grade science textbooks: The call for more informational texts in primary grades. In M. S. Khine (Ed.), *Critical analysis of science textbooks: Evaluating instructional effectiveness* (pp. 101–120). Dordrecht, the Netherlands: Springer.

Campanile, M. F., Lederman, N. G., & Kampourakis, K. (2015). Mendelian genetics as a platform for teaching about nature of science and scientific inquiry. *Science & Education*, *24*, 205–225.

Carnine, L., & Carnine, D. (2004). The interaction of reading skills and science content knowledge when teaching struggling secondary students. *Reading & Writing Quarterly*, *20*, 203–218.

Chambliss, M. J., & Calfee, R. C. (1998). *Textbooks for learning: Nurturing children's minds*. Malden, MA: Wiley.

Chiang-Soong, B., & Yager, R. E. (1993). The inclusion of STS material in the most frequently used secondary science textbooks in the U.S. *Journal of Research in Science Teaching*, *30*(4), 339–349.

Chiappetta, E. L., & Fillman, D. A. (2007). Analysis of five high school biology textbooks used in the United States for inclusion of the nature of science. *International Journal of Science Education*, *29*(15), 1847–1868.

Chiappetta, E. L., Ganesh, T. G., Lee, Y. H., & Phillips, M. C. (2006). *Examination of science textbook analysis research conducted on textbooks published over the past 100 years in the United States*. Paper presented at the annual meeting of the National Association for Research in Science Teaching, San Francisco, CA.

Chiappetta, E. L., & Koballa, T. (2002). *Science instruction in the middle and secondary schools* (5th ed.). Upper Saddle River, NJ: Prentice Hall.

Chiappetta, E. L., Sethna, G. H., & Fillman, D. A. (1991). A quantitative analysis of high school chemistry textbooks for scientific literacy themes and expository learning aids. *Journal of Research in Science Teaching, 28,* 939–951.

Chiappetta, E. L., Sethna, G. H., & Fillman, D. A. (1993). Do middle school life science textbooks provide a balance of scientific literacy themes? *Journal of Research in Science Teaching, 30,* 787–797.

DiGiuseppe, M. (2014). Representing nature of science in a science textbook: Exploring author-editor-publisher interactions. *International Journal of Science Education, 36*(7), 1061–1082.

Dunne, J., Mahdi, A. E., & O'Reilly, J. (2013). Investigating the potential of Irish primary school textbooks in supporting inquiry-based science education (IBSE). *International Journal of Science Education, 35*(9), 1513–1532.

Duschl, R. A., & Grandy, R. (2013). Two views about explicitly teaching nature of science. *Science & Education, 22,* 2109–2139.

Elgar, A. G. (2004). Science textbooks for lower secondary schools in Brunei: Issues of gender equity. *International Journal of Science Education, 26*(7), 875–894.

Erduran, S., & Dagher, Z. (2014). *Reconceptualising the nature of science in science education.* Dordrecht, the Netherlands: Springer.

Fang, Z., & Wei, Y. (2010). Improving middle school students' science literacy through reading infusion. *The Journal of Educational Research, 103,* 262–273.

Fillman, D. A. (1989). Biology textbook coverage of selected aspects of scientific literacy with implications for student interest and recall of text information. *Dissertation Abstracts International, 50,* 1618-A.

Ford, D. J. (2006). Representations of science within children's trade books. *Journal of Research in Science Teaching, 43*(2), 214–235.

Gericke, N. M., & Hagberg, M. (2010). Conceptual incoherence as a result of the use of multiple historical models in school textbooks. *Research in Science Education, 40,* 605–623.

Groves, F. H. (1995). Science vocabulary load of selected secondary science textbooks. *School Science and Mathematics, 95*(5), 231–235.

Guisasola, J., Almudí, J. M., & Furió, C. (2005). The nature of science and its implications for physics textbooks: The case of classical magnetic field theory. *Science & Education, 14,* 321–338.

Guthrie, J. T., & Wigfield, A. (2000). Engagement and motivation in reading. In M. L. Kamil, P. B. Mosenthal, P. D. Pearson, & R. Barr (Eds.), *Handbook of reading research* (pp. 403–422). Mahwah, NJ: Lawrence Erlbaum.

Helms, J. V., & Carlone, H. B. (1999). Science education and the commonplaces of science. *Science Education, 83*(2), 233–245.

Holliday, W. G. (1991). Helping students learn effectively from science text. In C. M. Santa & D. E. Alvermann (Eds.), *Science learning: Processes and applications* (pp. 38–47). Newark, NJ: International Reading Association.

Hubisz, J. (2003). Middle-school texts don't make the grade. *Physics Today, 56*(5), 50–54.

Irez, S. (2009). Nature of science as depicted in Turkish biology textbooks. *Science Education, 93*(3), 422–447.

Johnson, B. E., & Zabrucky, K. M. (2011). Improving middle and high school students' comprehension of science texts. *International Electronic Journal of Elementary Education, 4*(1), 19–31.

Kahveci, A. (2010). Quantitative analysis of science and chemistry textbooks for indicators of reform: A complementary perspective. *International Journal of Science Education*, *32*(11), 1495–1519.

Kampourakis, K. (2016). The "general aspects" conceptualisation as a pragmatic and effective means to introducing students to nature of science. *Journal of Research in Science Teaching*, *53*(5), 667–682.

Kesidou, S., & Roseman, J. E. (2002). How well do middle school science programs measure up? Findings from project 2061's curriculum review. *Journal of Research in Science Teaching*, *39*, 522–549.

King, C. J. H. (2010). An analysis of misconceptions in science textbooks: Earth science in England and Wales. *International Journal of Science Education*, *32*(5), 565–601.

Kloser, M. (2013). Exploring high school biology students' engagement with more or less epistemologically considerate texts. *Journal of Research in Science Teaching*, *50*(10), 1232–1257.

Knain, E. (2001). Ideologies in school science textbooks. *International Journal of Science Education*, *23*(3), 319–329.

Lederman, N. G., Abd-El-Khalick, F., Bell, R. L., & Schwartz, R. (2002). Views of nature of science questionnaire (VNOS): Toward valid and meaningful assessment of learners' conceptions of nature of science. *Journal of Research in Science Teaching*, *39*(6), 497–521.

Lee, O., Eichinger, D., Anderson, C. W., Berkheimer, G. D., & Blakeslee, T. D. (1993). Changing middle school students' conceptions of matter and molecules. *Journal of Research in Science Teaching*, *30*, 249–270.

Leite, L. (2002). History of science in science education: Development and validation of a checklist for analyzing the historical content of science textbooks. *Science & Education*, *11*, 333–359.

Lumpe, A. T., & Beck, J. (1996). A profile of high school biology textbooks using scientific literacy recommendations. *The American Biology Teacher*, *58*(3), 147–153.

McComas, W. F. (2008). Seeking historical examples to illustrate key aspects of nature of science. *Science & Education*, *17*, 249–263.

McDonald, C. V. (2016). Evaluating junior secondary science textbook usage in Australian schools. *Research in Science Education*, *46*, 481–509.

McKenzie, P., Kos, J., Walker, M., & Hong, J. (2008). *Staff in Australia's schools 2007*. Canberra: DEEWR.

Morris, B. J., Masnick, A. M., Baker, K., & Junglen, A. (2015). An analysis of data activities and instructional supports in middle school science textbooks. *International Journal of Science Education*, *37*(16), 2708–2720.

Morris, H. (2014). Socioscientific issues and multidisciplinarity in school science textbooks. *International Journal of Science Education*, *36*(7), 1137–1158.

National Research Council. (1996). *National science education standards*. Washington, DC: The National Academic Press.

National Research Council. (2012). *A framework for K-12 science education: Practices, crosscutting concepts, and core ideas*. Washington, DC: The National Academies Press.

NGSS Lead States. (2013). *Next generation science standards: For states, by states*. Washington, DC: The National Academies Press.

Niaz, M. (1998). From cathode rays to alpha particles to quantum of action: A rational reconstruction of structure of the atom and its implications for chemistry textbooks. *Science Education*, *82*, 527–552.

Niaz, M. (2000a). The oil drop experiment: A rational reconstruction of the Millikan—Ehrenhaft controversy and its implications for chemistry textbooks. *Journal of Research in Science Teaching, 37*, 480–508.

Niaz, M. (2000b). A rational reconstruction of the kinetic molecular theory of gases based on history and philosophy of science and its implications for chemistry textbooks. *Instructional Science, 28*, 23–50.

Niaz, M. (2001a). How important are the laws of definite and multiple proportions in chemistry and teaching chemistry? A history and philosophy of science perspective. *Science & Education, 10*, 243–266.

Niaz, M. (2001b). A rational reconstruction of the origin of the covalent bond and its implications for general chemistry textbooks. *International Journal of Science Education, 23*, 623–641.

Niaz, M., & Fernández, R. (2008). Understanding quantum numbers in general chemistry textbooks. *International Journal of Science Education, 30*, 869–901.

Niaz, M., Klassen, S., McMillan, B., & Metz, D. (2010). Reconstruction of the history of the photoelectric effect and its implications for general physics textbooks. *Science Education, 94*, 903–931.

Niaz, M., & Maza, A. (2011). *Nature of science in general chemistry textbooks.* Dordrecht, the Netherlands: Springer.

Norris, S., & Phillips, L. (2003). How literacy in its fundamental sense is central to scientific literacy. *Science Education, 87*, 224–240.

Ogan-Bekiroglu, F. (2007). To what degree do the currently used physics textbooks meet the expectations? *Journal of Science Teacher Education, 18*, 599–628.

Overman, M., Vermunt, J. D., Meijer, P. C., Bulte, A. M. W., & Brekelmans, M. (2013). Textbook questions in context-based and traditional chemistry curricula analyzed from a content perspective and a learning activities perspective. *International Journal of Science Education, 35*(17), 2954–2978.

Penney, K., Norris, S. P., Phillips, L. M., & Clark, G. (2003). The anatomy of high school science textbooks. *Canadian Journal of Science, Mathematics, and Technology Education, 3*(4), 415–436.

Reddy, V. (2005). State of mathematics and science education: Schools are not equal. *Perspectives in Education, 23*(3), 125–138.

Rodríguez, M. A., & Niaz, M. (2002). How in spite of the rhetoric, history of chemistry has been ignored in presenting atomic structure in textbooks. *Science & Education, 11*, 423–421.

Roseman, J. E., Stern, L., & Koppal, M. (2010). A method for analyzing the coherence of high school biology textbooks. *Journal of Research in Science Teaching, 47*(1), 47–70.

Rosenthal, D. B. (1984). Social issues in high school biology textbooks: 1963–1983. *Journal of Research in Science Teaching, 21*(8), 819–831.

Schmidt, W., McKnight, C., & Raizen, S. (1997). *A splintered vision: An investigation of U.S. science and mathematics education.* Lansing, MI: Michigan State University.

Sharma, A., & Buxton, C. A. (2015). Human-nature relationships in school science: A critical discourse analysis of a middle-grade science textbook. *Science Education, 99*, 260–281.

Shepardson, D. P., & Pizzini, E. L. (1991). Questioning levels of junior high schools science textbooks and their implications for learning textual information. *Science Education, 75*(6), 673–682.

Smith, M. U., & Scharmann, L. (2008). A multi-year program developing an explicit reflective pedagogy for teaching pre-service teachers the nature of science by ostention. *Science & Education, 17*, 219–248.

Stern, L., & Roseman, J. E. (2004). Can middle-school science textbooks help students learn important ideas? Findings from project 2061's curriculum evaluation study: Life science. *Journal of Research in Science Teaching, 41*(6), 538–568.

Unsworth, L. (1997). Some practicalities of a language-based theory of learning. *Australian Journal of Language and Literacy, 20*(1), 36–52.

Vesterinen, V-M., Akesla, M., & Lavonen, J. (2013). Quantitative analysis of representations of nature of science in Nordic upper secondary school textbooks using framework of analysis based on philosophy of chemistry. *Science & Education, 22*, 1839–1855.

Wei, B., Li, Y., & Chen, B. (2013). Representations of nature of science in selected histories of science in the integrated science textbooks in China. *School Science and Mathematics, 113*, 170–179.

Weis, A. M. (2013). *2012 National survey of science and mathematics education: Status of middle school science.* Chapel Hill, NC: Horizon Research.

Wilkinson, J. (1999). A quantitative analysis of physics textbooks for scientific literacy themes. *Research in Science Education, 29*(3), 385–399.

Wong, S. L., & Hodson, D. (2010). More from the horse's mouth: What scientists say about science as a social practice. *International Journal of Science Education, 32*(11), 1431–1463.

2   A Longitudinal Analysis of the Extent and Manner of Representations of Nature of Science in U.S. High School Chemistry, Biology, and Physics Textbooks

Fouad Abd-El-Khalick, Jeremy J. Belarmino, Jeanne L. Brunner, An-Phong Le, John Y. Myers, Ryan G. Summers, Nader Wahbeh, Noemi Waight, Mindy Waters, and Ava A. Zeineddin

This chapter presents results, and draws very heavily on text, from two published research studies that examined representations of NOS in high school chemistry (Abd-El-Khalick, Waters, & Le, 2008), as well as high school biology and physics textbooks (Abd-El-Khalick et al., 2016) in the United States.* It should be noted that data collection and analysis in the case of both studies were undertaken from the same analytical framework and used the same methodological approach, which rendered the findings from these two investigations compatible.

The goal of helping students develop informed conceptions of nature of science (NOS) is one of the major global themes in precollege science education (Lederman, 2007; Lederman & Lederman, 2014). In the United States this goal has been a continuous central focus for national reform efforts for the past six decades (American Association for the Advancement of Science [AAAS], 1971, 1990, 1993; National Research Council [NRC], 1996, 2000, 2012; National Science Teachers Association [NSTA], 1982, 2000; Rutherford, 1964; Wilson, 1954). Indeed, like their predecessors, the most recent U.S. reform efforts (NRC, 2012), which were embodied in the *Next Generation Science Standards* (NGSS) (NGSS Lead States, 2013), have explicitly emphasized several NOS themes as prominent curricular components and instructional outcomes. The themes emphasized in the NGSS are consistent with those targeted by reform documents over the past three decades (e.g., AAAS, 1990; NRC, 1996; NSTA, 1982). The themes include the lack of a universal scientific method ("scientific investigations use a variety of methods"); empirical and tentative nature of scientific claims ("scientific knowledge is based on empirical evidence" and "is open to revision"); nature of models, theories, and laws; and "science as a human endeavor." Many aspects under the latter dimension also have been emphasized in past reform efforts, including the creative ("scientific knowledge is a result of human endeavor, imagination, and creativity"), theory-laden ("scientists' backgrounds, theoretical commitments, and fields of endeavor influence the nature of their findings"), and social NOS, as well as social and cultural embeddedness of science ("Men and women from different social, cultural, and ethnic backgrounds work as scientists" and "science and engineering are influenced by society, and society is influenced by science and engineering") (see NGSS Lead States, 2013, pp. 98–100).

The longevity of the focus on NOS in science education has translated into sustained and intensive research and development efforts focused on gauging science students' and teachers' NOS understandings, and developing and assessing the impact of instructional approaches and materials aimed at improving those understandings. Progress toward achieving NOS-related goals has been, nonetheless, frustrating. Research consistently indicates that a majority of precollege students and their teachers continue to harbor naïve conceptions of several important dimensions of NOS, including those highlighted in the NGSS (see Lederman & Lederman, 2014). To be sure, a number of complex and intertwined factors serve to explain such less-than-desirable progress, which range from the nature of teachers' disciplinary scientific education in the academy, the culture of school science, to difficulties that often impede systemic change in precollege science curricula and instruction (Abd-El-Khalick, 2012a, 2013; Atkin & Black, 2007; Jones & Carter, 2007). Nonetheless, some evidence suggests that ways in which NOS is represented in commercial science textbooks is a major contributing factor to this state of affairs (Chiappetta & Fillman, 2007). The few empirical studies that specifically examined the treatment of NOS aspects emphasized in past and current reform documents in commercial science textbooks are limited in their number and scope (e.g., Irez, 2009; Vesterinen, Akesla, & Lavonen, 2013). In our first study (Abd-El-Khalick et al., 2008), for which we collected data about a decade ago, we found that U.S. high school chemistry textbooks conveyed explicitly naïve representations of several aspects of NOS. Moreover, counter to what would be expected given the discourse and emphases of science education reforms, we found that these naïve representations persisted over a period of several decades covered in the analysis. Our second study (Abd-El-Khalick et al., 2016) aimed to substantiate these initial findings and expand their scope, as well as examine possible underlying or contributing factors.

Rationale and Review of the Literature

A focus on commercial science textbooks is highly justified because of their undue influence on teaching and learning in school science classrooms. To be sure, science educators and science education researchers, as well as qualified and experienced science teachers view and/or use the science textbook as one of many other curricular and instructional resources available to them. Nonetheless, research has shown that science textbooks dictate, to a significant extent, the content and emphases of science curricula, as well as the nature and scope of instructional activities and discourse in a majority of science classrooms (Chiappetta, Sethna, & Fillman, 1991; Roseman, Stern, & Koppal, 2010; Shiland, 1997). Research also has shown, and continues to show, that these influences are exacerbated for science teachers who lack robust understandings of their content and/or strong pedagogical training in science teaching methods (e.g., Hashweh, 1987; McDonald, 2016). The latter concern is particularly relevant in the case of NOS, where a majority of science teachers hold naïve understandings of NOS, which are rather similar to the restricted NOS ideas held by their students (Abd-El-Khalick & Lederman, 2000a; Lederman, 2007).

The impact of textbooks has been deemed so important for the successful adoption and enactment of reform efforts in science education in the United States that the AAAS launched a wide-ranging effort to meticulously analyze commercial science textbooks for their alignment with the *Benchmarks for Science Literacy* (AAAS, 1993), including NOS benchmarks (e.g., Kesidou & Roseman, 2002; Stern & Roseman, 2004). The AAAS continues to advocate for the development and adoption of valid and reliable textbook analysis protocols to measure important dimensions of science textbooks, such as conceptual coherence, with an eye for improving the quality of these textbooks (Roseman et al., 2010). The express aim of the analyses spearheaded, and widely publicized among teachers, by the AAAS was to direct the attention of commercial publishers to reform-based standards when producing or revising science textbooks. The underlying assumption was that 'pressure' generated by teachers' demand for textbooks that are aligned with reform agendas would compel publishers to better address the relevant domains. The latter include, among other things, attention to depth versus breath in approaching disciplinary content, inquiry-oriented activities and resources, focus on science and engineering practices, and NOS (AAAS, 1990, 1993; NRC, 1996, 2012). Nonetheless, preliminary evidence suggests that the efficacy of this approach when it comes to the domain of NOS is, at best, questionable. For instance, our first study suggested that the effect of textbook authors might outweigh, probably to a substantial extent, that of textbook publishers. While admittedly limited by our sole focus on chemistry textbooks, we found that NOS scores for textbook series by the same group of authors produced by different publishers tended to have much less variability compared to scores of textbook series written by different authors and produced by the same publisher. We set out in the second study to examine if such an 'author effect' is, indeed, robust. Such an effect would have important implications for strategies aimed at improving the treatment of NOS in textbooks. In this context, it should be noted that, albeit based on a case study of the development of two chapters from a single high school chemistry textbook, DiGiuseppe (2014) reported a similar author effect, but claimed a rather significant publisher effect. Thus, further examination of the relative impact of authors versus publishers on NOS representations in science textbooks surely is worthwhile.

A focus on U.S. science textbooks is justified. The annual U.S. school textbook market is a multi-billion-dollar industry, with estimated sales for the 2012–13 school year of about 19 billion U.S. dollars (Association of American Publishers, 2013). Enormous investments in the U.S. school textbooks industry translate into a reach and impact that goes far beyond its national boundaries. In 2009, for instance, a consortium of publishers—including Pearson, McGraw-Hill, and Macmillan—was estimated to account for about 85 percent of the global print textbook market (Butler, 2009). Thus, it is reasonable to assume that trends in U.S. science textbooks likely will have major impacts on science teaching and learning across several global markets.

Relative to the impact of textbooks on school science curriculum and instruction, little empirical research has been dedicated to assessing the *quality* and *extent* of NOS representations in textbooks, or the extent to which textbook authors and publishers have been responsive to the consistent emphasis by reform documents on accurately depicting NOS for precollege students. The comprehensive review of the literature presented in Chapter 1 of this volume indicates that a few studies analyzed secondary science textbooks from a *broad* NOS perspective that focused on four literacy themes, including science as a way of thinking—the theme most aligned with NOS. These studies found that textbooks overemphasized content and paid little attention to science as a way of knowing (Chiappetta et al., 1991; Chiappetta & Fillman, 2007; Lumpe & Beck, 1996). Another set of studies examined the historical accuracy of the treatment in college level biology, chemistry, and physics textbooks of specific science concepts; and reported that textbooks either ignored or lacked coherent history and philosophy frameworks to address the development of theories and constructs, or highlight the role of competing frameworks in scientific progress (e.g., Brito, Rodriguez, & Niaz, 1995; Gericke & Hagberg, 2010; Niaz, 1998, 2000; Niaz, Klassen, McMillan, & Metz, 2010; Rodriguez & Niaz, 2002). Additionally, Irez (2009) found that 10 Turkish biology textbooks lacked a framework depicting science as a way of knowing, did not address several important NOS themes, and had mixed treatments (i.e., naïve and informed) of other themes. Vesterinen et al. (2013) reported that upper secondary Finnish and Swedish chemistry textbooks had little emphasis on science as a way of knowing, and that explicit and implicit NOS references in these textbooks mostly were focused on the tentative NOS, while other NOS dimensions received much less attention.

As noted earlier, our first study suggested that an 'author effect' outweighs a 'publisher effect' in accounting for the patterns we found regarding the treatment of NOS in secondary chemistry textbooks. Nonetheless, findings by DiGiuseppe (2014) suggest that this latter claim warrants further examination. In an 11-month case study, he examined the development of NOS representations in two chapters of a high school chemistry textbook slated for use in a Western Canadian province. DiGiuseppe focused on interactions between members of the textbook development team, which included the author, editor, publisher, and two reviewers/advisors. Team members also completed the *Views of Nature of Science Questionnaire—Form C* (VNOS-C) (Lederman, Abd-El-Khalick, Bell, & Schwartz, 2002) followed by semi-structured interviews to elucidate their NOS understandings. DiGiuseppe offered very limited information on how the team members fared in terms of their conceptions of NOS other than to assert that the author's and editor's "pre-study VNOS-C-based assessments were judged to be highly informed" (p. 1068).

DiGiuseppe (2014) reported a number of factors that influenced the development of NOS representations in the examined textbook chapters. These included considerations by the observed team for the developmental appropriateness of NOS representations for target students and grade levels, consistency of representations across the entire textbook, and their alignment with relevant provincially mandated curricula in Canada. DiGiuseppe also demonstrated the power of reviewers and editor over the author in wrestling over words (e.g., "infer" versus "indirectly measure") to the extent of potentially changing the meanings of some key NOS-related concepts. Relevant to the purposes of our second study, he reported that marketability—including perceived likeability and agreeableness of chapter contents to potential buyers—was major among the factors he identified, as well as the time, textbook pages, and expertise allotted by the publisher to the development process. DiGiuseppe (2014) corroborated our claim that there is, indeed, an author effect, but noted that his findings "also show that publishers, as chief administrators of textbook development, influence the process greatly" (p. 1078). There clearly is need for additional research to examine the relative impacts of authors versus publishers on the treatment of NOS in textbooks.

When it comes to commercial science textbooks, it is well understood that the 'authors' rarely are, if ever, limited to the lead authoring scientist(s). Textbooks mostly are authored by teams that vary widely in their sizes, but typically include—in addition to the lead author(s)—science writers, content reviewers, teacher reviewers, and safety and other consultants, all working together with—among many others—text, image, and art designers; copy, project, and managing editors, and a host of production personnel. Also, authors anecdotally report that they are accorded various levels of 'control' during development and production, ranging from complete oversight on all aspects of authorship to much lesser levels of engagement and oversight (D. DeCoste, personal communication, March 20, 2009; K. Deters, personal communication, October 14, 2008). While it is difficult to draw neat boundaries between the two groups engaged with developing a science textbook, for purposes of our work, 'authors' are taken to include all individuals with technical *scientific* expertise (whether content and/or pedagogically focused), while 'publishers' refer to those engaged with *production*, especially as it relates to decisions pertaining to—among other things—textbook marketability, time and resources dedicated to textbook development, as well as space, both in terms of total textbook pages and ratio of textual elements per page or across the whole textbook (e.g., relative proportion of words to images and illustrations).

Purpose and Research Questions

The two studies aimed to assess the manner (naïve versus informed, implicit versus explicit, and consistent versus inconsistent) in which several important aspects of NOS are represented in U.S. high school biology, chemistry, and physics textbooks. The studies also examined the extent to which: these representations have changed over the course of several decades; the NOS aspects were emphasized (in textbook pages) in the biology and physics textbooks; and any of the patterns observed in how textbooks address NOS were subject matter specific and/or impacted by textbook authors versus publishers.

Our research questions were: 1) How much emphasis, in textbook pages, are several NOS themes accorded in U.S. high school biology and physics textbooks? 2) How are the NOS themes represented in U.S. high school biology, chemistry, and physics textbooks? 3) Have these NOS representations changed over the course of the past several decades? 4) Are these representations dependent on subject matter, namely, biology, chemistry, and physics? 5) What is the relative impact or effect of 'author' versus 'publisher' on the observed patterns in NOS representations?

Method

The studies adopted a semi-structured, document analysis approach. We developed and validated a rubric to analyze a sample of U.S. high chemistry textbooks for their representation of NOS in the first study. We applied the same rubric in the second study toward analyzing a sample of U.S. high school biology and physics textbooks.

Analytical Framework

Nature of Science

NOS refers to the assumptions and values underlying the generation and validation of claims to scientific knowledge and incorporates the attributes of this body of knowledge (Lederman, 2007). NOS draws on scholarship in history, philosophy, sociology, and psychology of science (HPSPS); disciplines with ongoing and vigorous research activities. NOS, thus, necessarily remains an evolving domain with some contested areas. Nonetheless, at the level of generality needed for scientific literacy, several NOS aspects are virtually non-controversial and accessible to precollege students (Lederman, 2007; Lederman & Lederman, 2014). We adopted 10 of these NOS aspects in our analyses of science textbooks. These aspects, it should be noted, have been emphasized in recent and current science education reform documents (namely: AAAS, 1993; NGSS Lead States, 2013; NRC, 1996; NSTA, 1982), and almost all have—at some level of depth or another, been consistently emphasized in research on NOS in science education for close to 60 years (Abd-El-Khalick, 2014). These aspects are described in Table 2.1.

Table 2.1 Explication of the NOS Aspects Targeted in the Analysis of the Selected Textbooks

NOS aspect	Dimensions emphasized in textbook analysis
Empirical	Scientific claims are derived from, and/or consistent with, observations of natural phenomena. Scientists, however, do not have 'direct' access to most natural phenomena: Their observations are almost always filtered through the human perceptual apparatus, mediated by the assumptions underlying the functioning of 'scientific' instruments, and/or interpreted from within elaborate theoretical frameworks.
Inferential	There is a crucial distinction between observations and inferences. Observations are descriptive statements about natural phenomena that are accessible to the senses (or extensions of the senses) and about which observers can reach consensus with relative ease (e.g., objects released above ground level tend to fall to the ground). Inferences, on the other hand, are statements about phenomena that are not directly accessible to the senses (e.g., objects tend to fall to the ground because of 'gravity'). Scientific constructs, such as gravity, are inferential in the sense that they can only be accessed and/or measured through their manifestations or effects.
Creative	Science is not an entirely rational or systematic activity. Generating scientific knowledge involves human creativity in the sense of scientists inventing explanations and theoretical entities. The creative NOS, coupled with its inferential nature, entail that scientific entities (atoms, force fields, species, etc.) are functional theoretical models rather than faithful copies of 'reality.'
Theory-laden	Scientists' theoretical and disciplinary commitments, beliefs, prior knowledge, training, and expectations influence their work. These background factors affect scientists' choice of problems to investigate and methods of investigations, observations (both in terms of what is and is not observed), and interpretation of these observations. This (sometimes collective) individuality or mindset accounts for the role of theory in generating scientific knowledge. Contrary to common belief, science never starts with neutral observations. Like investigations, observations are always motivated and guided by, and acquire meaning in light of questions and problems derived from, certain theoretical perspectives.
Tentative	Scientific knowledge is reliable and durable, but never absolute or certain. All categories of knowledge ('facts,' theories, laws, etc.) are subject to change. Scientific claims change as new evidence, made possible through conceptual and technological advances, is brought to bear; as extant evidence is reinterpreted in light of new or revised theoretical ideas; or due to changes in the cultural and social spheres or shifts in the directions of established research programs.

NOS aspect	Dimensions emphasized in textbook analysis
Myth of 'The Scientific Method'	This myth is often manifested in the belief that there is a recipe-like step-wise procedure that typifies all scientific practice. This notion is erroneous: There is no single 'Scientific Method' that would guarantee the development of infallible knowledge. Scientists do observe, compare, measure, test, speculate, hypothesize, debate, create ideas and conceptual tools, and construct theories and explanations. However, there is no single sequence of (practical, conceptual, or logical) activities that will unerringly lead them to valid claims, let alone 'certain' knowledge.
Scientific theories	Scientific theories are well-established, highly substantiated, internally consistent systems of explanations, which (a) account for large sets of seemingly unrelated observations in several fields of investigation, (b) generate research questions and problems, and (c) guide future investigations. Theories are often based on assumptions or axioms and posit the existence of non-observable entities. Thus, direct testing is untenable. Only indirect evidence supports and validates theories: Scientists derive specific testable predictions from theories and check them against observations. An agreement between predictions and observations increases confidence in the tested theory.
Scientific laws	In general, laws are descriptive statements of relationships among observable phenomena. Theories, by contrast, are inferred explanations for observable phenomena or regularities in those phenomena. Contrary to common belief, theories and laws are not hierarchically related (the naïve view that theories become laws when 'enough' supporting evidence is garnered, or that laws have a higher status than theories). Theories and laws are different kinds of knowledge and one does not become the other. Theories are as legitimate a product of science as laws.
Social dimensions of science	Scientific knowledge is socially negotiated. This should not be confused with relativistic notions of science. This dimension specifically refers to the constitutive values associated with established venues for communication and criticism within the scientific enterprise, which serve to enhance the objectivity of collectively scrutinized scientific knowledge through decreasing the impact of individual scientists' idiosyncrasies and subjectivities. The double-blind peer-review process used by scientific journals is one aspect of the enactment of the NOS dimensions under this aspect.
Social and cultural embeddedness of science	Science is a human enterprise embedded and practiced in the context of a larger cultural milieu. Thus, science affects and is affected by various cultural elements and spheres, including social fabric, worldview, power structures, philosophy, religion, and political and economic factors. Such effects are manifested, among other things, through public funding for scientific research and, in some cases, in the very nature of 'acceptable' explanations of natural phenomena (e.g., differing stories of hominid evolution have resulted from the advent of feminist perspectives brought about by increased access, participation, and leadership of females in the biosocial sciences).

Note: Adopted from Abd-El-Khalick et al. (2008).

In this regard, two important attributes of the 10 NOS aspects need to be highlighted. First, the aspects are intricately interrelated: Abd–El–Khalick and Lederman (2000b) presented one possible configuration of these inter-relationships. Second, the target NOS aspects are focused on *epistemological* dimensions and, thus, exclude science process skills. Thus, textbook references to, or activities that entail engagement with, basic or integrated science process skills (observing, hypothesizing, controlling variables, measuring, interpreting data, designing experiments, etc.) were not deemed representations of certain NOS aspects unless coupled with relevant explicit or implicit textual messages. Indeed, research shows that the enactment of science process skills when conducting science inquiries does not necessarily enable students to develop understandings of the relevant NOS dimensions or underlying epistemological issues (Khishfe & Abd–El–Khalick, 2002; Sandoval & Morrison, 2003). Science process skills, if you will, would be included under Chiappetta et al.'s (1991) "investigative nature of science" dimension that is separate from (albeit related to) the "science as a way of knowing" dimension, which is closely aligned with NOS.

Explicit Versus Implicit Approaches to Addressing NOS

A substantial body of empirical research—including quasi-experimental, pretest-posttest comparison group design studies—has examined the relative impact of implicit versus explicit approaches to teaching about NOS. The resulting corpus of evidence indicates that explicit NOS instructional approaches are more effective in impacting learners' understandings than implicit ones (Abd–El–Khalick & Lederman, 2000a; Lederman, 2007; Lederman & Lederman, 2014). The latter mostly assume that engagement with inquiry-based science activities or the *doing* of science necessarily translates into enhanced NOS understandings (see Lederman & Lederman, 2014). Implicit approaches often lack structured opportunities to encourage learners to reflect on their science-based activities from within a NOS framework to enable them to build and internalize the desired understandings (Abd–El–Khalick & Lederman, 2000a). Thus, a distinction between explicit and implicit attention to NOS in the analyzed textbooks was built into the development of the scoring rubric used here. In this regard, it cannot be overemphasized that explicit attention to NOS is *not* equivalent to didactic teaching. Explicit NOS instruction specifically refers to (a) including NOS cognitive learning outcomes among those targeted by instruction, and (b) providing ample, structured opportunities for reflection to help students develop meta-understandings about the characteristics, development, and validation of scientific knowledge. Thus, our analytical framework intended to document whether textbooks addressed the target NOS aspects, how the aspects were represented (i.e., informed versus naïve), as well as the manner in which (i.e., explicit versus implicit; and consistent versus inconsistent) the textbooks approached these aspects.

It is important to clarify what we mean by implicit versus explicit representations of NOS aspects in textual materials. After all, it is reasonable to contend that a textbook either includes some identifiable element(s) (statements, figures, charts, images, etc.) that address a NOS aspect or it does not. In this specific sense, a textbook either explicitly addresses a NOS theme or it does not. The latter approach, we believe, is too restrictive because it fails to capture an essential difference between implicit and explicit instructional approaches to addressing NOS in science classrooms. This difference lies with the assumption that underlie implicit approaches, namely that *engagement* with various enactments of science instruction would necessarily entail learning some 'lessons' about NOS even in the absence of explicit and/or reflective prompts, which focus or draw learners' attention to relevant epistemological dimensions that might be embedded in these enactments. Thus, according to the implicit approach, conducting an inquiry activity, practicing a science process skill, reading a historical narrative on some scientific discovery (see Abd-El-Khalick & Lederman, 2000b) and, by extension, engagement with textual materials in a science textbook would necessarily result in learning about one or more elements of NOS. We noted that this assumption has been discredited by empirical research (see Abd-El-Khalick, 2012b; Abd-El-Khalick & Lederman, 2000a). In our approach, an explicit representation of a NOS aspect entailed the identification of some textual elements (statements, figure captions, etc.), or reflective prompts (questions, etc.), which convey messages that are epistemological in nature, or that invite students to think about the text in ways to help them draw some conclusions about the NOS aspect in question. An implicit representation of this NOS aspect, in comparison, was noted when relevant epistemological ideas could be *inferred* from textual materials. Consider the following illustrative example. In his 1974 textbook, Giancoli included an extended treatment of the theory-driven NOS and, specifically, about the theory-laden nature of observation. Giancoli (1974) wrote:

A scientist can never include everything in a description of what he observes; there is just too much happening (how could a scientist ever go anywhere, for example, if he insisted on knowing what every atom in the universe was doing at all times). He must judge what is relevant in a given situation, and his judgment is based partly on what he already knows and believes. The ancient Greeks, for example, studied the horizontal motion of objects along the ground. To them the relevant observations were that after an initial push an object always slowed down and came to rest [and] . . . concluded that objects are naturally at rest. Galileo saw it differently . . . What was relevant to Galileo was that different objects slowed down at different rates depending on their surfaces. Because he saw something different in the same 'facts,' Galileo established a whole new theory of motion. Thus we see that the practice of science is not an entirely objective activity. The subjective element is very important and, in fact, is indispensable if new theories are to develop. Being able to see old 'facts' in a new way as Galileo did requires a creative mind.

(pp. 5–6)

These statements were coded as an explicit (and informed) representation of the theory-driven NOS. Giancoli (1974) went to great lengths to explain that scientists' ideas or theories influence, to a significant extent, what they 'see' or observe; how they interpret or make sense of these observations; and what scientists say about how the world works in light of these observations (albeit, at times, these observations could be anchored in the exact same 'facts').

Consider, in comparison, the following statement from Biggs, Kapicka, and Lundgren (1995): "Before a scientist makes a hypothesis, he or she has some idea what the answer to a question might be because of experience, extensive reading, and previous experiments" (p. 27). This statement has the *potential* to help students develop understandings about the role that prior ideas or theory play in directing selective attention to particular 'answers' to scientific questions. However, Biggs et al. did not elaborate on this notion, nor did they follow up with a question or prompt to help students *infer* an epistemological lesson about the role of theory in shaping scientists' observations and interpretation of data. This instance was coded as an implicit (and informed) representation of the theory-driven NOS, specifically because it entails a conceptual jump, an inference, on the part of the reader, which might or might not actually occur.

Textbook Pages Dedicated to NOS

Our first study, like Irez (2009), attended to the qualitative representation of NOS in science textbooks. Both studies, nonetheless, did not address the quantitative emphasis accorded to NOS dimensions in the analyzed textbooks. Vesterinen et al. (2013) quantified the number of statements dedicated to certain NOS aspects in the textbooks they analyzed, and the percentage of these statements that were judged to be naïve or informed. Textual materials, nonetheless, are not necessarily restricted to narrative 'statements.' In the context of science textbooks, textual materials also include figures, illustrations (of models, processes, etc.), charts, mathematical notations and formulations, photos, tables, etc. (Khine, 2013). In our second study, we set out to capture the *extent* of representation or *emphasis* given to NOS in the analyzed textbooks. The number of textbook pages dedicated to addressing NOS aspects was used as a fairly reasonable proxy for gauging such extent of representation and emphasis.

Indeed, 'textbook pages' play a significant role in the process of authoring and structuring science textbooks. Among other criteria, authors report that publishers provide strict directives in terms of structuring their textbook pages. In addition to the total number of pages, which set an overall framework for developing a textbook, author directives include specific parameters, such as the specific percentages of each textbook page that should be dedicated to expository text or statements versus pictorial or illustrated textual elements (charts, photos, figures, tables, etc.). Balancing these directives often is translated into decisions about textbook emphases in terms of the content to be included and the extent or depth to which such content is addressed (D. DeCoste, personal communication, March 20, 2009). For example, textbook authors might find themselves having to choose between, on the one hand, dedicating statements to vignettes that accurately represent the historical development of atomic theory and associated NOS aspects and, on the other hand, the inclusion of text to elucidate the current status of the theory itself, as well as statements (e.g., in the form of captions) to integrate and reinforce these explanations with other *mandated* pictorial textual materials aimed at a multimodal representation of atomic theory. Taken altogether, the number of text pages dedicated to different topics and themes within these topics end up reflecting the relative emphases dedicated to each within the total framework of a textbook.

Textbook Sample

Sample Selection and Criteria

A major goal of our work was to assess the responsiveness of textbooks to the consistent calls of educational reforms to address NOS in precollege science classrooms. Responsiveness would be reflected in changes over time, if any, in the manner in which, and extent to which, secondary science textbooks addressed various NOS aspects that were highlighted in the most intensive and widely publicized U.S. national reform documents in science education over the course of the past several decades (i.e., AAAS, 1971, 1990, 2001; NGSS Lead States, 2013; NRC, 1996, 2012; 2012; NSTA, 1982). Thus, the first decision for sampling textbooks focused on the time frame of their publication. Toward achieving this goal, it was important to sample from among textbooks that, in the case of each study, came out before and around the times of, and then following, the publication of these reform documents. Nonetheless, the NRC (2012) report and NGSS (NGSS Lead States, 2013), which translated the NRC (2012) vision into performance indicators, were either not in existence in the case of the chemistry textbooks study, or had just been released in the case of the biology and physics textbooks study. In other words, at the time of data collection and analyses, the NRC (2012) and NGSS (2013) reform documents were not around, or had not been around long enough, to impact science textbooks' development.

Additionally, major publishers synchronize their decisions to update or issue new editions of their textbooks with the cycles of textbook adoption in the most populous states across the United States (i.e., California, Texas,

Florida, and New York) because school textbook markets in these states have an undue influence on the publishing industry (Collins, 2012). The textbook adoption cycles in these states vary from about five to seven years (e.g., California Department of Education, 2016; Texas Education Agency, 2016). It followed that the target time frame for textbook selection would extend from about seven years before to about seven after the publication of the abovementioned reform documents. Thus, the population of textbooks targeted here comprised secondary chemistry, biology, and physics textbooks published in the period from around 1965 to 2005. Textbooks published after 2005 would have been published about a decade following the release of the NRC (1996) document, which would make it hard to attribute observed changes in these textbooks to the influence of the latter reform or those that came before it.

The next set of sampling decisions were focused on selecting textbooks that had substantial impact on classroom science instruction as reflected in their market share, and which represented continuity over substantial periods of time in terms of their authors and/or publisher. The latter consideration was important to allow making reasonably robust claims about the responsiveness of the textbooks to reform efforts, as well as the relative impact of textbook authors versus publishers on the treatment of NOS. Thus, we set out to sample textbook series as compared to individual textbooks. To meet all of the above considerations, we used three criteria to select textbooks for analysis: 1) Having a significant share of the U.S. science textbook market; 2) being part of a 'connected textbook series,' which meant several editions of the same textbook, or a set of textbooks having the same title and/or author(s) and produced by the same publisher; and 3) being part of a connected textbook series that span, at least, one decade and up to several decades, and which roughly fall in the period from 1965 to 2005.

Accessing accurate market share figures for the U.S. textbook industry is a very difficult and costly prospect. Nonetheless, *Reports of the 2000 and 2012 National Survey of Science and Mathematics Education* (Banilower et al., 2013; Weiss, Banilower, McMahon, & Smith, 2001), provided indirect access to these figures. The reports are "based on a national probability sample of science and mathematics schools and teachers in grades K-12 in the 50 states . . . [which] . . . allow national estimates of science and mathematics course offerings and enrollment, . . . [and] textbook usage" (Banilower et al., 2013, p. 2). The reports also identified the most used textbooks in U.S. science classrooms. The application of the above selection criteria resulted in identifying several candidate textbook series. Of those, the 12 most prominent in terms of market share, inclusion of the most used textbooks in science classrooms, and those series with the larger time spans and/ or textbooks per series, were selected for analysis. As will become evident below, the time and labor-intensive nature of the analyses necessitated the selection of a subset of all the series that were identified. Thus, a total of 48 textbooks (16 biology, 14 chemistry, and 18 physics) in 12 series (3 biology, 5 chemistry, and 4 physics) were included in the analysis. In the case of extended series—especially *Modern Biology*, which has been in continuous production since the first edition was published in 1921 under the title, *Biology for Beginners* (Moon, 1921)—one textbook was randomly selected from each decade. The three biology textbook series included: 1) seven textbooks from the *Modern Biology* series published by Holt and associates (Feldkamp, 2002; Moon, Mann, Otto, Kuntz, & Dury, 1958; Moon, Otto, & Towle, 1963; Otto & Towle, 1973; Otto, Towle, & Bradley, 1981; Towle, 1991, 1999); 2) the Biological Sciences Curriculum Study (BSCS) *Blue Version* series first published by Houghton Mifflin and later by D.C. Heath and associates (BSCS, 1963, 1968, 1973, 1980, 1985, 1990, 1996); and 3) *Biology: The Dynamics of Life* series published by Glencoe and associates (Biggs et al., 2004; Biggs, Kapicka, & Lundgren, 1995).

The five chemistry textbook series included: 1) the *Modern Chemistry* series published by Holt, Rinehart and Winston (Davis, Metcalfe, Williams, & Castka, 2002; Metcalfe, Williams, & Castka, 1966, 1982); 2) four textbooks published by Holt, Rinehart, and Winston (Bolton, Lamphere, Menesini, & Huang, 1973; Myers, Oldham, & Tocci, 2004; Tocci & Viehland, 1996; Toon, Ellis, & Brodkin, 1968); 3) three *ChemCom: Chemistry in the Community* textbooks (American Chemical Society [ACS], 1988, 1993, 2002); 4) two *Chemistry Concepts and Applications* textbooks by Glencoe McGraw-Hill (Phillips, Strozak, & Wistrom, 1997, 2005); and 5) two *Chemistry* textbooks by the same group of authors (Wilbraham, Staley, Matta, & Waterman, 2005; Wilbraham, Staley, Simpson, & Matta, 1997).

The four physics textbook series were: 1) the *Conceptual Physics* series (Hewitt, 1971, 1977, 1987, 1992, 1998) first published by Little, Brown, and Company, and later by Addison-Wesley; 2) the *Physics: Principles and Problems* series first published by Merrill and later by Glencoe and associates (Murphy & Smoot, 1972, 1977; Murphy, Zitzewitz, & Hollon, 1986; Zitzewitz, 2002; Zitzewitz, Davids, & Neff, 1992); 3) a series of six textbooks authored by Giancoli and published by Harcourt Brace Jovanovich and Prentice Hall (Giancoli, 1974, 1980, 1984, 1986, 1995, 2000); and 4) the *Holt Physics* series (Serway & Faughn, 1999, 2006). It could be seen that the selected textbook series spanned a range from a single decade (e.g., *Biology: The Dynamics of Life*) up to five decades (e.g., *Modern Biology*).

Seven of the 12 selected series were published over the course of at least three decades. Taken together, the selected chemistry, biology, and physics textbook series commanded about 83 percent of the U.S. high school science textbooks' market. Additionally, the analyzed textbooks included the two most commonly used physics textbooks in U.S. high school classrooms, namely, *Conceptual Physics* and *Physics: Principles and Problems*; and the two most commonly used biology textbooks that are published by Houghton Mifflin (now Houghton Mifflin Harcourt) and Addison-Wesley, which currently is a subsidiary of Pearson Education (cf. Banilower et al.,

2013); as well as two of the three most widely used high school chemistry textbooks, namely *Addison-Wesley—Chemistry* and *Modern Chemistry* (cf. Weiss et al., 2001).

Selection of Chapters and Sections for Analysis

The 48 selected textbooks comprised a total of about 38,000 pages of text. Applying the meticulous analyses employed in our work to all textbooks in their entirety would have been a prohibitively difficult undertaking, even for a team of 10 researchers. Thus, materials were sampled from within each text-book for analysis. In this regard, it should be noted that well-justified sampling from within textbooks is common practice in textual analysis studies (see Khine, 2013). In sampling within the selected textbooks, we included the fol-lowing materials for purposes of data analysis: First, the textbook chapters or sections titled 'the scientific method,' 'the scientific process,' 'science as inquiry,' 'how science works,' 'the science of biology,' 'biology: the scientific study of living things,' etc., or any materials that addressed the nature of disciplinary research in biology, chemistry, or physics. The analyzed materials also included all chapters related to genetics, photosynthesis, and the circulatory and nervous systems in the biology textbooks; atomic structure, kinetic molecular theory, and gas laws in the chemistry textbooks; and to heat, electricity, and New-ton's laws of motion in the physics textbooks. These chapters and sections were selected because of their direct relevance to NOS (e.g., chapter on the 'scientific method') and because high school biology, chemistry, and physics textbooks often include some historical treatment of the development of the selected topics (genetics, atomic theory, heat, etc.), thus, providing a context for addressing several NOS aspects. Also, these materials were selected because analyses were focused not only on how NOS is addressed in the generic, content-lean introductory chapter often included in textbooks, but also attended to whether and the ways in which target NOS aspects were addressed in the context of the biology, chemistry, and physics *content* covered in the selected textbooks. Finally, the detailed textbook tables of content and subject indexes were thoroughly examined for topics and/or key terms, which were relevant to NOS, including 'inference,' 'laws,' 'models,' 'observation,' 'scientific method,' 'scientific thinking,' 'scientific publications,' 'scientific process,' 'scientific the-ory,' 'scientific law,' 'social,' 'society,' etc. The corresponding sections or pages were then identified and included in the analysis. This selection process of textbook materials resulted in a total of about 6,100 pages of text—16.3 per-cent of the total number of pages in the 48 selected textbooks—which were photocopied, indexed, and included in data analysis.

Data Analysis Procedures

Textbooks were analyzed for the ways in which they addressed the 10 NOS themes along two dimensions. The first is whether the representation of a NOS aspect in an analyzed textbook was informed, partially informed, or naïve; that is, the extent to which such representation was consistent or incommensurate with HPSPS scholarship, and/or with the ways in which this aspect is represented in the aforementioned reform documents (e.g., AAAS, 1990; NGSS Lead States, 2013; NRC, 1996). Obviously, a textbook could remain silent on a certain NOS aspect, that is, it does not offer any or enough textual elements to allow making an informed judgment on the representation of this NOS aspect. The second dimension of manner of representation was whether the treatment of a NOS aspect in textual materials was implicit or explicit. The latter dimension, as explained above, is grounded in a robust body of evidence, which showed a differential positive effect favoring explicit approaches in impacting learners' understandings of NOS (see Bell, Lederman, & Abd-El-Khalick, 1998).

Thus, the analysis of NOS representations was approached with a sort of two-dimensional matrix with the accuracy of these representations (i.e., informed, partially informed, silent, or naïve) along one axis, and the manner in which the textual materials addressed the NOS aspects (i.e., implicit or explicit) on the other. Another important element along the latter axis was the extent to which textual elements pertaining to a certain NOS aspect or closely related aspects across a textbook were consistent or not. For example, a textbook could include statements to the effect that developing scientific knowledge entails human creativity. The same textbook would then affirm that all scientists follow the steps of a universal 'Scientific Method' to develop claims to scientific knowledge. Such a textbook would have conveyed inconsistent messages about the creative NOS because it acknowledges a role for creativity, and then advances a formulaic method for doing science. Similarly, a textbook would be coded as having put forth inconsistent messages about the tentative NOS if it states that scientific knowledge is subject to change with the advent of new evidence or theory, and then claims that scientific laws are 'facts' that are proven beyond doubt. These dimensions and elements of analyzing representations of aspects of NOS in the analyzed textbooks are captured in our scoring rubric, which is described below.

A team comprising 10 science education researchers and graduate research assistants analyzed the data. For both studies, analyses proceeded in two phases. The first involved establishing inter-rater reliability using a randomly selected sub-sample of textbook materials. Next, all selected textbook materials were distributed among a subset of researchers and analyzed. The remaining researchers were involved in the second phase of analysis, which also commenced with establishing inter-rater reliability among coders. Next, first-phase analyses were distributed among the latter coders, who validated the coding and scoring. The process involved reading all textual materials again, checking those segments deemed relevant to the target NOS aspects, and examining the associated scores, which were assigned by the first group of coders. Discrepancies in scoring were resolved through discussion between the primary author and second group of coders and often entailed consultation of original textual materials and reference to the rubric. For biology and physics textbooks, both phases of data analysis involved generating estimates of the numbers of pages dedicated to addressing the target NOS aspects in the analyzed textbooks.

Scoring Rubric

Data analysis targeted the aforementioned 10 aspects of NOS. Analysis started by carefully reading textual materials and color-coding all sections that were relevant to one or more aspects of NOS. Sections included charts of the 'scientific method' or scientific process and associated text, historical narratives or vignettes related to the development of scientific concepts or theories, narratives on the interactions between science and society, activity boxes, etc. Coded sections from a textbook were *not* analyzed or scored independently. Instead, all coded sections, materials, and references targeting the same NOS aspect were grouped together and examined holistically. The score assigned to the representation of a specific NOS aspect within a textbook was based on an examination of all sections relevant to that aspect across the textbook materials. In some cases, assigning a score for a certain NOS aspect also took into consideration the representation of a closely related aspect or a set of aspects. The representation of each target NOS aspect within a textbook was assigned a score on a scale ranging from -3 to +3 points, which reflected the accuracy (i.e., naïve, silent, partially informed, or informed) and manner (i.e., implicit or explicit; consistent or inconsistent) of such representation as articulated in the rubric (see Table 2.2). With 10 NOS aspects targeted in the analysis, the overall score for a textbook could range from -30 to +30 points. Scores were assigned in accordance with the following rubric (see Abd-El-Khalick et al., 2008, 2016 for illustrative examples of textual materials and associated scores):

a)   Three points = Explicit, informed, and consistent representation of the target NOS aspect: (i) explicit statements that convey an informed representation, (ii) consistency across the selected chapters or sections in addressing the target NOS aspect, and (iii) consistency in addressing other directly related NOS aspects. For example, to receive a score of '3' for the 'tentative NOS,' textbook materials should explicitly convey the notion that all categories of scientific knowledge are subject to change. An example of the lack of consistency in this case would be stating that scientific theories are subject to change while emphasizing that scientific laws are 'facts' or 'truths.' Representations of a target NOS aspect *could* include supportive examples, such as accurate historical vignettes or other accurate examples (e.g., "that the sun rises ... every day" [Phillips et al., 1997, p. 59] is not an accurate example of a scientific law).

b)   Two points = Explicit, partially informed representation of the target NOS aspect: (i) explicit statements that convey an informed, but incomplete representation, and (ii) consistency across the selected chapters or sections in representing the target NOS aspect. An incomplete representation derives from the textbook materials remaining silent in terms of addressing other related NOS aspects that ensure a complete informed representation. For example, emphasizing the role of observation or evidence in science while remaining silent on other related aspects, such as the theory-driven NOS or the role of interpretation in generating scientific claims, would not constitute a complete and informed representation of the 'empirical NOS.' Representations of a target NOS aspect *could* include supportive examples, such as accurate historical vignettes or other accurate examples.

c) One point = Implicit, informed, and consistent representation of the target NOS aspect: (i) an informed representation of the target NOS aspect could be *inferred* from the textbook materials (e.g., relevant explanations, activities, examples, or historical episodes *lacking* structured, reflective prompts or explicit statements), and (ii) absence of other explicit or implicit messages that are inconsistent with the inferred implicit representation.

d) Zero points = The target NOS aspect is not addressed: (i) no explicit or implicit treatment of the target NOS aspect, or (ii) not enough materials (statements, examples, historical vignettes, etc.) to make an informed judgment or to convey to the textbook reader a sense about the target aspect of NOS one way or the other.

e) Negative one point = Implicit misrepresentation of the target NOS aspect: A naïve representation could be *inferred* from the textbook materials.

f) Negative two points = The textbook materials convey mixed explicit and/or implicit messages about the target NOS aspect: (i) implicit, informed representations that could be inferred from some parts of the textbook materials are countered by explicit, naïve statements in other parts, or (ii) explicit statements that convey conflicting messages about the same NOS aspect. For example, a historical vignette about the development of atomic model, which could convey a sense of the tentativeness of scientific knowledge (the vignette is an 'implicit' instance because it lacks structured, reflective prompts or explicit statements about this NOS aspect) is countered with an explicit statement, such as: "Certain facts in science always hold true. Such facts are labeled as scientific laws" (Tocci & Viehland, 1996, p. 20).

g) Negative three points = Explicit, naïve representation of the target NOS aspect: Explicit statement or statements that clearly communicate a naïve representation of the target NOS aspect, such as, "A scientific law is simply a fact of nature that is observed so often that it becomes accepted as truth" (Phillips et al., 2005, p. 59).

Estimating Textbook Pages Dedicated to NOS

As selected textbook materials were analyzed for their representation of various NOS aspects, coders kept track of biology and physics textbook pages or parts of pages dedicated to addressing these aspects. If a textbook featured a whole chapter or section dedicated to NOS, then all associated textbook pages were counted. Additionally, each analyzed page of a text-book was color-coded as addressing, if any, one or more of the target NOS themes. A measuring ruler was then used to gauge how much space was dedicated to *all* highlighted NOS aspects on that page. The corresponding space was coded as a whole page or fraction of a page (¼ page, ½ page, etc.) and recorded at the bottom of that page.

It should be noted that no attempt was made to determine emphases in terms of textbook pages dedicated to each of the 10 individual NOS aspects targeted in the analysis. This decision was based on research that examined the balance of scientific literacy themes in secondary science textbooks (e.g., Chiappetta et al., 1991; Chiappetta & Fillman, 2007; Vesterinen et al., 2013), which suggested that the number of pages in a given secondary science text-book dedicated to NOS would highly likely be rather small. As a result, our analysis focused on estimating the total number of textbook pages dedicated to addressing all target NOS aspects. Yet, as will become evident in the results section below, textbook emphases on NOS when estimated as the number of textbook pages addressing NOS themes still came out to be surprisingly minuscule.

Next, all pages and page fractions addressing NOS were summed to gen-erate two figures: the total number of pages in the chapter or sections dedi-cated to NOS (mostly the introductory chapter or some sections of such a chapter), and number of pages dedicated to NOS in the remaining textbook materials (mostly related to content, such as genetics and Newton's laws of motion). Next, based on the assumption that the treatment of NOS in the analyzed content chapters would be representative of how NOS is addressed in other content chapters within the same textbook, the actual number of pages addressing NOS in the analyzed materials was extrapolated to esti-mate the total number of pages possibly dedicated to NOS across an entire textbook.

Establishing Inter-Rater Reliability

While very structured, our scoring rubric required coders to make infer-ences. Certain factors and measures, thus, were needed to ensure its reli-able use. First, with a single exception, all co-authors hold B.S. and/or M.S. degrees in the respective science disciplines, and had experience with teach-ing secondary and/or middle school science. The one co-author who did not hold a science degree or teach school science had deep expertise in philosophy and history of science. Second, the nine researchers who assisted with data analysis had completed a graduate level course on NOS taught by the primary author. The course, which draws on scholarship in HPSPS and science education, was empirically shown to help participants develop robust NOS understandings (Abd-El-Khalick, 2005). Thus, all authors shared sophisticated understandings of the NOS aspects targeted in the analysis. Third, a formal process was undertaken to establish inter-rater reliability in using the rubric to analyze textbook materials.

As noted earlier, data were analyzed in two phases, each of which involved a subset of the researchers. Similar procedures were followed in each phase to establish inter-rater reliability. First, all coders independently analyzed and scored materials from two randomly selected biology, chemistry, and/ or physics textbooks. Each coder's scores were supported by direct quotes or descriptions of relevant charts, tables, sections, activities, etc., drawn from the materials analyzed. Then, scores were compared and differences were resolved through discussion and reference to the analyzed materials and supporting evidence. Once a shared, nuanced understanding of applying the rubric was developed, a different set of two randomly selected textbooks was independently scored by each researcher. In our second study, inter-rater agreement for the first phase of analysis was measured using Fleiss's Kappa, which extends Cohen's Kappa (Cohen, 1968) to measure agreement between multiple raters (Fleiss, 1971; Fleiss, Cohen, & Everitt, 1969). The resulting value of 0.76 indicated strong coder agreement (Fleiss, 1981). Next, all textbook materials were divided between coders for analysis and scoring. A similar process was used with the second group of coders and resulted in a Kappa value of 0.74, which still reflected strong inter-rater agreement. Next, as noted above, the second group of coders closely examined all the analyses and scores generated by the first group. The result was a high degree of coder agreement of about 86 percent for the first and 88 percent for the second study. The remaining differences were scrutinized by the primary author and resolved by further discussion and interrogation of the analyzed materials.

Tabulated textbook scores were examined to discern patterns to answer the guiding research questions related to: 1) the accuracy of NOS representations, and changes in these representations over the course of the decade(s) during which the analyzed textbook series were published; 2) whether an author effect (versus a publisher effect) associated with the observed representations from the first study was corroborated by data from the second study; and 3) possible relationships between disciplinary focus (i.e., biology, chemistry, and physics) and representations of the target NOS aspects. Finally, the reader is reminded that the analyzed secondary science textbooks and textbook series commanded a sizable majority (about 83 percent) of the U.S. market share, and included the most used textbooks in secondary science classrooms. Thus, claims derived from systematic comparisons of descriptive statistics characterizing the analyzed textbooks (e.g., relative NOS aspect scores, relative percentages of pages dedicated to NOS themes in various textbooks) still speak volumes to ways in which textbooks represent and emphasize NOS for the larger majority of secondary science students in the United States.

Results and Discussion

Extent of the Representation of NOS in the Analyzed Biology and Physics Textbooks

Table 2.2 presents the data on the extent of NOS representations. The data, illustrated here by reference to *Physics: Principles and Problems* (Murphy & Smoot, 1977), include the: 1) total number of pages in a textbook (497 pages), including number of pages in the introductory or first chapter (15 pages) that is typically aligned with NOS with titles, such as 'how science works' or 'science as inquiry'; 2) total number of pages analyzed (170 pages, 34 percent of the textbook), which includes all pages in the first chapter (15 pages), selected content pages (153 pages), and 'other' pages identified by examining the detailed table of contents and index for NOS-related terms and phrases (2 pages); 3) number of pages that addressed NOS themes within the introductory chapter (1 page), selected content chapters (2.25 pages), and 'other' pages (1 page); 4) extrapolated number of pages dedicated to NOS within all content pages (7.09 pages), that is, in all textbook pages less the first chapter; 5) extrapolated total number of pages addressing NOS (9.09 pages), that is, the sum of actual NOS pages in the first chapter and 'other' pages, and extrapolated NOS pages in content chapters; and 6) percent of textbook pages addressing NOS themes (1.83 percent), and the percentage of these total NOS pages that are contained in the introductory chapter (11.00 percent).

Prior research has documented imbalances in the treatment of scientific literacy themes in secondary science textbooks: 'Science as a way of knowing' (a theme roughly aligned with NOS) has consistently received substantially less emphasis than other themes, such as knowledge of science, investigative nature of science, and interactions between science, technology, and society (e.g., Chiappetta et al., 1991; Vesterinen et al., 2013). Nonetheless, our work would be the first to document the extent—in textbook pages, to which U.S. secondary biology and physics textbooks addressed specific aspects of NOS that have been consistently emphasized in science education reform documents over the past six decades (see Abd-El-Khalick, 2014). Even against the rather pessimistic backdrop gleaned from prior research, our findings still are *very* disconcerting and clearly demonstrate the dismal attention accorded to NOS in secondary science textbooks. Since our estimates were not conservative and erred on the side of textbooks, the present data represent a best-case scenario in terms of the pages dedicated to NOS in these textbooks.

Table 2.2 shows that the analyzed textbooks dedicated between 0.37 percent to 4.57 percent of their pages to the target NOS themes, with an overall weighted average of 2.42 percent. Only four textbooks (12 percent) had between 4 and 5 percent of their pages (about 31 to 52 pages) dedicated to NOS, and eight textbooks (24 percent) with 3 to 4 percent of their pages (22

Table 2.2 Number of Pages Analyzed and Number of Actual and Estimated Pages Addressing NOS-related Themes in Biology and Physics Textbooks

Textbook	Total pp.	No. of pp. analyzed				No. of pp. addressing NOS				Total estimated pp. addressing NOS		Percent estimated pp. addressing NOS	
	Book[1]	Intro[2]	Content[3]	Other[4]	Total	Intro[2]	Content[3]	Other[4]	Total	Content[3]	Book[1]	Intro[2]	Book[1]
Physics													
Giancoli (1974)	444	12	137	3	152	6.50	1.50	0.50	8.50	4.73	11.73	55.41	2.64
Giancoli (1980)	794	6	133	0	139	2.35	1.00	0	3.35	5.92	8.27	28.40	1.04
Giancoli (1984)	877	11	101	0	112	1.75	1.65	0	3.40	14.15	15.90	11.01	1.81
Giancoli (1986)	598	10	91	0	101	3.30	2.45	0	5.75	15.83	19.13	17.25	3.20
Giancoli (1995)	1008	17	128	0	145	3.20	2.45	0	5.65	18.97	22.17	14.43	2.20
Giancoli (2000)	1171	15	125	0	140	1.60	1.00	0	2.60	9.25	10.85	14.75	0.93
Hewitt (1971)	555	5	63	6	74	2.50	1.00	0.50	4.00	8.73	11.73	21.31	2.11
Hewitt (1977)	656	5	79	0	84	2.00	1.00	0	3.00	8.24	10.24	19.53	1.56
Hewitt (1987)	632	6	118	0	124	3.50	1.25	0	4.75	6.63	10.13	34.55	1.60
Hewitt (1992)	676	9	119	3	131	3.75	1.25	0.50	5.50	7.01	11.26	33.31	1.67
Hewitt (1998)	729	15	124	5	144	3.90	1.25	0.10	5.25	7.20	11.20	34.83	1.54
Murphy and Smoot (1972)	450	15	81	2	98	1.00	2.00	1.00	4.00	10.74	12.74	7.85	2.83
Murphy and Smoot (1977)	497	15	153	2	170	1.00	2.25	1.00	4.25	7.09	9.09	11.00	1.83
Murphy et al. (1986)	569	14	100	0	114	2.75	0.75		3.50	4.16	6.91	39.78	1.21
Zitzewitz et al. (1992)	653	9	85	0	94	2.25	0.75	0	3.00	5.68	7.93	28.36	1.21
Zitzewitz (2002)	716	31	105	0	136	4.50	1.50	0	6.00	9.79	14.29	31.50	2.00
Serway and Faughn (1999)	989	34	148	0	182	3.00	0.10	0	3.10	0.65	3.65	82.30	0.37
Serway and Faughn (2006)	958	34	135	0	169	4.15	0.10	0	4.25	0.68	4.83	85.84	0.50
Biology													
Biggs et al. (1995)	1184	49	108	0	157	9.50	1.50	0	11.00	15.76	25.26	37.60	2.13
Biggs et al. (2004)	1042	27	143	0	170	6.75	2.25	0	9.00	15.97	22.72	29.71	2.18
BSCS (1963)	689	13	102	0	115	5.00	2.50	0	7.50	16.57	21.57	23.18	3.13

(Continued)

Table 2.2 (Continued)

Textbook	Total pp.	No. of pp. analyzed				No. of pp. addressing NOS				Total estimated pp. addressing NOS		Percent estimated pp. addressing NOS	
	Book¹	Intro²	Content³	Other⁴	Total	Intro²	Content³	Other⁴	Total	Content³	Book¹	Intro²	Book¹
BSCS (1968)	819	22	156	0	178	6.27	3.39	0	9.66	17.32	23.59	26.58	2.88
BSCS (1973)	745	18	117	0	135	4.12	3.76	0	7.88	23.36	27.48	14.99	3.69
BSCS (1980)	765	17	100	0	117	5.22	2.80	0	8.02	20.94	26.16	19.95	3.42
BSCS (1985)	769	15	125	0	140	2.24	2.02	0	4.26	12.18	14.42	15.53	1.88
BSCS (1990)	789	19	131	0	150	5.49	1.58	0	7.07	9.29	14.78	37.15	1.87
BSCS (1996)	789	19	102	0	121	4.89	3.01	0	7.90	22.72	27.61	17.71	3.50
Moon et al. (1958)	756	15	118	0	133	3.40	3.30	0	6.70	20.72	24.12	14.09	3.19
Moon et al. (1963)	738	13	95	13	121	4.00	2.75	2.50	9.25	20.99	27.49	14.55	3.72
Otto and Towle (1973)	842	18	88	0	106	6.25	3.25	0	9.50	30.43	36.68	17.04	4.36
Otto et al. (1981)	743	8	89	0	97	3.75	3.25	0	7.00	26.84	30.59	12.26	4.12
Towle (1991)	879	8	101	1	110	4.25	3.80	0.25	8.30	32.77	37.27	11.40	4.24
Towle (1999)	1120	9	117	0	126	4.13	3.40	0	7.53	32.29	36.42	11.34	3.25
Feldkamp (2002)	1120	9	85	0	94	4.13	3.60	0	7.73	47.05	51.18	8.07	4.57

¹ Overall textbook.

² Typically the first or introductory chapter (with titles such as 'the scientific process,' 'science as inquiry,' 'how science works,' 'the science of biology').

³ Selected content chapters (e.g., chapters related to genetics, photosynthesis, heat, Newton's laws of motion).

⁴ All other textbooks pages identified by examining the detailed tables of content and subject indexes for topics and/or key terms relevant to NOS (e.g., inference, models, scientific thinking, scientific theory, social, society).

to 28 pages) addressing NOS. Less than 3 percent of pages in the remaining majority of textbooks (22 of 34 textbooks, or 62 percent) addressed NOS, which translated to a total of 4 to 25 pages in these 22 textbooks. Indeed, 70 percent of the analyzed textbooks dedicated 25 pages or less to NOS. This dismal attention accorded to NOS, which becomes glaring when one considers that we targeted 10 NOS themes, is manifested in two ways. First, many textbooks did not address, neither explicitly nor implicitly, many NOS aspects. A total of 480 instances of addressing the target NOS aspects were possible in the 48 textbooks examined in both studies. Only 315 instances (65 percent) were documented; 57 percent, 66 percent, and 70 percent of all possible instances in the case of physics, chemistry, and biology textbooks, respectively. For example, Table 2.3 shows that only five physics (28 percent) and four biology (25 percent) textbooks addressed the social and creative NOS, respectively. Second, in most cases, far from a thorough or even a reasonable treatment, a NOS aspect received no more than a single isolated or passing mention in an entire textbook, which rendered the associated NOS scores very sensitive to minor changes in the various editions of an analyzed series. For example, a few additional statements in Hewitt (1992) resulted in a +2 score for the creative NOS versus a zero in other *Conceptual Physics* textbooks (Hewitt, 1971, 1977, 1998). Similarly, omitting a single, extended, explicit reference to the myth of a universal 'Scientific Method' entailed replacing a +3 score for this aspect in the Giancoli (1974, 1980) textbooks with a zero in his other analyzed textbooks (Giancoli, 1984, 1986, 1995, 2000). Also, the total percentages of pages addressing NOS in the analyzed textbooks were highly and negatively correlated ($r = -.61, p < .0001$) with the percentage of the total pages contained in introductory chapters. In other words, textbooks that tended to 'heavily' address NOS in their introductory chapters, seemed less likely to address NOS in the context of their content chapters.

The extent—in number of pages—to which a textbook addressed NOS was not, however, indicative of the degree to which it conveyed informed representations of the target aspects. Indeed, with a mere 1.04 percent of its pages (about 9 pages) dedicated to NOS, the Giancoli (1980) textbook got the second highest overall NOS score (+21 points) among all analyzed textbooks. The Giancoli textbooks featured explicit, historically and philosophically informed treatments of several target aspects of NOS. In comparison, even with 3.72 percent of its pages (about 28 pages) addressing NOS, the Moon et al. (1963) textbook earned the lowest overall score of -4 points.

Representations of NOS in the Analyzed Biology, Chemistry, and Physics Textbooks

Table 2.3 presents scores for the target NOS aspects and cumulative NOS scores for the biology, chemistry, and physics textbooks. Overall, the analyzed textbooks did not fare well in their NOS representations. With a possible

Table 2.3 Textbook Series Scores on the Target Aspects of NOS Sorted by Content Area and Series

Textbook content and series	NOS aspect										Total score
	Empirical	Inferential	Creative	Theory-driven	Tentative	Scientific method	Theories	Laws	Social	Social, cultural	
Biology											
Dynamics of Life											
Biggs et al. (1995)	2	0	0	1	−2	−2	2	−1	−1	1	0
Biggs et al. (2004)	2	0	0	1	−2	−2	2	−1	−1	0	−1
BSCS											
BSCS (1963)	2	1	2	1	1	0	2	0	0	1	10
BSCS (1968)	2	1	2	0	2	0	2	1	0	1	11
BSCS (1973)	2	1	1	1	1	0	2	0	1	1	10
BSCS (1980)	2	2	2	0	1	0	2	0	0	1	10
BSCS (1985)	2	1	0	0	0	0	2	0	1	0	6
BSCS (1990)	2	0	0	0	2	1	3	0	0	3	11
BSCS (1996)	2	1	0	0	2	1	2	0	0	3	11
Modern Biology											
Moon et al. (1958)	2	1	0	1	−2	−2	1	−2	0	1	0
Moon et al. (1963)	−2	1	0	−2	−2	−2	1	1	0	1	−4
Otto and Towle (1973)	1	1	0	1	−2	−2	1	1	1	1	3
Otto et al. (1981)	1	1	0	−2	1	−2	1	1	0	1	2
Towle (1991)	−2	1	0	1	1	−2	−2	2	2	0	4
Towle (1999)	1	1	0	1	−2	−2	2	1	2	1	1
Feldkamp (2002)	1	1	0	1	1	−2	2	0	2	0	6
Chemistry											
Modern Chemistry											
Metcalfe et al. (1966)	2	3	2	1	−1	−2	2	2	0	0	9
Metcalfe et al. (1982)	2	1	0	0	2	−2	2	2	0	0	7

	Col1	Col2	Col3	Col4	Col5	Col6	Col7	Col8	Col9	Col10	Col11
Davis et al. (2002)	2	2	0	0	0	-2	2	2	1	0	7
Holt Chemistry											
Toon et al. (1968)	2	1	0	0	3	2	2	2	0	0	12
Bolton et al. (1973)	1	3	2	0	0	-2	1	0	1	0	6
Tocci and Viehland (1996)	2	3	-3	-3	-2	-3	2	-3	1	0	-6
Myers et al. (2004)	1	2	-3	-2	-2	-3	2	-3	1	0	-7
ChemCom											
ACS (1988)	1	2	0	0	1	-1	0	0	0	0	3
ACS (1993)	1	3	-1	-1	1	-1	2	2	0	0	6
ACS (2002)	1	3	-1	0	0	-1	1	0	1	0	4
Chemistry											
Concepts and Applications											
Phillips et al. (1997)	1	0	0	1	-2	-3	3	-3	0	0	-3
Phillips et al. (2005)	1	1	0	1	-2	-3	3	-3	0	1	-1
Chemistry											
Wilbraham et al. (1997)	1	0	0	1	1	-3	3	3	0	0	6
Wilbraham et al. (2005)	1	1	0	0	1	-3	3	2	2	1	8
Physics											
Giancoli											
Giancoli (1974)	3	3	3	1	1	3	3	2	1	2	22
Giancoli (1980)	2	3	3	0	3	3	3	3	1	0	21
Giancoli (1984)	2	1	3	0	3	0	3	3	0	0	15
Giancoli (1986)	2	1	3	1	3	0	3	3	1	1	18
Giancoli (1995)	2	1	3	0	3	0	3	3	1	1	17
Giancoli (2000)	2	1	3	0	3	0	3	3	0	0	15
Conceptual Physics											
Hewitt (1971)	1	0	0	0	2	3	2	0	0	0	8
Hewitt (1977)	1	0	0	0	2	3	2	0	0	0	8
Hewitt (1987)	2	0	0	1	3	-2	3	-1	0	0	6

(Continued)

Table 2.3 (Continued)

Textbook content and series	NOS aspect										Total score
	Empirical	Inferential	Creative	Theory-driven	Tentative	Scientific method	Theories	Laws	Social	Social, cultural	
Hewitt (1992)	2	0	2	1	3	-2	3	-1	0	0	8
Hewitt (1998)	2	0	0	1	3	-2	3	-1	0	0	6
Principles and Problems											
Murphy and Smoot (1972)	1	2	0	0	0	-3	1	0	0	0	1
Murphy and Smoot (1977)	1	2	0	0	0	-3	1	-1	0	1	1
Murphy et al. (1986)	1	0	0	0	1	-3	1	0	0	0	0
Zitzewitz et al. (1992)	1	0	3	0	0	3	1	1	0	1	10
Zitzewitz (2002)	2	0	0	0	1	2	3	1	1	2	11
Holt Physics											
Serway and Faughn (1999)	1	0	0	0	0	-3	0	0	0	0	-2
Serway and Faughn (2006)	1	0	0	0	0	-2	0	0	0	0	-1

range of -30 to +30 cumulative points, scores for biology textbooks ranged from -4 to +11 points, with two textbooks (12.5 percent) earning negative cumulative scores, and scores for 10 of 16 textbooks (62.5 percent) falling in the narrow range of-4 to +6 points. The chemistry textbooks cumulative scores ranged from-7 to +12 points, with the overwhelming majority of the textbooks (79 percent) falling in the range from-7 to +7 points. Four textbooks (29 percent) had negative, and 10 (71 percent) had positive, cumulative scores ranging from 3 to 12 points. With the exception of the Giancoli series, total scores for physics textbooks similarly ranged from-2 to +11 points, with two textbooks (11 percent) earning negative cumulative scores, and scores for 9 of 18 textbooks (50 percent) falling in the range from-2 to +8 points.

By far, Giancoli's series achieved the highest cumulative NOS scores (+15 to +22 points), and featured informed explicit or implicit representations of most target NOS aspects. Specifically, almost all Giancoli textbooks had explicit, accurate, and consistent representations of the tentative and creative NOS, and nature of scientific theories and laws. The inferential and empirical NOS also were well represented across this series. Giancoli (1974, 1980) explicitly debunked the myth of 'The Scientific Method' while keeping silent on this aspect in the other textbooks. In contrast, his textbooks mostly remained silent on the theory-driven NOS, and remained silent or conveyed implicit, informed representations of the social NOS and social-cultural embeddedness of science.

The Giancoli series surely was an outlier among physics textbooks. Indeed, 75 to 100 percent of the other physics textbooks remained silent on the inferential, creative, theory-driven, social, and social-cultural NOS. A third of these textbooks presented implicit, naïve representations of the nature of laws, while the remainder kept silent on this NOS aspect. A single 'Scientific Method' was expressly and naively confirmed in two-thirds of these physics textbooks, with only 4 of 12 textbooks (33 percent) explicitly dismissing this myth. The textbooks fared better in representing the empirical NOS, nature of theories, and to a lesser extent, the tentative NOS (7 of 12 textbooks).

None of the chemistry textbooks attended to (accurately or otherwise) all target aspects of NOS. For instance, the first *ChemCom* textbook in the series (ACS, 1988) did not address 6 of the 10 NOS aspects. Even Toon et al. (1968), which featured the highest cumulative score of +12 points, remained silent on four NOS aspects. The social and cultural embeddedness of science and social aspects of the scientific enterprise were not addressed in 86 percent and 57 percent of the chemistry textbooks, respectively. Similarly, the theory-driven NOS was not addressed or inadequately addressed in 71 percent of the analyzed textbooks. Most disturbing was the fact that, with one exception (Toon et al., 1968), all 14 textbooks scored a -3 or -2 with regards to the diehard myth of the 'Scientific Method.' Toon et al. (1968) was the *only* textbook that provided more informed views of this NOS aspect emphasizing certain attitudes and habits of mind that typify scientists' work rather than detailing a prescribed way for 'doing science.' Chemistry textbooks did better in terms of addressing the inferential and empirical NOS, as well as explanatory, predictive, and well-supported nature of theories. For instance, while two textbooks remained silent on the inferential NOS, four (29 percent) addressed this aspect implicitly, and the remaining eight (57 percent) addressed it in explicit and consistent ways. All chemistry textbooks adequately addressed the empirical NOS. Textbook treatment of the nature of laws, and creative and tentative NOS were mixed, but leaned more toward naïve than informed views. Half of the chemistry textbooks either did not address (21 percent) or inadequately addressed (29 percent) the nature of laws. The latter four textbooks scored a -3 (Table 2.3) for explicitly equating laws with 'facts' or attributing 'certainty' to them.

Table 2.3 shows similar disconcerting patterns in the treatment of NOS in the biology textbooks. Nine of 16 textbooks (56 percent) explicitly confirmed the myth of 'The Scientific Method' while five textbooks (31 percent) remained silent on this aspect. A majority of biology textbooks (75 percent) also did not address the creative NOS, and only four (25 percent) conveyed more informed views in this regard. Most textbooks featured implicit, informed representations of the nature of theories (94 percent), inferential NOS (81 percent), and social-cultural NOS (75 percent). Treatment of the tentative, theory-driven, and social NOS, as well as nature of laws was mixed with equal subsets of textbooks remaining silent on, or conveying implicit naïve or informed explicit representations of, these NOS aspects. The cumulative NOS scores for the *BSCS* series (+6 to +11 points) were substantially higher than those for the *Biology: Dynamics of Life* (-1 to 0 points) and *Modern Biology* (-4 to +6 points) series. However, the majority of *BSCS* textbooks remained silent on the theory-driven and social NOS, myth of 'The Scientific Method,' and nature of laws, while the rest conveyed only implicit informed messages about these NOS aspects.

Changes in NOS Representations During the Past Several Decades

Table 2.3 indicates that, in most cases, the individual NOS aspects and cumulative NOS scores for the biology, chemistry, and physics textbook series were markedly 'stable' over the course of several decades. It was common for the same NOS aspect to be represented in the exact same manner over an extended period of time. For instance, the *Modern Biology* series received a score of -2 owing to naïve affirmations of a single 'Scientific Method' over the course of 44 years (1958 to 2002). This period, it is noteworthy, is inclusive of the publication of several seminal philosophical works that specifically debunked this notion (e.g., Feyerabend, 1975; Kuhn, 1962). Similarly, over the course of these 44 years, this series conveyed implicit informed messages of the inferential, and remained silent on the creative, NOS. Table 2.3 shows that similar patterns are discernable in other textbook series. The same applies for cumulative NOS scores. For example, scores for the seven *BSCS* textbooks ranged from +6 to +11 points over the course of more than 30 years. Indeed, with the *BSCS* (1985) textbook aside, these scores would range from +10 to +11 points over the same period. Similarly, the total scores for the three *Modern Chemistry* and five *Conceptual Physics* textbooks ranged from +7 to +9 and +6 to +8 points over the course of about three decades, respectively. Indeed, on the 60-point scale that ranged from -30 to +30 points, the total change in cumulative NOS scores for 8 of the 12 analyzed textbooks series, which spanned one to four decades, ranged from 1 to 3 points (i.e., a 1.7 to 5 percent total change in scores).

Relatively larger changes were evident in the case of the remaining four series. The total NOS score for the *Holt Chemistry* textbooks decreased from +12 for the 1968 edition to -7 points for the 2004 edition (32.7 percent change). This change owed to the reversal from explicit or implicit informed, to explicit or implicit naïve representations of several NOS aspects, including the nature of laws, and creative and tentative NOS. A positive change was evident in the case of the *Physics: Principles and Problems* series, where scores increased from +1 to +11 points from 1972 to 2002 (16.7 percent change). This change was mostly due to a major reversal (-3 to +2) in addressing the myth of 'The Scientific Method' and speaking to the nature of theories (+1 to +3). Total NOS scores for the *Modern Biology* series vacillated between -4 to +6 points (16.7 percent change) over the course of four decades, but mostly kept in the range of 0 to 6 points. Scores for the Giancoli series decreased from +22 to +15 points over the course of 26 years (11 percent change). This difference owed largely to keeping silent on the myth of the method in the post-1980 textbooks *versus* having explicitly debunked this notion in earlier textbooks. It could be seen that, where evident, larger changes in overall NOS scores for the analyzed textbook series did not exhibit a consistent pattern.

Finally, an examination of the data, with scores for individual NOS aspects and cumulative NOS scores pooled by content area and for all textbooks, did not reveal any particularly major or persistent patterns. In effect, to the extent that the selected textbooks represent the space of U.S. secondary biology, chemistry, and physics textbooks, it could be claimed that representations of NOS in these textbooks did not significantly change over the course of about five decades.

Representations of NOS by Content Area

As Table 2.3 shows, almost all analyzed textbooks conveyed informed (albeit sometimes implicit and at others explicit) representations of the empirical NOS and nature of theories. In comparison, with a few exceptions, almost all textbooks conveyed explicit naïve affirmations of the myth of a single 'Scientific Method.' The majority of all textbooks did not address the social NOS. Most biology and physics textbooks remained silent on the creative NOS, while several chemistry textbooks had naïve representations of this aspect. The treatment of scientific laws spanned the gamut in the case of each content area, with a majority of the textbooks either not addressing or naively representing this NOS aspect. Physics textbooks largely remained silent on, while biology and chemistry textbooks conveyed naïve views of, the tentative and theory-driven NOS. Finally, while almost all chemistry and the majority of physics textbooks did not address the sociocultural NOS, almost all biology textbooks fared better in representing this NOS aspect.

With a few exceptions, cumulative NOS scores were not substantially different when the analyzed textbooks were grouped by content area. However, physics textbooks had substantially higher scores than the other two content areas for the creative and tentative NOS. In comparison, scores for the inferential NOS were higher for chemistry textbooks when compared to the biology and physics textbooks, while the biology textbooks seemed to have the upper hand when it came to the sociocultural embeddedness of science. Thus, no consistent pattern was evident in terms of the few differences in scores for a subset of NOS aspects across textbooks by content area.

Author Versus Publisher Effect

Our first study suggested a much stronger 'author effect' compared to a 'publisher effect' in shaping NOS representations in secondary chemistry textbooks. While acknowledging an author effect, DiGiuseppe (2014) argued that textbook publishers also have a substantial influence. It might as well be the case that both author and publisher teams influence messages about NOS conveyed in the final product. Still, the question remains as to which group exhibits the larger influence. As noted above, in the following analyses, a textbook's lead authors were taken to stand as proxy for the authoring team (lead authors, science writers, content and teacher reviewers, etc.) that brings technical scientific and pedagogical expertise to bear on the development process. The publishing company stood as proxy for a publisher's team (designers, editors, and production personnel) that mainly speaks to textbook marketability, time and resources devoted to the development process, and design and production of the various textbook elements.

Some data from our second study (see Table 2.3) were not revealing of the relative impact of publisher versus author on textbook NOS representations due to possible interaction effects. For example, total NOS scores for the first three *Physics: Principles and Problems* textbooks (Murphy et al., 1986; Murphy & Smoot, 1972, 1977) by Charles E. Merrill Publishing went virtually unchanged at +1, +1, and 0 points. Next, under Glencoe/McGraw-Hill, scores for textbooks in this series substantially increased by 10 points (Zitzewitz, 2002; Zitzewitz et al., 1992). Nonetheless, the latter change was not necessarily evidence of a more substantial publisher effect, because it was coupled with a simultaneous change in author leadership from Murphy to Zitzewitz. Other data, however, were much more telling about the relative impact of author versus publisher.

To start with, the NOS scores for textbooks by the same author(s) or overlapping groups of authors and same publisher were markedly stable irrespective of the number of editions or overall duration of these partnerships. Total differences in cumulative NOS scores for such textbooks were on the order of one or two points on the 60-point scale for series that spanned one to four decades. For example, the overall NOS scores for the: two *Biology: Dynamics of Life* textbooks by Biggs et al. (1995, 2004) published by Glencoe/McGraw-Hill were 0 and -1; three *Physics: Principles and Problems* textbooks by Murphy and colleagues (Murphy & Smoot, 1972, 1977; Murphy et al., 1986) published by Charles E. Merrill were +1, +1, and 0; and three *Modern Chemistry* textbooks by Metcalf and colleagues (Metcalfe et al., 1966, 1982, 2002) published by Holt Rinehart and Winston were +9, +7, and +7 (see Table 2.3). Second, albeit released by different publishers, overall scores for textbooks in series by the same author(s) or sponsoring organizations also remained strikingly stable. For example, scores for the two *ChemCom* textbooks published by Kendall Hunt (ACS, 1988, 1993) and the third published by W.H. Freeman (ACS, 2002) ranged from +3 to +6 points. Scores for four *BSCS* textbooks published by Houghton Mifflin (BSCS, 1963, 1968, 1973, 1980) and two later textbooks in the series published by D.C. Heath (BSCS, 1990, 1996) were +10 or +11 points, with the exception of BSCS (1985) at +6 points. Similarly, NOS scores for the five *Conceptual Physics* textbooks published by Little Brown and Company (Hewitt, 1971, 1977) and Addison-Wesley (Hewitt, 1987, 1992, 1998) ranged from +6 to +8 points. Finally, albeit featuring wider variability (+15 to +22 points), all six physics textbooks by Giancoli earned the highest total NOS scores among all textbooks despite having been released by different publishers (Harcourt Brace Jovanovich *versus* Prentice Hall). Thus, it could be seen that an authors' group or sponsoring organization's framework for NOS as conveyed in their textbooks remained virtually unchanged across long spans of time, irrespective of concurrent changes in scholarship on HPSPS or emphases related to NOS in contemporaneous science education reform documents.

In comparison, total NOS scores for textbooks in the same series, carrying the same title, and released by the same publisher were more substantially varied when taken on by different authors. For example, between 1968 and 2004, Holt Rinehart and Winston released at least four textbooks under the title of *Holt Chemistry*. Overall NOS scores for these textbooks varied widely as different groups handled authorship: from +12 points for Toon et al. (1968) to +6 points for Bolton et al. (1973), then sharply down to -6 points when Tocci and Viehl (1996) served as authors. Note that the latter score reversal persisted with a score of -7 points into the 2004 edition (Myers, Oldham, & Tocci, 2004) with Tocci overlapping between the last two author groups. Similarly, Holt Rinehart and Winston released at least six *Modern Biology* textbooks between 1963 and 2002. Scores for these textbooks varied from -4 to +6 points under different author groups with most substantial changes evident when author groups were mutually exclusive, as was the case with the Moon et al. (1963) score of -4 versus the Feldkamp (2002) scores of +6 points.

Another interesting pattern also is illuminating when it comes to the relative impact of authors versus publishers on textbook NOS representations. If we assumed that publishers have some systematic mindset, framework, or a set of criteria or policies (as these might pertain to time, textbook pages, expertise allotted to the textbook development process, marketability, alignment with pertinent standards, etc.) by which to approach decisions related to how NOS is represented in a science textbook, then it is reasonable to expect that the *same* publishing company developing two secondary science textbooks around the *same* time period would produce textbooks with fairly similar NOS representations. There are several data points that suggest this not to be the case (see Table 2.3). For example, *Holt Chemistry* (Myers et al., 2004), *Modern Biology* (Feldkamp, 2002), and *Holt Physics* (Serway & Faughn, 2006) featured widely different total NOS scores (-7, +6, and -1 points, respectively), even though all three textbooks were published by Holt Rinehart and Winston within the short span of four years. Similarly, *Modern Biology* (Moon et al., 1963) and *Modern Chemistry* (Metcalfe et al., 1966), both published by Holt Rinehart and Winston, featured radically different overall scores of -4 and +9 points, respectively. This also was the case for *Biology: Dynamics of Life* (Biggs et al., 1995; 0 points) and *Physics: Principles and Problems* (Zitzewitz et al., 1992; +10 points), which were both published by Glencoe/McGraw-Hill.

One could argue though that the above assumption is not reasonable because there might be substantial and consistent differences in terms of NOS representations by content area. Our data, as noted above, did not reveal any such differences. However, even if we were to set this finding aside and proceed with the much narrower prediction—that is, that the *same* publisher developing two secondary science textbooks around the *same* time period and addressing the *same* content area would produce textbooks with fairly similar NOS representations—we still find that the present data do not support this narrow expectation. For instance, *Modern Chemistry* (Davis et al., 2002) and *Holt Chemistry* (Myers et al., 2004) both published by Holt Rinehart and Winston within the span of two years, have drastically different cumulative NOS scores of +7 and -7, respectively. Authors, again, emerge as the major factor that would explain observed differences in NOS scores. Put together, the above lines of evidence and arguments show very convincingly that, as substantial as a publisher's impact might be on the representations of NOS conveyed in secondary science textbooks, this impact is outweighed by the impact of the textbook authors. This differential impact, it will be argued in the following section, is not trivial and has significant implications for addressing major shortcomings as far as addressing NOS in secondary science textbooks.

Implications and Recommendations

Our studies make for some very disconcerting findings. The analyzed secondary biology, chemistry, and physics textbooks dominate the U.S. market and impact science teaching and learning for the greater majority of U.S. secondary students and, highly likely, students of other nations given the global reach of the massive U.S. textbook industry (Butler, 2009). The textbooks devote miniscule attention (as measured in pages) to epistemological dimensions of scientific knowledge and the workings of the scientific enterprise. It is very hard to imagine that students would engage in any meaningful thinking about NOS themes, which have been consistently touted as central to precollege science education reform efforts of the past 60 years, when a 1000-page biology textbook (e.g., Serway & Faughn, 2006) dedicates a mere five pages (0.5 percent of its content) to NOS. Equally disconcerting is the fact that, in several cases, this minimal content only conveyed naïve messages about NOS. In the case of the latter textbook, the single clear message conveyed in those five pages was that scientific practice follows a prescribed set of sequential steps.

The landscape of the analyzed textbooks, nonetheless, did feature some bright spots, which could be meaningfully expanded and strengthened. For instance, Giancoli's textbooks presented articulate-explicit or implicit informed treatments of several NOS themes. In earlier editions (e.g., Giancoli, 1974), most of the NOS content (about 55 percent) was concentrated in a few (about 6) pages of the introductory chapter and sparsely revisited or reinforced in later chapters. Explicit, informed messages about NOS in an introductory chapter would serve as a robust advance organizer for promoting learning about NOS. However, students would hardly internalize rich and lasting NOS understandings if these introductory messages were not revisited and discussed in the context of, as well as anchored in, learning about specific concepts, theories, practices, and/or historical vignettes (Abd-El-Khalick, 2013, 2014; Wahbeh & Abd-El-Khalick, 2014). Later editions of Giancoli's textbooks featured more of the latter approach where, for instance, the 1995 edition had about 15 percent of the NOS pages in the introductory chapter, while the remaining pages were spread across the physics content. Still, NOS was addressed in only about 2.2 percent of this edition's pages.

Another interesting case was the BSCS textbooks, which featured consistent messages about the empirical, inferential, and tentative NOS, the nature of theories, and the social-cultural embeddedness of science. The messages were explicit and partially informed, or implicit informed, and none were naïve in any respect. Additionally, some of these textbooks (BSCS, 1963, 1973, 1980, 1996) dedicated about 3 to 3.5 percent of their pages to NOS, which placed them on the higher end among the analyzed textbooks. Nonetheless, there surely is much room for improvement as this series remained largely silent on other NOS aspects, particularly the theory-driven and social NOS, as well as the myth of 'The Scientific Method.' Arguably, internalizing the latter aspects are crucial for the meaningful engagement of students with several scientific practices (NRC, 2012).

The above two series serve to show that there are some tangible and informed efforts to address NOS in secondary science textbooks, albeit the efforts remained rather steady as compared to featuring improvements over the past four decades. The overall picture emerging from our findings, however, is that one of the more powerful factors influencing school science instruction (Chiappetta et al., 1991; Hashweh, 1987; McDonald, 2016) most likely has been, and continues to be, one of the major *obstacles* to realizing a persistent and central theme for U.S. precollege science education. Similar results from analyses undertaken in other nations (e.g., DiGiuseppe, 2014; Irez, 2009; Vesterinen et al., 2013) strongly suggest this to be the case beyond the borders of the United States. This state of affairs, namely, the dismal attention accorded to epistemological dimensions of science in commercial science textbooks, forms the backdrop for current reform efforts in the United States (i.e., NGSS Lead States, 2013) and those around the world, which continue to ascribe centrality to NOS as a valued instructional outcome for precollege education (Lederman & Lederman, 2014). The question remains: how to address or ameliorate this state of affairs?

First, the present findings empirically and convincingly demonstrate that unequivocal and strong emphasis on the teaching and learning about NOS in the rhetoric and documents of national reform efforts most likely has had very little impact on the respective content of textbooks. The 12 secondary science textbook series analyzed in this study, literally, survived *unscathed* four decades of widely publicized and circulated national reform documents (e.g., AAAS, 1971, 1990, 1993; NRC, 1996, 2000; NSTA, 1982). Overall, cumulative NOS scores for textbooks within each series either remained largely unchanged or decreased over the course of the decades, which featured the aforementioned contemporaneous reform efforts. Indeed, our findings indicate that textbook authors continue to address NOS in practically the same manner over the course of decades with little regard to contemporaneous science education reforms or changes in scholarship on HPSPS. Second, the same evidence strongly suggests that concerted and sustained efforts, which are explicitly intended to draw the attention of textbook publishers to the curricular imperatives of reforms (e.g., Kesidou & Roseman, 2002; Roseman et al., 2010; Stern & Roseman, 2004) equally are unlikely to impact the content of commercial science textbooks when it comes to NOS. The latter approach attempted to impact the marketability of textbooks by alerting consumers (i.e., science teachers, and school district and state personnel) to the alignment, or lack thereof, of the textbooks with specific reforms documents (i.e., AAAS, 1990, 1993, in which NOS serves as one of the main organizing principles). In a sense, the inertia associated with the massive nature and enormity of the school textbook industry renders such efforts almost futile.

In our first study, we had called for a focus on assessment as a means to move this domain forward. We argued that shaping performance assessments relative to NOS—which are primary drivers of classroom instruction—could serve as a powerful tool to focus textbook authors' and publishers' attention on generating broader and more informed treatments of NOS in commercial science textbooks. Over and above, interestingly enough, the most significant finding of our second study might suggest an equally, or even more, fruitful pathway to impact this treatment. Our findings demonstrate that, no matter what impact is exercised by a textbook publisher on its treatment of NOS, the impact of authors clearly outweighs that of the publishers. Thus, instead of targeting our efforts toward 'publishers,' who in essence are likely impenetrable corporate entities, the science education community would be better served to direct these efforts toward the authors. The latter are scientists, science teachers, and science writers, who deeply care about science, and science teaching and learning, as well as share our ethos of promoting scientific literacy among precollege students, which entail an informed understanding of the epistemological underpinnings of scientific knowledge and science practices. Science education organizations could develop evidence-based position papers, which are then communicated to textbook authors, and coupled with making available to those authors resources—including materials and personnel, to provide feedback on a textbook's treatment of NOS themes, as well as ways in which such treatment could be broadened and deepened, and then anchored to the textbook's scientific content and associated science processes and practices.

Note

* Used here with permission from Wiley publishers.

References

Abd-El-Khalick, F. (2005). Developing deeper understandings of nature of science: The impact of a philosophy of science course on preservice science teachers' views and instructional planning. *International Journal of Science Education, 27*(1), 15–42.

Abd-El-Khalick, F. (2012a). Nature of science in science education: Toward a coherent framework for synergistic research and development. In B. J. Fraser, K. Tobin, & C. McRobbie (Eds.), *Second international handbook of science education* (Vol. 2, pp. 1041–1060). Dordrecht, the Netherlands: Springer.

Abd-El-Khalick, F. (2012b). Examining the sources for our understandings about science: Enduring conflations and critical issues in research on nature of science in science education. *International Journal of Science Education, 34*(3), 353–374.

Abd-El-Khalick, F. (2013). Teaching *with* and *about* nature of science, and science teacher knowledge domains. *Science & Education, 22*(9), 2087–2107.

Abd-El-Khalick, F. (2014). The evolving landscape related to assessment of nature of science. In N. G. Lederman & S. K. Abell (Eds.), *Handbook of research on science education* (2nd ed., pp. 621–650). Mahwah, NJ: Lawrence Erlbaum.

Abd-El-Khalick, F., & Lederman, N. G. (2000a). Improving science teachers' conceptions of the nature of science: A critical review of the literature. *International Journal of Science Education, 22*(7), 665–701.

Abd-El-Khalick, F., & Lederman, N. G. (2000b). The influence of history of science courses on students' views of nature of science. *Journal of Research in Science Teaching, 37*(10), 1057–1095.

Abd-El-Khalick, F., Myers, J. Y., Summers, R., Brunner, J., Waight, N., Wahbeh, N., Zeineddin, A., & Belarmino, J. (2016). A longitudinal analysis of the extent and manner of representations of nature of science in U.S. high school biology and physics textbooks. *Journal of Research in Science Teaching, 54*(1), 82–120.

Abd-El-Khalick, F., Waters, M., & Le, A. (2008). Representations of nature of science in high school chemistry textbooks over the past four decades. *Journal of Research in Science Teaching, 45*(7), 835–855.

American Association for the Advancement of Science. (1971). *A guide to inservice instruction*. Lexington, MA: Xerox Education Services.

American Association for the Advancement of Science. (1990). *Science for all Americans*. New York: Oxford University Press.

American Association for the Advancement of Science. (1993). *Benchmarks for science literacy*. New York: Oxford University Press.

American Association for the Advancement of Science. (2001). *Project 2061: Atlas of science literacy*. Washington, DC: American Association for the Advancement of Science.

American Association of Publishers: PreK-12 Learning Group. (2013, September 8). *Sales, enrollment, and market trends in K-12.* Retrieved from www.aepweb.org/aepweb/?p=3261&option=com_wordpress&Itemid=68

American Chemical Society. (1988). *ChemCom: Chemistry in the community*. Dubuque, IA: Kendall Hunt.

American Chemical Society. (1993). *ChemCom: Chemistry in the community* (2nd ed.). Dubuque, IA: Kendall Hunt.

American Chemical Society. (2002). *Chemistry in the community: ChemCom* (4th ed.). New York: W. H. Freeman.

Atkin, J. M., & Black, P. (2007). History of curriculum reform in the United States and United Kingdom. In S. K. Abell & N. G. Lederman (Eds.), *Handbook of research on science education* (pp. 781–806). Mahwah, NJ: Lawrence Erlbaum.

Banilower, E. R., Smith, P. S., Weiss, I. R., Malzahn, K. A., Campbell, K. M., & Weis, A. M. (2013). *Report of the 2012 national survey of science and mathematics education*. Chapel Hill, NC: Horizon Research.

Bell, R. L., Lederman, N. G., & Abd-El-Khalick, F. (1998). Implicit and explicit approaches to teaching the nature of science: An explicit response to Palmquist and Finley. *Journal of Research in Science Teaching, 35*(9), 1057–1061.

Biggs, A., Hagins, W. C., Kapicka, C., Lundgren, L., Rillero, P., Tallman, K. G., & Zike, D. (2004). *Biology: The dynamics of life* (teacher wrap-around ed.). New York: Glencoe/McGraw-Hill.

Biggs, A., Kapicka, C., & Lundgren, L. (1995). *Biology: The dynamics of life*. New York: Glencoe/McGraw-Hill.

Biological Sciences Curriculum Study. (1963). *Biological science: Molecules to man* (blue version). Boston, MA: Houghton Mifflin Company.

Biological Sciences Curriculum Study. (1968). *Biological science: Molecules to man* (blue version, revised ed.). Boston, MA: Houghton Mifflin Company.

Biological Sciences Curriculum Study. (1973). *Biological science: Molecules to man: BSCS blue version* (3rd ed.). Boston, MA: Houghton Mifflin Company.

Biological Sciences Curriculum Study. (1980). *Biological science: A molecular approach: BSCS blue version* (4th ed.). Boston, MA: Houghton Mifflin Company.

Biological Sciences Curriculum Study. (1985). *Biological science: A molecular approach: BSCS blue version* (5th ed.). Lexington, MA: D.C. Heath and Company.

Biological Sciences Curriculum Study. (1990). *Biological science: A molecular approach: BSCS blue version* (6th ed., teacher's annotated ed.). Lexington, MA: D.C. Heath and Company.

Biological Sciences Curriculum Study. (1996). *Biological science: A molecular approach: BSCS blue version* (7th ed.). Lexington, MA: D.C. Heath and Company.

Bolton, R. P., Lamphere, E.V., Menesini, M., & Huang, P. C. (1973). *Action chemistry: Matter, energy, change.* New York: Holt, Rinehart and Winston.

Brito, A., Rodriguez, M. A., & Niaz, M. (1995). A reconstruction of development of the periodic table based on history and philosophy of science and its implications for general chemistry textbooks. *Journal of Research in Science Teaching, 42,* 84–111.

Butler, D. (2009, April 2). The textbook of the future. *Nature, 458,* 568–570.

California Department of Education. (2016). *Curriculum framework & instructional materials: Instructional materials adoption.* Retrieved May 25, 2016, from www.cde.ca.gov/ci/cr/cf/imagen.asp

Chiappetta, E. L., & Fillman, D. A. (2007). Analysis of five high school biology textbooks used in the United States for inclusion of the nature of science. *International Journal of Science Education, 29*(15), 1847–1868.

Chiappetta, E. L., Sethna, G. H., & Fillman, D. A. (1991). A quantitative analysis of high school chemistry textbooks for scientific literacy themes and expository learning aids. *Journal of Research in Science Teaching, 30,* 787–797.

Cohen, J. (1968). Weighted kappa: Nominal scale agreement with provision for scaled disagreement or partial credit. *Psychological Bulletin, 70*(4), 213–220.

Collins, G. (2012, June 21). How Texas inflicts bad textbooks on us. *The New York Review of Books.* Retrieved May 25, 2016, from www.nybooks.com/articles/2012/06/21/how-texas-inflicts-bad-textbooks-on-us/

Davis, R. E., Metcalfe, H. C., Williams, J. E., & Castka, J. F. (2002). *Modern chemistry.* Austin, TX: Holt, Rinehart and Winston.

DiGiuseppe, M. (2014). Representing nature of science in a science textbook: Exploring author-editor-publisher interactions. *International Journal of Science Education, 36,* 1061–1082.

Feldkamp, S. (Exec. Ed.). (2002). *Modern biology.* Austin, TX: Holt, Rinehart, and Winston.

Feyerabend, P. (1975). *Against method.* New York: New Left Books.

Fleiss, J. L. (1971). Measuring nominal scale agreement among many raters. *Psychological Bulletin, 76,* 378–382.

Fleiss, J. L. (1981). *Statistical methods for rates and proportions* (2nd ed.). New York: John Wiley.

Fleiss, J. L., Cohen, J., & Everitt, B. S. (1969). Large sample standard errors of kappa and weighted kappa. *Psychological Bulletin, 72,* 323–327.

Gericke, N. M., & Hagberg, M. (2010). Conceptual incoherence as a result of the use of multiple historical models in school textbooks. *Research in Science Education, 40,* 605–623.

Giancoli, D. C. (1974). *The ideas of physics*. New York: Harcourt Brace Jovanovich.

Giancoli, D. C. (1980). *Physics: Principles with applications*. Englewood Cliffs, NJ: Prentice Hall.

Giancoli, D. C. (1984). *General physics*. Englewood Cliffs, NJ: Prentice Hall.

Giancoli, D. C. (1986). *The ideas of physics* (3rd ed.). New York: Harcourt Brace Jovanovich.

Giancoli, D. C. (1995). *Physics: Principles with applications* (4th ed.). Englewood Cliffs, NJ: Prentice Hall.

Giancoli, D. C. (2000). *Physics for scientists & engineers with modern physics* (3rd ed.). Upper Saddle River, NJ: Prentice Hall.

Hashweh, M. (1987). Effects of subject-matter knowledge in the teaching of biology and physics. *Teaching and Teacher Education, 3*(2), 109–120.

Hewitt, P. G. (1971). *Conceptual physics: A new introduction to your environment*. Boston, MA: Little, Brown and Company.

Hewitt, P. G. (1977). *Conceptual physics: A new introduction to your environment* (3rd ed.). Boston, MA: Little, Brown and Company.

Hewitt, P. G. (1987). *Conceptual physics: A high school physics program*. Menlo Park, CA: Addison-Wesley.

Hewitt, P. G. (1992). *Conceptual physics: The high school physics program* (2nd ed.). Menlo Park, CA: Addison-Wesley.

Hewitt, P. G. (1998). *Conceptual physics* (8th ed.). Menlo Park, CA: Addison-Wesley.

Irez, S. (2009). Nature of science as depicted in Turkish biology textbooks. *Science Education, 93*, 422–447.

Jones, M. G., & Carter, G. (2007). Science teacher attitudes and beliefs. In S. Abell & N. G. Lederman (Eds.), *Handbook of research in science education* (pp. 1067–1104). Mahwah, NJ: Lawrence Erlbaum.

Kesidou, S., & Roseman, J. E. (2002). How well do middle school science programs measure up? Findings from project 2061's curriculum review. *Journal of Research in Science Teaching, 39*(6), 522–549.

Khine, M. S. (Ed.). (2013). *Critical analysis of science textbooks: Evaluating instructional effectiveness*. Dordrecht, the Netherlands: Springer.

Khishfe, R., & Abd-El-Khalick, F. (2002). Influence of explicit reflective versus implicit inquiry-oriented instruction on sixth graders' views of nature of science. *Journal of Research in Science Teaching, 39*(7), 551–578.

Kuhn, T. S. (1962). *The structure of scientific revolutions*. Chicago: University of Chicago Press.

Lederman, N. G. (2007). Nature of science: Past, present, and future. In S. K. Abell & N. G. Lederman (Eds.), *Handbook of research on science education* (pp. 831–879). Mahwah, NJ: Lawrence Erlbaum.

Lederman, N. G., Abd-El-Khalick, F., Bell, R. L., & Schwartz, R. (2002). Views of nature of science questionnaire (VNOS): Toward valid and meaningful assessment of learners' conceptions of nature of science. *Journal of Research in Science Teaching, 39*(6), 497–521.

Lederman, N. G., & Lederman, J. (2014). Research on teaching and learning of nature of science. In N. G. Lederman & S. K. Abell (Eds.), *Handbook of research on science education* (Vol. 2, pp. 600–620). Mahwah, NJ: Lawrence Erlbaum.

Lumpe, A. T., & Beck, J. (1996). A profile of high school biology textbooks using scientific literacy recommendations. *American Biology Teacher, 58*(3), 147–153.

McDonald, C. V. (2016). Evaluating junior secondary science textbook usage in Australian schools. *Research in Science Education, 46*, 481–509.

Metcalfe, H. C., Williams, J. E., & Castka, J. F. (1966). *Modern chemistry*. New York: Holt, Rinehart and Winston.

Metcalfe, H. C., Williams, J. E., & Castka, J. F. (1982). *Modern chemistry*. New York: Holt, Rinehart and Winston.

Moon, T. J. (1921). *Biology for beginners*. New York: Henry Holt and Company.

Moon, T. J., Mann, P. B., Otto, J. H., Kuntz, J. A., & Dury, E. J. (1958). *Modern biology: Gregor Mendel edition*. New York: Henry Holt and Company.

Moon, T. J., Otto, J. H., & Towle, A. (1963). *Modern biology*. New York: Holt, Rinehart, and Winston.

Murphy, J. T., & Smoot, R. C. (1972). *Physics: Principles and problems*. Columbus, OH: Charles E. Merrill Publishing Co.

Murphy, J. T., & Smoot, R. C. (1977). *Physics: Principles and problems* (teacher's annotated ed.). Columbus, OH: Charles E. Merrill Publishing Co.

Murphy, J. T., Zitzewitz, P. W., & Hollon, J. M. (1986). *Physics: Principles and problems*. Columbus, OH: Charles E. Merrill Publishing Co.

Myers, R. T., Oldham, K. B., & Tocci, S. (2004). *Holt chemistry: Visualizing matter*. Austin, TX: Holt, Rinehart and Winston.

National Research Council. (1996). *National science education standards*. Washington, DC: The National Academic Press.

National Research Council. (2012). *A framework for K-12 science education: Practices, crosscutting concepts, and core ideas*. Washington, DC: The National Academies Press.

National Science Teachers Association. (1982). *Science-technology-society: Science education for the 1980s* (An NSTA position statement). Washington, DC: Author.

National Science Teachers Association. (2000). *NSTA position statement: The nature of science*. Retrieved March 18, 2003, from www.nsta.org/159&psid=22

NGSS Lead States. (2013). *Next generation science standards: For states, by states*. Washington, DC: The National Academies Press.

Niaz, M. (1998). From cathode rays to alpha particles to quantum of action: A rational reconstruction of structure of the atom and its implications for chemistry textbooks. *Science Education, 82*, 527–552.

Niaz, M. (2000). A rational reconstruction of the kinetic molecular theory of gases based on history and philosophy of science and its implications for chemistry textbooks. *Instructional Science, 28*, 23–50.

Niaz, M., Klassen, S., McMillan, B., & Metz, D. (2010). Reconstruction of the history of the photoelectric effect and its implications for general physics textbooks. *Science Education, 94*, 903–931.

Otto, J. H., & Towle, A. (1973). *Modern biology*. New York: Holt, Rinehart, and Winston.

Otto, J. H., Towle, A., & Bradley, J.V. (1981). *Modern biology* (teacher's ed.). New York: Holt, Rinehart, and Winston.

Phillips, J. S., Strozak, V. S., & Wistrom, C. (1997). *Chemistry concepts and applications*. New York: Glencoe/McGraw Hill.

Phillips, J. S., Strozak, V. S., & Wistrom, C. (2005). *Chemistry concepts and applications*. Chicago: Glencoe/McGraw-Hill.

Rodriguez, M. A., & Niaz, M. (2002). How in spite of the rhetoric, history of chemistry has been ignored in presenting atomic structure in textbooks. *Science & Education, 11*, 423–421.

Roseman, J. E., Stern, L., & Koppal, M. (2010). A method for analyzing the coherence of high school biology textbooks. *Journal of Research in Science Teaching, 47*(1), 47–70.

Rutherford, F. J. (1964). The role of inquiry in science teaching. *Journal of Research in Science Teaching, 2*(2), 80–84.

Sandoval, W. A., & Morrison, K. (2003). High school students' ideas about theories and theory change after a biological inquiry unit. *Journal of Research in Science Teaching, 40*(4), 369–392.

Serway, R. A., & Faughn, J. S. (1999). *Holt physics.* Austin, TX: Holt, Rinehart, and Winston.

Serway, R. A., & Faughn, J. S. (2006). *Holt physics* (teacher ed.). Austin, TX: Holt, Rinehart, and Winston.

Shiland, T. W. (1997). Quantum mechanics and conceptual change in high school chemistry textbooks. *Journal of Research in Science Teaching, 34,* 535–545.

Stern, L., & Roseman, J. E. (2004). Can middle-school science textbooks help students learn important ideas? Findings from project 2061's curriculum evaluation study: Life science. *Journal of Research in Science Teaching, 41*(6), 538–568.

Texas Education Agency. (2016). *Curriculum & instructional materials: Review and adoption process proclamations.* Retrieved May 25, 2016, from http://tea.texas.gov/interiorpage.aspx?id=2147486662

Tocci, S., & Viehland, C. (1996). *Holt chemistry: Visualizing matter.* Austin, TX: Holt, Rinehart and Winston.

Toon, E. R., Ellis, G. L., & Brodkin, J. (1968). *Foundations of chemistry.* New York: Holt, Rinehart and Winston.

Towle, A. (1991). *Modern biology* (annotated teacher's ed.). New York: Holt, Rinehart, and Winston.

Towle, A. (1999). *Modern biology.* New York: Holt, Rinehart, and Winston.

Vesterinen, V-M., Akesla, M., & Lavonen, J. (2013). Quantitative analysis of representations of nature of science in Nordic upper secondary school textbooks using framework of analysis based on philosophy of chemistry. *Science & Education, 22,* 1839–1855.

Wahbeh, N., & Abd-El-Khalick, F. (2014). Revisiting the translation of nature of science understandings into instructional practice: Teachers' nature of science pedagogical context knowledge. *International Journal of Science Education, 36*(3), 425–466.

Weiss, I. R., Banilower, E. R., McMahon, K. C., & Smith, P. S. (2001). *Report of the 2000 national survey of science and mathematics education.* Chapel Hill, NC: Horizon Research.

Wilbraham, A. C., Staley, D. D., & Matta, M. S. (1997). *Chemistry* (4th ed.). New York: Addison-Wesley.

Wilbraham, A. C., Staley, D. D., Matta, M. S., & Waterman, E. L. (2005). *Chemistry* (6th ed.). Upper Saddle River, NJ: Pearson/Prentice Hall.

Wilson, L. L. (1954). A study of opinions related to the nature of science and its purpose in society. *Science Education, 38*(2), 159–164.

Zitzewitz, P. W. (2002). *Glencoe physics: Principles and problems.* New York: Glencoe/McGraw-Hill.

Zitzewitz, P. W., Davids, M., & Neff, R. F. (1992). *Merrill physics: Principles and problems.* New York: Glencoe/McGraw-Hill.

3 Relationship Between Domain-Specific and Domain-General Aspects of Nature of Science in Science Textbooks

Mansoor Niaz

Introduction

Students' and teachers' understanding of nature of science (NOS) has been the subject of considerable research in science education. This research shows that both students and teachers in most parts of the world lack an adequate understanding of many domain-general NOS aspects, including: theory-laden nature of experimental observations, tentative nature of scientific theories, competition among rival theories, alternative interpretations of the same experimental data leading to controversies, relationship between scientific constructs (models) and reality, relationship between scientific theories and laws, a universal or step-wise scientific method, inconsistent nature of scientific theories, objectivity in science, and scientific ideas are affected by their social and historical milieu (Dogan & Abd-El-Khalick, 2008; Erduran & Dagher, 2014; Hodson, 2014; Lederman, Bartos, & Lederman, 2014; McComas, 2014; Niaz, 2012, 2016). The relationship between NOS and history and philosophy of science (HPS) has been recognized in the literature (Abd-El-Khalick, 2005). Similarly, the role of history and philosophy of science in science textbooks has been the subject of considerable research (Niaz, 2014). The objective of this chapter is to present some of the NOS aspects (domain-general) along with historical episodes (domain-specific) as found in science textbooks, in order to facilitate a better understanding of the scientific enterprise. Most of these historical episodes form part of the science curriculum, and are included in high school and introductory level college science textbooks.

At this stage it is important to note that the science curriculum is itself a compendium of domain-specific aspects of NOS. However, these aspects by themselves lack the 'glue' necessary for facilitating students' understanding of the scientific enterprise. This glue is provided precisely by the domain-general aspects of NOS. Consequently, integration can be beneficial for the advancement of science education. Looking back, I am reminded of the debates at the National Association for Research in Science Teaching (NARST) conferences in the 1980s with respect to domain-general reasoning (Lawson-Piaget) and domain-specific prior knowledge (Novak-Ausubel). Those were heated debates that involved various members of the science education community. I recall having contributed to some aspects of this debate (cf. Niaz, 1993, 1995). What was the upshot of that debate? Perhaps both sides were wrong, as at present the science education community recognizes the importance of both scientific reasoning and prior content knowledge. According to Sternberg (1989), domain-generality and domain-specificity is a false dichotomy as it is much more fruitful to explore how the two interact. In a similar vein, Abd-El-Khalick (2012) has discussed the pitfalls involved in emphasizing only the domain-specific approach to NOS, instead of integrating the two. Despite some differences, Erduran and Dagher (2014) have also endorsed a similar thesis:

> Although school science is dominated by theories, laws and models, often characterized as 'content knowledge', there is little in the way of building students' understanding of how various forms of scientific knowledge relate to each other, and how they contribute to scientific explanations in a given scientific discipline.
>
> (p. 114)

Interestingly, a recent study (Cracolice & Busby, 2015) has recapitulated the previous debates in science education and concluded that success in general chemistry requires both prior content knowledge (domain-specific) and scientific reasoning (domain-general). I hope the science education community does not make the same mistake again by emphasizing one aspect and leaving out the other (for further details, see Niaz, 2016). In the following sections I provide examples of how domain-general NOS aspects can be integrated with the domain-specific historical episodes found in most science textbooks. It is plausible to suggest that a presentation and discussion in textbooks of historical episodes (domain-specific) within a domain-general framework can provide a more motivating and congenial understanding of the scientific enterprise.

Theory-Laden Nature of Experimental Observations

As early as the middle of the nineteenth century Charles Darwin had drawn attention to this aspect of NOS in clear terms: "How odd it is that anyone should not see that all observations must be for or against some view if it is to be of any service" (Letter to Henry Fawcett, September 18, 1861 in Charles Darwin, Collected Correspondence, Cambridge University Press, Vol 9, p. 269). Most historians and philosophers of science would agree with some form of the thesis that experimental observations are theory-laden. According to Schwab (1962), scientists generally formulate heuristic principles before doing an experiment, which provide the rationale of the experiment based on presuppositions/theoretical rationale/guiding assumptions.

One of the best examples of this thesis is provided by Robert Millikan's presuppositions with respect to the atomic nature of electricity, which led to a bitter controversy with Felix Ehrenhaft that lasted for many years. Early in his research program, Millikan (1917) asked a thought-provoking question: "Do all atoms possess similar constituents? In other words, is there a primordial sub-atom out of which atoms are made?" (p. 41). Millikan explicitly acknowledged that this question was based on the early experiments of Thomson (1897), Townsend, and others, that helped to establish the existence of a universal charged particle in cathode rays. With this background, Millikan (1917) postulated the atomic nature of electricity as a heuristic principle/guiding assumption of his research program:

> whether electricity in gases and solutions is actually built up out of electrical atoms, each of which has exactly the same value, or whether the electron which had first made its appearance in Faraday's experiments on solutions and then in Townsend's and Thomson's experiments on gases is after all only a *statistical mean* of charges which are themselves greatly divergent.
>
> (p. 58, original italics)

Indeed, this constituted the dilemma faced by Millikan while working on the oil drop experiment: The charge on the oil drop could have been a statistical mean of particles having varying charges or a discrete particle with a definite charge in all experiments. Interestingly, it is generally ignored that just like Millikan, Ehrenhaft also had a presupposition (guiding assumption) based on the anti-atomist theories of Ernst Mach that led him to believe that charge on the oil drops was a statistical mean of varying charges. Holton (1978) has attributed the controversy between Millikan and Ehrenhaft precisely to their perseverance with different presuppositions.

Based on a history and philosophy of science framework, Niaz (2000a) developed six criteria and analyzed 31 college chemistry textbooks published in the United States. Results obtained showed that none of textbooks mentioned the Millikan-Ehrenhaft controversy or the difficulties involved in doing the experiment. Furthermore, none of the textbooks mentioned one of the most important aspect of Millikan's methodology, namely in the face of anomalous data, a scientist perseveres with his presuppositions, holding its falsification in abeyance—in other words, suspension of disbelief. It can be argued that college chemistry textbooks are not supposed to teach research methodology. Although it may seem surprising, this is what most textbooks do. For example, most textbooks emphasize the traditional scientific method, namely scientists do experiments which help them to elaborate hypotheses, enunciate laws, and formulate theories. In the case of the oil drop experiment, if the traditional scientific method had been followed, Ehrenhaft's (with impeccable credentials as an experimentalist) results and not Millikan's would have been accepted by the scientific community. Of course, as the textbooks generally ignore this controversy, in this case Ehrenhaft's role has been conveniently forgotten.

Rodríguez and Niaz (2004a), based on the same criteria as Niaz (2000a) analyzed 43 college physics textbooks published in the United States and found that none referred to the Millikan-Ehrenhaft controversy. However, two textbooks (Olenick, Apostol, & Goodstein, 1985; Urone, 2001) mentioned Millikan's heuristic principle in the context of his guiding assumption. Olenick et al. (1985) reproduced the following quote from Millikan's laboratory notebook (dated 15 March, 1912; see Holton, 1978 for Millikan's laboratory notebooks): "One of the best ever [data] . . . almost exactly *right.* Beauty—publish" (original italics). After reproducing the quote, the textbook authors asked a very thought-provoking question: "What's going on here? How can it be right if he's supposed to be measuring something he doesn't *know?* One might expect him to publish everything!" (p. 244, original italics). These are important issues related to nature of science, namely, can a scientist know beforehand what he is going to find and what is even more difficult to understand is how can a scientist know the right answer before doing the experiment. Interestingly, the authors themselves provided further insight and advice for students:

> Now, you shouldn't conclude that Robert Millikan was a bad scientist . . . What we see instead is something about how real science [cutting-edge] is done in the real world. What Millikan was doing was not cheating. He was applying scientific judgment . . . But experiments must be done in that way. Without that kind of judgment, the journals would be full of mistakes, and we'd never get anywhere. So, then, what protects us from being misled by somebody whose 'judgment' leads to wrong results? Mainly, it's the fact that someone else with a different prejudice can make another measurement . . . Dispassionate, unbiased observation is supposed to be the hallmark of the scientific method. Don't believe everything you read. Science is a difficult and subtle business, and there is no method that assures success.
>
> (Olenick et al., 1985, p. 244)

This is a good illustration of how Millikan's presuppositions and heuristic principle can facilitate students' understanding of nature of science: 1) Doing experiments means gathering data and its interpretation (scientific judgment); 2) without such judgments journals would be full of mistakes, 3) some scientists can be misled in their judgments; 4) another scientist with a different heuristic principle can present an alternative interpretation, namely science is self-correcting; and 5) there are no dispassionate, unbiased observations as suggested by the scientific method, namely observations are theory-laden.

Based on the same criteria as Niaz (2000a), 27 college chemistry textbooks published in Turkey have been analyzed by Niaz and Coştu (2013).

Similar to the textbooks published in the United States, none of the textbooks mentioned the Millikan-Ehrenhaft controversy. One of the textbooks implicitly mentioned Millikan's guiding assumption in the following terms:

> Millikan measured charges on the charged droplets. In the experiments, charges of the droplets were found to be, q = a. 1.6×10^{-19}C. In this equation, a = 1, 2, 3, . . . and so forth were integer numbers. These numbers showed that there is no charge lower than 1.6×10^{-19}C on the droplets. [Thus] Millikan assumed that the charge on the electron has to be 1.6×10^{19}C.
>
> (Yavuz, 1978, pp. 5–6)

Of the remaining 26 textbooks that made no mention of Millikan's guiding assumption, the following excerpt is an example, "In 1909 R.A. Millikan measured successfully both the charge and mass of an electron by performing an experiment known as the oil drop experiment (see Fig)" (Hazer, 1997, p. 22).

The difference between the two types of presentations can easily be appreciated by a science teacher. Presentation classified as mention attempts to provide some background reasons, such as 'Millikan assumed the charge on the electron' (of course, it could have been better) and thus convince the students. On the other hand, the presentation classified as no mention is simply prescriptive and the student has simply to memorize it. Such presentations can easily be interpreted as an inductive generalization. In other words, the experimental results led Millikan to deduce the elementary electrical charge and his guiding assumptions played no part.

To summarize, discussion of the oil drop experiment and its presentation in textbooks (domain-specific) can help students to understand that in the face of anomalous data, a scientist perseveres with his presuppositions, namely an understanding of the theory-laden nature of experimental observations (domain-general).

Alternative Interpretations of the Same Experimental Data Leading to Controversies

It is well known that E. Rutherford (1911) postulated his nuclear model of the atom based on the alpha particle experiments of Geiger and Marsden (1909). However, what is not well known is that soon after the publication of Geiger and Marsden (1909), J.J. Thomson conducted similar experiments (later published by Crowther, 1910) in his Cavendish laboratory at Cambridge. Although results from both laboratories were similar, the interpretations of Thomson and Rutherford were entirely different. Thomson propounded the hypothesis of *compound scattering*, according to which large angle deflection of an alpha particle resulted from successive collisions between the alpha particles and the positive charges distributed throughout the atom. Rutherford, in contrast, propounded the hypothesis of *single scattering*, according to which a large angle deflection resulted from a single collision between the alpha particle and the massive positive charge in the nucleus. The rivalry between Thomson and Rutherford led to a bitter dispute between the proponents of the two hypotheses. At one stage, Rutherford even accused Crowther (1910), a colleague of Thomson, of having 'fudged' the data in order to provide support for Thomson's model of the atom (Wilson, 1983). Heilbron (1981) has provided a succinct account of this controversy.

Based on a history and philosophy of science framework, Niaz (1998) analyzed 23 college chemistry textbooks published in the United States and found that none of the textbooks mentioned the alternative interpretations of alpha particle experiments. In a later study, Rodríguez and Niaz (2004b) analyzed 41 college physics textbooks published in the United States and found two textbooks (Cooper, 1970; Krane, 1996) presented a satisfactory account of the alternative interpretations to explain alpha particle experiments. Cooper (1970), a Nobel Laureate in physics presented the following excerpt:

> Rutherford calculated that from the large Thomson positive charge distribution particles should never be deflected more than 0.03 degrees in a single collision; in undergoing multiple collisions they should have about an equal chance of being deflected one way as another. Therefore, large deflections as a result of many deflections in the same direction were very improbable. (It had been calculated on the basis of the Thomson model that a total deflection greater than $90°$ in traversing gold foil would have only one chance in 10^{3500} of occurring).
>
> (p. 321)

This excerpt clearly shows how arguments based on the probability of many deflections (multiple scattering) played a crucial role in the bitter Thomson-Rutherford controversy. Based on the same criteria, Niaz and Coştu (2009) analyzed 21 Turkish college chemistry textbooks, and Niaz, Kwon, Kim, and Lee (2013) analyzed 16 college physics textbooks published in South Korea. In both these studies none of the textbooks referred to the alternative interpretations of alpha particle experiments.

Importantly, a discussion of the interpretations of alpha particle experiments (domain-specific) can help students to understand that the same experimental data can be interpreted differently leading to controversies (domain-general). Later, based on the intervention of the scientific community, a consensus is achieved.

There is No Universal Step-Wise Scientific Method

Most science and methodology courses emphasize the importance of the scientific method and the same framework is repeated in science textbooks, in the form of flow diagrams, such as: Observations → Hypotheses → Experiments → Analysis of data → Conclusions (based on theories and laws). Windschitl (2004) considers such presentations as the unproblematic scientific method. Most textbooks generally emphasize the role of observations in science, endorse inductive reasoning and ignore that all observations are theory-laden. Lederman et al. (2002) have clearly traced its origin to Francis Bacon's *Novum Organum*, and its unhealthy influence on science education.

Irez (2008) analyzed the depiction of nature of science in Turkish secondary school biology textbooks and found that authors often appeared not to understand the processes that underlie the scientific enterprise. Following are two examples of how textbooks presented the scientific method:

> Scientific problems emerge as result of scientific observations and answers are found through the scientific method . . . The scientific method is the way scientists follow in an investigation of a scientific problem.
>
> (Sagdic et al., 2006, p. 15)

> In order to solve scientific problems in a successful way, the scientific method should be applied step by step.
>
> (Ozet, Arpaci, & Uslu, 2006, p. 15)

Indeed, such presentations are frequently found in most science textbooks published in different parts of the world. Interestingly, the textbook by Sagdic et al. (2006) has been assigned by the Turkish Ministry of National Education as the primary textbook in all secondary schools and is used by millions of students as the primary source of nearly all information about NOS. Based on the results of this study, Irez (2008) concluded:

> science was generally portrayed as a collection of facts, not as a *dynamic process of generating and testing alternative explanations about nature* . . . analysis showed that the majority of these inadequate descriptions were concentrated on two aspects of NOS: the scientific method and the tentative nature of scientific knowledge.
>
> (p. 443, italics added)

Lack of a dynamic process of generating and testing alternative explanations about nature is frequently found in most science textbooks published in many parts of the world (cf. Niaz, 2014).

Niaz and Maza (2011) analyzed 75 college chemistry textbooks published in the United States and found that five textbooks presented the scientific method satisfactorily, as in the following example:

> One last word about the scientific method: some people wrongly imagine science to be a strict set of rules and procedures that automatically lead to inarguable, objective facts. This is not the case. Even our diagram [quite similar to that presented in most textbooks] of the scientific

method is only an idealization of real science, useful to help us see the key distinctions of science. Doing real science requires hard work, care, creativity, and even a bit of luck. Scientific theories do not just fall out of data—they are crafted by men and women of great genius and creativity. A great theory is not unlike a master painting and many see a similar kind of beauty in both. (For more on this aspect of science, see the box entitled *Thomas S. Kuhn and Scientific Revolutions*).

(Tro, 2008, p. 6, italics in original)

Tro (2008) provides the traditional diagram of the scientific method and then points out that it is an idealization of real science. Furthermore, the author emphasizes that theories do not 'fall out of data' but on the contrary require a considerable amount of hard work and creativity. Of all the textbooks analyzed in this study, Tro (2008) was the only one to not only cite Kuhn (1962), but also discuss some implications. This should be a cause of concern to science educators, as Kuhn's major work was published almost 50 years ago, and it is timely for students to be introduced to his ideas. Of course, reading Kuhn does not mean that one has to agree with him.

To conclude, it is important to provide students with examples of how science is not a simple collection of facts and data drawn from specific historical contexts (domain-specific), to facilitate their understanding that there is no universal step-wise scientific method (domain-general).

The Role of Refutation and Falsification

The role of refutations and falsifications has been the subject of considerable debate in the history and philosophy of science literature. According to Lakatos (1970), a scientist generally does not abandon his 'hard-core' of beliefs or presuppositions in the face of anomalous data. An interesting example is provided by Millikan's rejection of Einstein's hypothesis of lightquanta. After working on the photoelectric effect for many years, Millikan (1916) provided an experimental value of Planck's constant h, which was widely accepted by the scientific community. However, Millikan (1916) accepted Einstein's photoelectric equation and at the same time rejected the underlying hypothesis of lightquanta:

This hypothesis [Einstein's] may well be called reckless first because an electromagnetic disturbance which remains localized in space seems a violation of the very conception of an electromagnetic disturbance, and second because it flies in the face of the thoroughly established facts of interference—interpreted satisfactorily in terms of classical theory.

(p. 355)

In other words, Millikan strongly believed in the classical wave theory of light as it explained interference and hence Einstein's hypothesis of lightquanta was considered reckless. Actually, Millikan did not accept Einstein's hypothesis of lightquanta, even as late as his Nobel Prize acceptance speech in 1924. This clearly shows how empirical data (Millikan's determination of *h*) did not provide instant rationality for refuting the classical wave theory of light. Based on a history and philosophy of science framework, Niaz, Klassen, McMillan, and Metz (2010a) analyzed 103 college physics textbooks published in the United States and found that only three textbooks satisfactorily described Millikan's rejection of Einstein's hypothesis of lightquanta. Hecht (1998) pointed out that the photoelectric effect, "was so disconcerting to people educated in classical wave theory that it was especially slow to be accepted" (p. 1028).

The Michelson-Morley experiment is another good example that can be utilized to understand the role of refutations in the history of science. First conducted in 1887, this experiment provided a 'null' result with respect to the ether-drift hypothesis, namely, no observable velocity of the earth with respect to the ether. Despite considerable experimental evidence, it took almost 25 years for this hypothesis to be refuted and recognized as the "greatest negative experiment in the history of science" (Lakatos, 1970, p. 162).

Thus, a discussion of how Millikan's successful determination of Planck's constant *h* did not lead to the refutation of the classical wave theory of light— a theory that Millikan held while testing Einstein's hypothesis of lightquanta (domain-specific). This example shows how experimental evidence does not necessarily lead to the refutation of a theory (domain-general).

Inconsistent Nature of Scientific Theories

Maxwell's (1860) seminal paper on the kinetic theory is a good example of a research program progressing on inconsistent foundations. On the one hand, it was based on 'strict mechanical principles' derived from Newtonian mechanics, however at least two of Maxwell's simplifying assumptions (referring to the movement of particles and the consequent generation of pressure) were in contradiction with Newton's hypothesis explaining the gas laws based on repulsive forces between particles. Brush (1976) pointed out the contradiction explicitly: "Newton's laws of mechanics were ultimately the basis of the kinetic theory of gases, though this theory had to compete with the repulsive theory attributed to Newton" (p. 14). Based on a history and philosophy of science framework, Niaz (2000b) analyzed 22 college chemistry textbooks published in the United States and found that all ignored the inconsistent nature of Maxwell's research program. Many textbooks explicitly invoke Newtonian mechanics along with Maxwell's presentation of the kinetic theory (constant random motion), without realizing an inherent contradiction; the following is an example:

> The molecules of a gas are in a *constant random motion*, and since the molecules are material bodies (in the sense that they possess a mass, m) they obey *Newton's laws of motion.*
> (Quagliano & Vallarino, 1969, p. 113, italics added)

Based on the same criteria, Niaz and Coştu (2013) analyzed 22 Turkish college chemistry textbooks and found that none described that Maxwell's program, although successful, was also based on an inconsistent foundation.

Bohr's (1913) model of the atom incorporated Planck's 'quantum of action' to the classical electrodynamics of Maxwell. For many of Bohr's contemporaries and philosophers of science, this represented a contradictory 'graft' or an inconsistent foundation, and even a 'deep philosophical chasm.' Based on a history and philosophy of science framework, Niaz (1998) analyzed 23 college chemistry textbooks published in the United States and found only two textbooks satisfactorily described the inconsistent nature of Bohr's model of the atom, as in the following example:

> There are two ways of proposing a new theory in science, and Bohr's work illustrates the less obvious one. One way is to amass such an amount of data that the new theory becomes obvious and self-evident to any observer. The theory then is almost a summary of the data. The other way is to make a bold new assertion that initially does not seem to follow from the data, and then to demonstrate that the consequences of this assertion, when worked out, explain many observations. With this method, a theorist says, "You may not see why, yet, but please suspend judgment on my hypothesis until I show you what I can do with it." Bohr's theory is of this type. Bohr said to classical physicists: "You have been misled by your physics to expect that the electron would radiate energy and spiral into the nucleus. Let us assume that it does not, and see if we can account for more observations than by assuming that it does."
> (Dickerson, Gray, Darensbourg, & Darensbourg, 1984, p. 264)

Based on the same criteria, Rodríguez and Niaz (2004b) analyzed 41 college physics textbooks published in the United States, and found only one textbook provided a satisfactory presentation:

> In 1913 Niels Bohr proposed his famous theory of the hydrogen atom. One cannot say that he resolved the problems raised by Rutherford. In a sense he crystallized the dilemma in an even more dramatic form. Focusing his attention entirely on the construction of a nuclear atom, Bohr took what principles of classical physics he needed and added several nonclassical hypotheses almost without precedent; the mélange was not consistent. But they formed a remarkably successful theory of the hydrogen atom. It would be years before it could be said that one had a consistent theory again.
> (Cooper, 1970, p. 325)

Again, based on the same criteria, Niaz and Coştu (2009) analyzed 21 Turkish college chemistry textbooks and found that none referred to the inconsistent nature of Bohr's model of the atom. Similarly, Niaz, Kwon, Kim, and

Lee (2013) analyzed 16 college physics textbooks published in South Korea and found that only one referred to the inconsistent nature of Bohr's model of the atom.

To summarize, contradictions in Maxwell's simplifying assumptions of the kinetic theory and Bohr's model of the atom (domain-specific) can help students to understand the inconsistent nature of scientific theories (domain-general). Furthermore, at times the scientific community accepts theories, even if they are inconsistent, with the expectation that the contradictions would be resolved over time.

Tentative Nature of Scientific Theories

History of science shows that a continual critical appraisal of the scientific endeavor generally leads to theories and models with greater explanatory power. In the case of atomic structure, even in the twentieth century scientists have developed a series of models that continue to provide increasing explanatory power, such as: Thomson, Rutherford, Bohr, Bohr-Sommerfeld, and wave-mechanical, among others (Niaz & Cardellini, 2011a, 2011b).

Based on a history and philosophy of science framework, Niaz and Maza (2011) analyzed 75 college chemistry textbooks published in the United States and found that 13 textbooks presented a satisfactory account of the tentative nature of scientific theories; the following is an example:

> Experimental data and observations also lead to the development of chemical concepts, theories and models which help us to understand our observations. For example, the first modern concept of an atom and the atomic theory were developed by John Dalton. Atoms are far too small to be observed directly. The best we can do is to develop a tentative mental picture of the concept. These mental pictures, called *models*, help scientists to understand and explain abstract concepts. Although this model [Dalton's] is extremely useful both then and now, it is important to avoid taking models too literally. They all have limitations and fall short of reality. The model of atoms has been modified many times since Dalton's time as a result of the work and discoveries of many scientists. The evolution of the atomic model from Dalton's simple 'billiard ball atoms' to the highly mathematical, abstract and sophisticated wave-mechanical model illustrates the importance of experimental investigation. As new evidence accumulates, theories and models must be modified accordingly. It should be noted however, that no matter how refined a model of atoms become, it can never depict a true atomic system.
>
> (Toon and Ellis, 1978, pp. 6–10, emphasis in original)

This presentation has many important features that can be of interest to not only students but also researchers in science education, such as: developing a tentative mental picture, avoiding taking models too literally, appreciating models have limitations and fall short of reality, recognizing the importance of experimental investigation, and understanding that as evidence accumulates models must be modified. It is not far-fetched to suggest that this passage in a textbook can provide students with insights into how science is done whilst examining the topic of atomic structure (domain-specific), thus facilitating an understanding of the tentative nature of science (domain-general). To provide an example from a different cultural context, Vesterinen, Aksela, and Lavonen (2013) found that the tentative nature of scientific theories was the most common aspect of NOS emphasized in all five upper secondary school textbooks published in Finland and Sweden. Some of the examples used to explain this aspect were: development of atomic models, discovery of the unknown elements, creation of the periodic table, and synthesis of new substances in drug discovery. Interestingly, the Swedish core curriculum explicitly includes the tentative nature of scientific knowledge.

Social and Cultural Embeddedness of Science

Development of scientific knowledge is socially negotiated within a historic milieu; however, this need not be confused with relativistic notions of science. According to Longino (2004):

> Establishing what the data are, what counts as acceptable reasoning, which assumptions are legitimate, and which are not become in this view a matter of social, discursive interactions as much as of interaction with the material world. Since assumptions are, by their nature, usually not explicit but taken-for-granted ways of thinking, the function of critical interaction is to make them visible.
>
> (p. 133)

It is important to note that Abd-El-Khalick, Waters, and Le (2008) consider the double-blind peer-review process used by scientific journals as an important component of this NOS aspect.

Evolution is one of the most difficult and controversial topics in biology textbooks. Interestingly, its coverage in textbooks varies according to the prevailing sociopolitical environment. For example, during the Cold War (1950s), the coverage of evolution decreased in high school biology textbooks published in the United States. According to Skoog (2005), this lack of attention could be attributed to the following: "The 1950s were characterized by growing social unrest and insecurity as the Cold War and anti-communist fervor were building. Communism was associated with godlessness as was evolution by some" (p. 404). Barberá, Zanón, and Pérez-Plá (1999) have traced the developments in the Spanish biology curriculum in the twentieth century (period of 100 years) based on the official publications of the nine national curricula and main textbooks used in this period. Authors found the political, social, and religious beliefs held by powerful and influential social groups to be particularly important in the elaboration of curriculum guidelines for the topic of evolution and other socially controversial issues in biology textbooks. Recent reviews have endorsed similar difficulties in effectively presenting evolution (Kampourakis & Nehm, 2014; Smith, 2010).

Based on a history and philosophy of science framework, Niaz and Maza (2011) analyzed 75 college chemistry textbooks published in the United States and found that five textbooks provided a satisfactory description of the interactions among scientists, their peers, and the sociopolitical structure of society. The following is an example from one of the textbooks:

> The development of scientific theories does not always happen easily, quickly, or smoothly. Evolution of thought takes time. The modern view of the solar system, for example, took thousands of years and countless astronomical observations to develop. At times, new ideas meet significant resistance. The famous Italian scientist Galileo Galilei (1564–1642) was forced by church authorities to retract his views that Earth moved around the sun ... In the early 1900s, Marie Curie, a Polish-born French scientist, was a pioneer in the newly discovered field of radioactivity. Despite her many honors, including two Nobel prizes, she was never elected to the French Academy of Sciences. Apparently she was slighted because she was Polish born and a woman. In the 1950s, Linus Pauling, an American chemist, had his passport restricted by the government and was not allowed to travel out of the United States. In the 1970s and 1980s, Andrei Sakharov, a Russian physicist, was exiled to a small Russian city and not allowed to talk with other scientists. Recently, the Catholic Church admitted that Galileo was treated unfairly in the 1600s, and Marie Curie's remains were moved to an honorary grave in the Pantheon of Paris 60 years after her death.
>
> (Dickson, 2000, p. 6)

This presentation is particularly interesting as it provides students with a wide spectrum of historical episodes that involved astronomers, church authorities, rights of women scientists, and scientists involved in promoting peace and banning nuclear weapons. Discussion of such episodes from the history of science can provide students with an opportunity to appreciate the complexity of the scientific enterprise, and acknowledge how construction of knowledge requires assumptions that support reasoning within a social and cultural context (Longino, 2004).

Cooper (1970) has attributed some of the difficulties students have in learning science to the lack of a historical perspective both in the textbooks and the curriculum. Students often wonder why an experiment was conducted at a particular time in history and how it created difficulties for the protagonists. According to Cooper (1970), a satisfactory answer can only be given if we provide students with the *milieu of the time*—namely, the opinions of the scientists involved, examining the alternatives, and the ensuing controversies and struggles. Indeed, in order to understand the importance and significance of an experiment (or for that matter, a scientific theory), it needs to be understood and interpreted within the context of the *milieu of the time*. For example, in order to understand the controversy between Millikan and Ehrenhaft, it is essential that students be provided the historical context based on the guiding assumptions in their respective research programs. Without that information, students will simply believe that Ehrenhaft was wrong, while Millikan (a genius) was right.

A discussion of a wide spectrum of historical episodes that involved astronomers, church authorities, rights of women scientists, banning of nuclear weapons, amongst others (domain-specific) can facilitate students' understanding of how the construction of scientific knowledge requires assumptions that support reasoning within a social and cultural context (domain-general).

Conclusion

In this chapter I have explored the relationship between historical episodes (domain-specific) as presented in science textbooks in most parts of the world, and the underlying domain-general NOS aspects. It is recommended that in order for the two NOS conceptualizations to be meaningful for students, an integration of perspectives is essential. In order to understand the controversial nature of the oil drop experiment, it is important to emphasize that both Millikan and Ehrenhaft worked with different presuppositions, namely the theory-laden nature of experimental observations (for a study based on actual classroom practice, see Niaz and Rivas, 2016). Similar data from the alpha particle experiments led to a controversy between Thomson and Rutherford as they had alternative interpretations of the experimental data. Millikan's successful experimental determination of Planck's constant h did not provide evidence for the refutation of the classical wave theory of light. Maxwell's simplifying assumptions for the kinetic theory and Bohr's atomic model were based on inconsistent foundations and still the scientific community accepted these formulations. Over the last two hundred years atomic models have changed continuously which shows the tentative nature of scientific theories. Finally, the construction of scientific knowledge requires assumptions that are embedded within a social and cultural context, and do not follow a step-wise scientific method.

It is plausible to suggest that science textbooks published in different countries and cultures follow a very similar empiricist epistemology that ignores the underlying rationale of how science progresses. According to Holton (2014), understanding science must include, "*knowledge* of science, plus an acquaintance with how science is done, plus a view of science as part of the cultural development of humanity" (p. 1876). It is concluded that in order to facilitate a better understanding of the scientific enterprise, it is essential to integrate domain-general and domain-specific NOS aspects based on a history and philosophy of science framework.

References

Abd-El-Khalick, F. (2005). Developing deeper understandings of nature of science: The impact of a philosophy of science course on preservice science teachers' views and instructional planning. *International Journal of Science Education, 27*, 15–42.

Abd-El-Khalick, F. (2012). Examining the sources for our understandings about science: Enduring conflations and critical issues in research on nature of science in science education. *International Journal Science Education, 34*(3), 353–374.

Abd-El-Khalick, F., Waters, M., & Le, A. (2008). Representations of nature of science in high school chemistry textbooks over the past four decades. *Journal of Research in Science Teaching, 45*, 835–855.

Barberá, O., Zanón, B., & Pérez-Plá, J. F. (1999). Biology curriculum in twentieth century Spain. *Science Education, 83*(1), 97–111.

Bohr, N. (1913). On the constitution of atoms and molecules. *Philosophical Magazine, 26*, 1–25.

Brush, S. G. (1976). *The kind of motion we call heat: A history of the kinetic theory of gases in the 19th century.* New York: North-Holland.

Cooper, L. N. (1970). *An introduction to the meaning and structure of physics* (short ed.). New York: Harper & Row.

Cracolice, M. S., & Busby, B. D. (2015). Preparation for college general chemistry: More than just a matter of content knowledge acquisition. *Journal of Chemical Education, 92*(11), 1790–1797.

Crowther, J. G. (1910). *Proceedings of the royal society* (Vol. lxxxiv). London: Royal Society.

Dickerson, R. E., Gray, H. B., Darensbourg, M. Y., & Darensbourg, D. J. (1984). *Chemical principles* (4th ed.). Menlo Park, CA: Benjamin/Cummings.

Dickson, T. R. (2000). *Introduction to chemistry* (8th ed.). New York: Wiley.

Dogan, N., & Abd-El-Khalick, F. (2008). Turkish grade 10 students' and science teachers' conceptions of nature of science: A national study. *Journal of Research in Science Teaching, 45*(10), 1083–1112.

Erduran, S., & Dagher, Z. R. (2014). *Reconceptualizing the nature of science for science education.* Dordrecht, the Netherlands: Springer.

Geiger, H., & Marsden, E. (1909). On a diffuse reflection of the alpha particles. In *Proceedings of the royal society* (Vol. lxxxii). London: Royal Society.

Hazer, B. (1997). *Genel kimya.* Trabzon: Akademi Ltd. Şti.

Hecht, E. (1998). *Physics: Algebra/trig* (2nd ed.). Pacific Grove, CA: Brooks/Cole.

Heilbron, J. L. (1981). *Historical studies in the theory of atomic structure.* New York: Arno Press.

Hodson, D. (2014). Nature of science in the science curriculum: Origin, development, implications and shifting emphases. In M. R. Matthews (Ed.), *International handbook of research in history, philosophy and science teaching* (Vol. II, pp. 911–970). Dordrecht, the Netherlands: Springer.

Holton, G. (1978). Subelectrons, presuppositions, and the Millikan-Ehrenhaft dispute. *Historical Studies in the Physical Sciences, 9*, 161–224.

Holton, G. (2014). The neglected mandate: Teaching science as part of our culture. *Science & Education, 23*, 1875–1877.

Irez, S. (2008). Nature of science as depicted in Turkish biology textbooks. *Science Education, 93*, 422–447.

Kampourakis, K., & Nehm, R. H. (2014). History and philosophy of science and the teaching of evolution: Students' conceptions and explanations. In M. R. Matthews (Ed.), *International handbook of research in history, philosophy and science teaching* (Vol. I, pp. 377–421). Dordrecht, the Netherlands: Springer.

Krane, K. S. (1996). *Modern physics* (2nd ed.). New York: Wiley.

Kuhn, T. S. (1962). *The structure of scientific revolutions*. Chicago: University of Chicago Press.

Lakatos, I. (1970). Falsification and the methodology of scientific research programmes. In I. Lakatos & A. Musgrave (Eds.), *Criticism and the growth of knowledge* (pp. 91–195). Cambridge: Cambridge University Press.

Lederman, N. G., Abd-El-Khalick, F., Bell, R. L., & Schwartz, R. (2002). Views of nature of science questionnaire: Toward valid and meaningful assessment of learners' conceptions of nature of science. *Journal of Research in Science Teaching, 39*, 497–521.

Lederman, N. G., Bartos, S. A., & Lederman, J. S. (2014). The development, use, and interpretation of nature of science assessments. In M. R. Matthews (Ed.), *International handbook of research in history, philosophy and science teaching* (Vol. II, pp. 971–997). Dordrecht, the Netherlands: Springer.

Longino, H. E. (2004). How values can be good for science. In P. Machamer & G. Wolters (Eds.), *Science, values and objectivity* (pp. 127–142). Pittsburgh, PA: University of Pittsburgh Press.

Maxwell, J. C. (1860). Illustrations of the dynamical theory of gases. *Philosophical Magazine, 19*, 19–32.

McComas, W. F. (2014). Nature of science in the science curriculum and in teacher education programs in the United States. In M. R. Matthews (Ed.), *International handbook of research in history, philosophy and science teaching* (Vol. III, pp. 1993–2023). Dordrecht, the Netherlands: Springer.

Millikan, R. A. (1916). A direct photoelectric determination of Planck's "*h*". *Physical Review, 7*, 355–388.

Millikan, R. A. (1917). *The electron*. Chicago: University of Chicago Press.

Niaz, M. (1993). "Progressive problemshifts" between different research programs in science education: A Lakatosian perspective. *Journal of Research in Science Teaching, 30*(7), 757–765.

Niaz, M. (1995). Enhancing thinking skills: Domain specific/domain general strategies—a dilemma for science education. *Instructional Science, 22*, 413–422.

Niaz, M. (1998). From cathode rays to alpha particles to quantum of action: A rational reconstruction of structure of the atom and its implications for chemistry textbooks. *Science Education, 82*, 527–552.

Niaz, M. (2000a). The oil drop experiment: A rational reconstruction of the Millikan-Ehrenhaft controversy and its implications for chemistry textbooks. *Journal of Research in Science Teaching, 37*, 480–508.

Niaz, M. (2000b). A rational reconstruction of the kinetic molecular theory of gases based on history and philosophy of science and its implications for chemistry textbooks. *Instructional Science, 28*, 23–50.

Niaz, M. (2012). *From 'science in the making' to understanding the nature of science: An overview for science educators*. New York: Routledge.

Niaz, M. (2014). Science textbooks: The role of history and philosophy of science. In M. R. Matthews (Ed.), *International handbook of research in history, philosophy and science teaching* (Vol II, pp. 1411–1441). Dordrecht, the Netherlands: Springer.

Niaz, M. (2016). *Chemistry education and contributions from history and philosophy of science.* Dordrecht, the Netherlands: Springer.

Niaz, M., & Cardellini, L. (2011a). What can the Bohr-Sommerfeld model show students of chemistry in the 21st century? *Journal of Chemical Education, 88,* 240–243.

Niaz, M., & Cardellini, L. (2011b). Why has the Bohr-Sommerfeld model of the atom been ignored by general chemistry textbooks? *Acta Chimica Slovenica, 58,* 876–883.

Niaz, M., & Coştu, B. (2009). Presentation of atomic structure in Turkish general chemistry textbooks. *Chemistry Education Research and Practice, 10,* 233–240.

Niaz, M., & Coştu, B. (2013). Analysis of Turkish general chemistry textbooks based on a history and philosophy of science perspective. In M. S. Khine (Ed.), *Critical analysis of science textbooks: Evaluating instructional effectiveness* (pp. 199–218). Dordrecht, the Netherlands: Springer.

Niaz, M., Klassen, S., McMillan, B., & Metz, D. (2010a). Reconstruction of the history of the photoelectric effect and its implications for general physics textbooks. *Science Education, 94,* 903–931.

Niaz, M., Kwon, S., Kim, N., & Lee, G. (2013). Do general physics textbooks discuss scientists' ideas about atomic structure? A case in Korea. *Physics Education, 48*(1), 57–64.

Niaz, M., & Maza, A. (2011). *Nature of science in general chemistry textbooks.* Dordrecht, the Netherlands: Springer.

Niaz, M., & Rivas, M. (2016). *Students' understanding of research methodology in the context of dynamics of scientific progress.* Dordrecht, the Netherlands: Springer.

Olenick, R. P., Apostol, T. M., & Goodstein, D. L. (1985). *Beyond the mechanical universe. From electricity to modern physics.* New York: Cambridge University Press.

Ozet, M., Arpaci, O., & Uslu, A. (2006). *Biology 10th grade.* Turkey: Zambak Publishing.

Quagliano, J. V., & Vallarino, L. M. (1969). *Chemistry* (3rd ed.). Englewood Cliffs, NJ: Prentice Hall.

Rodríguez, M. A., & Niaz, M. (2004a). The oil drop experiment: An illustration of scientific research methodology and its implications for physics textbooks. *Instructional Science, 32,* 357–386.

Rodríguez, M. A., & Niaz, M. (2004b). A reconstruction of structure of the atom and its implications for general physics textbooks. *Journal of Science Education and Technology, 13,* 409–424.

Rutherford, E. (1911). The scattering of alpha and beta particles by matter and the structure of the atom. *Philosophical Magazine, 21,* 669–688.

Sagdic, D., Bulut, O., Korkmaz, S., Boru, S., Ozturk, E., & Cavak, S. (2006). *Biology 10.* Turkey: Saray Publishing.

Schwab, J. J. (1962). *The teaching of science as enquiry.* Cambridge, MA: Harvard University Press.

Skoog, G. (2005). The coverage of human evolution in high school biology textbooks in the 20th century and in current state science standards. *Science & Education, 14*(3–5), 395–422.

Smith, M. U. (2010). Current status of research in teaching and learning evolution: Philosophical/epistemological issues. *Science & Education, 19,* 523–538.

Sternberg, R. J. (1989). Domain-generality versus domain-specificity: The life and impending death of a false dichotomy. *Merrill-Palmer Quarterly, 35*(1), 115–130.

Toon, E. R., & Ellis, G. L. (1978). *Foundations of chemistry.* New York: Holt, Rinehart & Winston.

Thomson, J. J. (1897). Cathode rays. *Philosophical Magazine, 44,* 293–316.

Tro, N. J. (2008). *Chemistry: A molecular approach*. Upper Saddle River, NJ: Prentice Hall.

Urone, P. P. (2001). *College physics* (2nd ed.). Pacific Grove, CA: Brooks/Cole.

Vesterinen, V-M., Aksela, M., & Lavonen, J. (2013). Quantitative analysis of representations of nature of science in Nordic upper secondary school textbooks using framework of analysis based on philosophy of chemistry. *Science & Education, 22*(7), 1839–1855.

Wilson, D. (1983). *Rutherford: Simple genius*. Cambridge, MA: MIT Press.

Windschitl, M. (2004). Folk theories of 'inquiry': How preservice teachers reproduce the discourse and practices of an atheoretical scientific method. *Journal of Research in Science Teaching, 41*, 481–512.

Yavuz, O. (1978). *Genel kimya*. Erzurum, Turkey: Atatürk Üniversitesi Basimevi.

4 The Portrayal of Nature of Science in Lebanese Ninth Grade Science Textbooks

Saouma BouJaoude, Zoubeida R. Dagher, and Sara Refai

Introduction

Despite the proliferation of multimedia tools and resources available to support teaching and learning in school classrooms, textbooks remain the main curricular resource utilized in many classrooms around the world. This is especially the case in Lebanon where the centralized curriculum guidelines are expressed in the official national textbooks, which in turn circumscribe the disciplinary content that gets taught in schools. The purpose of this chapter is to explore the extent to which nature of science (NOS) content is portrayed in ninth grade Lebanese science textbooks, and to propose a set of recommendations to guide future textbook development. In the following sections, we describe the context of the study, review NOS studies focused on textbooks, present the analytical framework and methodology, followed by the findings, conclusion, and implications.

Science Textbooks in Lebanese Schools

In Lebanon, textbooks typically follow curricular mandates set by the central Ministry of Education and Higher Education (MEHE). These textbooks are published by MEHE or by private publishers based on the stipulation that the textbooks align with the Lebanese curriculum guides. Teachers tend to rely heavily on the science textbook to guide their teaching (Georg Eckert Institute for International Textbook Research, 2009). This is especially true for Lebanon where country-wide exams administered at the culminating years of middle and high school (ninth and twelfth grades, respectively) determine the promotion or retention of students, as well as their eligibility to join higher education institutions.

In science, the Ministry of Education and Higher Education has specified 15 objectives of which several address some aspects of NOS (Center for Educational Research and Development [CERD], 1997). In addition to the central focus on understanding scientific knowledge and its applications, the objectives also address scientific values, the relationship between science and technology, and the historical, social, and cultural dimensions of scientific knowledge (see Dagher, 2009 for details). As in other subject areas, the national objectives are intended to set curriculum expectations and provide focus and guidance to textbook writers.

The purpose of this study is to utilize a new analytical framework aimed at capturing the extent to which Grade 9 Lebanese textbooks portray NOS. Specifically, the study focuses on the following research questions: 1) What NOS concepts, if any, are addressed in the textbooks, and which ones are not? 2) What suggestions can be offered based on the analysis to improve the books current coverage of NOS?

Studies on NOS in Science Textbooks

Why study science textbooks? Hurd (2000) reports on a study in which researchers found that 80 percent of the science curriculum was dependent on a single textbook. The same study also reported that most science teachers in the middle or high school level were not adequately prepared to teach at those grade levels. Furthermore, the surveyed teachers expressed their desire for a stronger background in science, more pre-service experience, more courses in science teaching methods, and more classes on early adolescence behavior management. Another study found that middle school teachers with a stronger background in education than in science tend to rely on their textbooks for guidance and content understanding (Stern & Roseman, 2004). The situation is no different in Lebanon where the textbook is also the main source of information, especially in Grades 9 and 12 when students sit for high-stakes national exams.

Studies on science textbooks in the last two decades have been relatively meager. Those studies have either focused on exploring the coverage of science concepts, the balance of scientific literacy themes in textbooks, or, to a lesser extent, the nature of scientific knowledge (see, for example, Chiappetta, Sethna, & Fillman, 1991, 1993; de Posada, 1999; Lumpe & Beck, 1996; Stern & Roseman, 2004).

Studies that explored how science textbooks portray NOS have reported similarly disappointing results. For example, in an early study of U.S. high school and college biology textbooks, Gibbs and Lawson (1992) found reference to scientific thinking to be bound into discussions about the 'scientific method' and commonly confined to the introductory chapter or beginning of examined books. Additionally, most books were found to lack discussion on the variety of scientific methods, with only a few texts including a sentence or two dedicated to stating that the scientific method is not a rigid list of rules. Rodríguez and Niaz (2002) found that chemistry textbooks' reference to the history and philosophy of science with respect to the presentation of atomic structure was not satisfactory, thus denying readers the opportunity to achieve a better understanding of scientific progress.

In the same vein, Chinn and Malhotra (2002) found that even when textbooks attempt to present "science as inquiry", the inquiries contained in them tend to be simplistic and suffer from a lack of authenticity, giving students a superficial understanding of scientific thinking and processes. Another study by Cohen and Dagher (2005) found that a sample of widely used middle school science textbooks in the United States were especially weak on several NOS themes such as communicating: 1) the diversity of scientific thinking, 2) the creative side of science, 3) the role of questioning in scientific work, and 4) distinctions between causal and correlational explanations. They also found that the disciplinary focus of the books impacted the frequency of coverage of themes that pertain to such content standards as: science as inquiry, history and nature of science standards, and science in personal perspective.

Abd-El-Khalick, Waters, and Le (2008) assessed the representations of NOS in 14 high school chemistry textbooks, and the extent to which these representations have changed in the past 40 years. Data were collected from chapters or sections of textbooks that have direct relevance to NOS such as those on the scientific method and the processes of science and topics related to atomic structure, kinetic molecular theory, and gas laws. Results showed that the textbooks either did not address NOS, or, when they did, presented naïve conceptions of NOS. Similar findings were reported in Turkey, when Irez (2009) investigated the nature and the quality of the treatment given to NOS in five Grade 10 biology textbooks, by analyzing the content of the textbooks and generating cognitive maps regarding NOS for each textbook. Results showed that NOS was discussed in one part of the first unit of each of the textbooks, and all but one of the textbooks described science as an objective body of knowledge that is 'out there' waiting to be discovered.

The limited number of studies on science textbooks in Lebanon focused on issues similar to those investigated worldwide. Boutros (1994) analyzed the content of a Grade 11 chemistry textbook using Klopfer's taxonomy of science teaching objectives and found that the textbook authors placed undue emphasis on knowledge and comprehension level objectives, as well as observation and measurement of science process skills, while neglecting higher level objectives. Hajj (1997) investigated the representation of cause-effect forms of reasoning in biology textbooks and found that the textbooks presented a limited number of references to sequential connections between events, and did not explicitly model causal and deductive reasoning.

Harbali (2000) used Chiappetta et al.'s (1991) framework to investigate the balance of scientific literacy themes in Lebanese middle school life and earth science, chemistry, and physics textbooks. Results showed that the textbooks emphasized science as a body of knowledge and science as a way of investigation, and neglected science as a way of thinking and the interaction among science, technology, and society. A more recent comparative study between Lebanese and Egyptian textbooks (Dagher, BouJaoude, & Alameh, 2010) used an analytical framework based on NOS ideas identified by Osborne, Collins, Ratcliffe, Millar, and Duschl (2003). The authors found that both ninth grade Egyptian and Lebanese textbooks did not address most of the NOS ideas offered by Osborne et al. (2003).

A recent book edited by Khine (2013) investigated the quality of textbooks from a variety of perspectives. This book, featuring contributions from Europe, Australia, the United States, and South America, included chapters on the methodology of textbook analysis and others on textual, language, and content analysis of science textbooks. Findings reported in the book suggest that even though textbooks may be guided by reform documents, they do not reflect real reform in the teaching of science, especially at the primary level, as they do not incorporate new theories of learning (Valanides, Papageorgiou, & Rigas, 2013). Moreover, textual analysis of linguistic resources used in textbooks in a study from Australia showed that there are differences in the way subjects are represented in the textbooks. For example, while physics and chemistry knowledge is typically represented in the form of rules and procedures with content being structured around unifying concepts, biology and geology are generally presented through description, elaboration, and persuasion (Muspratt & Freebody, 2013). By explicitly differentiating textual resources employed in textbooks of different science disciplines, teachers can provide multiple points of access to disciplinary literacy, which by default, includes understandings of NOS.

Context and Justification

The Lebanese Ministry of Education and Higher Education (MEHE) has the primary responsibility of overseeing the development of curriculum guides and textbooks through the CERD. In addition, it has the responsibility of supervising the implementation of appropriate services to support the delivery and enactment of curriculum directives. The educational system of Lebanon follows a structure of six elementary education years (Grades 1–6), followed by three middle school years (Grades 7–9), and three high school years (Grades 10–12). Lebanese students take chemistry, life and earth science, and physics as separate subjects in Grades 7–9. In Grade 7 they take three, 50-minute periods of life science and three, 50-minute periods of chemistry and physics per week (1.5 periods each on average). At the Grade 8 and 9 levels, students take two, 50-minute periods of life and earth science and four 50-minute periods of chemistry and physics per week (2 periods each on average). Students in Lebanon undergo high-stakes state-administered exit exams at the end of Grade 9 and Grade 12. Schools may choose to teach science in Arabic, English, or French in Grades 1–6; however, the majority of schools typically switch the language of instruction in science to English or French, starting in the seventh grade.

There are two reasons why studying ninth grade textbooks is important. First, ninth grade is the last year of middle school, at the end of which students take a national high-stakes assessment prior to entering high school.

Second, the middle school phase is a critical period where students' attitudes toward science have been shown to begin to decline (Osborne, & Dillon, 2008; Tai, Liu, Maltese, & Fan, 2006). Analysis of textbooks in relation to NOS content may help illuminate how the textbooks' representation of science might contribute to the noted decline.

The most recent reform of science curriculum objectives in Lebanon took place over two decades ago and was mainly focused on the development of students' scientific and technological literacy (CERD, 1994, 1995), a goal shared by other reform efforts in the United States and Canada. Textbooks developed around national science curriculum goals emphasize conceptual knowledge and applications, with little attention to the epistemic and social basis of scientific knowledge. Despite a disproportionate focus on science content and its applications, Lebanese students perform poorly on international tests such as Trends in Mathematics and Science Study (TIMSS)[1] (2003, 2007, 2011), a matter that is likely to trigger a new round of reform.

This study focuses on analyzing the English language versions of three official Lebanese textbooks used in Grade 9, titled after the disciplines: "chemistry", "life and earth science," and "physics" to determine the NOS concepts that are addressed in the textbooks, and offer suggestions to improve the books' coverage of NOS. An analysis of textbooks focusing on broader NOS perspectives is a timely endeavor because it can potentially inform future efforts focused on revising the science curriculum goals, in addition to the textbooks.

Methodology

In this section, we describe the textbooks, present the analytical framework, describe the process of content analysis, and report on inter-rater reliability.

Description of the Textbooks

The ninth grade textbooks are taught concurrently and share some structural attributes. It is important to note that none of the textbooks begins with a chapter specifically focused on NOS. Where NOS is addressed, it is scattered throughout the chapters of the textbook.

The chemistry textbook (CERD, 2000a) is 174 pages long and is divided into five units containing a total of eight chapters. Unit 1, The atom (2 chapters), Unit 2, Chemical bonding (1 chapter), Unit 3, Electrochemistry (1 chapter), Unit 4, Organic Chemistry (3 chapters), and Unit 5 Chemistry and Environment (1 chapter). Each chapter contains the following sections: *Activity, Glossary, Remark, Safety, Chapter Summary, Insights, Science and Society, Questions and Exercises* (CERD, 2000a, p. 8).

The life and earth science textbook (CERD, 2000b) is 199 pages long and consists of three parts which are equivalent to units: Part 1, Nutrition and Metabolism (5 chapters), Part 2, Nervous Communication and Human Behavior (1 chapter), Part 3, Reproduction and Genetics (4 chapters). Each chapter consists of smaller divisions titled Activities, a summing up and concept map page, exercise pages, and sections titled *Info Plus* that connect the topic discussed in the chapter with current events. Contrary to its title, this textbook is entirely focused on life science and does not contain any earth science concepts.

The physics textbook (CERD, 2000c) is 190 pages long and consists of four units: Optics (4 chapters), Electricity (5 chapters), Heat (2 chapters), and Mechanics (4 chapters). Each chapter contains the following parts: *Objectives, Activities Illustrating Big Ideas, Concept Review, Exercises, Further Study* (typically dealing with application of concepts). It is worth noting that only six out of the 15 chapters include a section entitled "Further Study."

Analytical Framework

Determining what NOS ideas ought to be included in textbooks, and therefore analyzed, is essential. The literature review highlights diverse orientations and inevitably, the reported findings reflect the extent to which the textbooks address the targeted NOS ideas. The choice of an analytical framework involves a value judgment regarding what is important to capture in the analysis. For example, in a comparative analysis of Egyptian and Lebanese textbooks (Dagher et al., 2010) the authors used an analytical framework derived from Osborne et al.'s (2003) findings, focusing on three dimensions that involve seven components pertaining to nature of scientific knowledge, 10 ideas pertaining to methods of science, and four ideas pertaining to the institutions and social practices in science. The outcomes regarding the three dimensions and the 21 categories they subsume revealed the extent to which the textbooks addressed nature of science ideas as defined within these specific dimensions.

Rather than use the same analytical framework for this study or adapt an existing one, we decided to base our analysis on a recent nature of science account captured by the Expanded Family Resemblance Approach (FRA) to NOS (Erduran & Dagher, 2014). This account, adopts Irzik and Nola's (2014) view of science as a cognitive-epistemic and social-institutional system, and adapts their original eight categories to include three additional ones, representing the relationship between the 11 categories visually as an FRA Wheel (Figure 4.1).

The Expanded Family Resemblance Approach (FRA) to NOS recognizes that a comprehensive understanding of the natural sciences demands recognition of shared and distinct elements among different science domains that include cognitive, epistemic, social, and institutional factors. As authors, we find the multidimensional categories expressed in the Expanded FRA to NOS to capture a set of understandings about science that are valuable

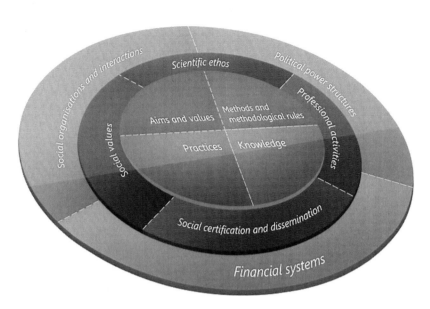

Figure 4.1 The FRA Wheel Capturing the 11 Categories of the Expanded Family Resemblance Approach to Nature of Science (Reprinted from Erduran & Dagher, 2014, p. 28)

to teach and therefore valuable to detect and analyze in this study. A brief description of these categories follows:

Scientific Aims and Values category comprises a number of cognitive values that include among other things, objectivity, novelty, accuracy, and empirical adequacy.

Scientific Methods category addresses the idea that scientists use many methods of true experiments involving the testing of hypothesis or not, thought experiments, or observations that include the testing of hypotheses or not.

Scientific Knowledge category pertains to addressing how scientific knowledge is expressed in multiple forms such as theories, laws, models that are used to explain and predict phenomena. How these forms of knowledge relate to one another and to scientific methods and practices affect the growth of knowledge over time.

Scientific Ethos category focuses on understanding that for scientific knowledge and practices to be credible and ethical, there are a number of norms that scientists are expected to abide by such as intellectual honesty, respect for and protection of human subjects, respect for colleagues and the environment, responsible publication, etc.

Social Values category includes an understanding of respecting the environment, social utility, and freedom.

Social Certification category describes the role of peer review, evaluation, and criticism with an understanding that scientific findings get reviewed, criticized, and evaluated by peers.

Professional Activities category focuses on understanding the role of attending professional conferences, presenting findings, writing research proposals, and conducting peer reviews of papers and proposals.

Financial Systems category acknowledges the roles of funding priorities, commercial and special interests in enabling, controlling or limiting scientific knowledge.

Political Power structures addresses gender issues, colonial interests, ideological influences on scientific knowledge and practices and who benefits from them.

Social Organization and Interactions category addresses the organizational structures and relational transactions within and among scientific communities.

The 11 categories described embody classes of ideas that contextualize and enrich science content. They are not imposed on science concepts but they coexist with these concepts—as they are naturally an inherent part of them. When properly integrated, they allow a broad set of nature of science ideas to emerge within any given content area, and then emerge similarly or differently across other content areas thus straddling the domain-specific and domain-general understanding of science.

In addition to the above considerations, using the Expanded FRA as the analytical framework for this study elucidates a comprehensive set of considerations about science, which are either partially addressed, or not addressed by other NOS frameworks. For example, it includes scientific practices which are ignored in some of the reviewed frameworks. It expands what students should understand about scientific knowledge by addressing growth in scientific knowledge and relationships between laws, theories, models, and explanations. It honors the aims and values of science and attends to specific social-institutional aspects of science that are worthy of articulation in school science, that are often left out of other frameworks.

In this study, we examine the extent to which all 11 categories of NOS ideas, deemed worthy of inclusion in a science curriculum, are addressed in the official ninth grade Lebanese textbooks. This analysis of the degree and quality of NOS coverage in ninth grade Lebanese science textbooks is guided by these research questions: 1) Which nature of science categories, if any, are addressed in the textbooks and which ones are not? 2) What suggestions can be offered based on the analysis to improve the books current coverage of NOS?

Description of Content Analysis

Each textbook was read in its entirety according to its naturally occurring thematic chunks (chapters within units) against the 11 NOS categories described in the analytical framework section. In other words, each chapter and its subsections were examined against these categories noting if any of them were depicted in the narrative, activities, exercises, or science-society connections, as well as noting the quality of such coverage. Presence of the category, whether it occurs once or more, in each chapter was marked with a tally mark. Then tallies across chapters pertaining to the same unit were consolidated for the whole textbook. In sum, the NOS ideas articulated by the analytical framework were tracked as they occurred in each chapter.

Recognizing the quality of NOS articulation might vary, we revisited the chapters' content to classify each as meeting one of four levels: 0-(F) *Failure* to address the target category; 1-(S) reference to NOS category is *superficial*, is implicit, or mentioned in passing, 2-(D) refers to NOS category in some *detail*, 3-(E) refers to the NOS category in an *exemplary* way. Determining the quality of coverage is important for achieving the second goal of the study aimed at offering constructive suggestions for improving the textbooks' articulation of NOS.

Anticipating that many of these categories may not be represented adequately or at all in the three targeted textbooks, we decided to read the entire textbooks instead of sampling their content for two reasons: 1) choosing random chapters may miss connections that made sense only when chapters and the concepts represented in them were read sequentially within an entire unit, and 2) selecting random units, while preserving the chapter sequence within the unit, may miss units that lend themselves more to some aspects of the framework than others—especially since the number of units concerned in each book is relatively small, ranging from three to five units. Given that we are using a new framework that is holistic and comprehensive, it seemed only reasonable to examine the books' chapters as part of a larger content-continuous unit so as to capture the NOS storyline, should there be one. Thus, we placed a higher value on maximizing the identification of a wide spectrum of NOS coverage than risking loss of information due to random sampling.

Reliability

Reliability was established through inter-rater agreement at the beginning of textbook analysis and checked again at the end of the analysis. First, the three researchers: a senior science educator and researcher who participated in the development the FRA Wheel, a senior science educator in the country where the analyzed textbooks are used, and a graduate student, met to discuss the analytical framework and ensure that they had a shared understanding of its components. They revisited and discussed the theoretical underpinnings for the analytical framework by reviewing the original work from which it was derived (Erduran & Dagher, 2014) in order to orient themselves adequately for the analysis. Subsequently, the three researchers applied the framework to one chapter from the life and earth science textbook independently and met to discuss the results and resolve any differences. Following this, the three researchers analyzed three randomly selected chapters, one from each of the three textbooks, independently, then compared the results and resolved any differences until consensus was reached. A full analysis of the textbooks was conducted by two of the researchers. Percentage agreement on each of the books was calculated on each of the three books. The results of inter-rater agreement were: life and earth science textbook: $\alpha = 0.94$ (10 chapters, inter-rater agreement of chapters ranged between $\alpha = 0.82$ and $\alpha = 1.0$), chemistry textbook: $\alpha = 0.86$ (8 chapters, inter-rater agreement of chapters ranged between $\alpha = 0.82$ and $\alpha = 0.91$), physics textbook: $\alpha = 0.83$ (15 chapters, inter-rater agreement of chapters ranged between $\alpha = 0.73$ and $\alpha = 1.0$).

Findings and Discussion

The goal of this study was to determine the extent of NOS coverage in ninth grade Lebanese textbooks and to provide constructive suggestions for improving the coverage of NOS. In this section, we summarize the overall findings, then delve into the specifics of the analysis for each textbook by first presenting the findings, and then offering suggestions for improving the integration of NOS into the textbook's content.

The main findings that emerge from the analysis are:

1)   The chemistry and life and earth science textbooks address at least once, four and five of the 11 categories explored in the analytical framework, respectively.
2)   Except for one instance where the quality of NOS content is ranked at level 2, all noted instances are at level 1, indicating brief or limited treatment of NOS content.
3)   The physics textbook did not address any of the 11 categories.

Table 4.1 provides a comparative overview of the frequency of instances in which NOS content is addressed in the three textbooks.

Having established that the textbooks give sporadic attention to some of the NOS categories included in this framework, it is important to note that this coverage varies across the disciplines. For example, six out of 10 chapters of the life and earth science textbook discuss some aspect of scientific methods, but they focus on hypothesis testing involving experiments, thus missing opportunities to call attention to experiments that do not involve hypothesis testing, or to observations that might or might not involve hypothesis testing. The physics textbook, on the other hand, does not address scientific methods but is replete with activities that do not include reflective or metacognitive components that address scientific practices or scientific methodology.

Table 4.1 Overview of the Results Showing the Frequency of Chapter Coverage of Each NOS Category Across the Ninth Grade Science Textbooks in Lebanon

NOS Dimension	NOS Category	Chemistry (8 chapters)	Life and Earth Science (10 chapters)	Physics (15 chapters)
Cognitive-Epistemic Aspects (CE)	Aims & values	0	1	0
	Practices	0	7	0
	Methods	3	6	0
	Knowledge	2*	2	0
Social-Institutional (SI-A)	Scientific Ethos	1	0	0
	Social Values	8	7	0
	Social Certification	0	0	0
	Professional Activities	0	0	0
Social-Institutional (SI-B)	Financial Systems	0	0	0
	Political Power Structures	0	0	0
	Social Organizations and Interactions	0	0	0

*One of the two instances where growth of scientific knowledge is addressed in the chemistry textbook is at level 2. All other frequencies are at Level 1.

Chemistry Textbook

Under the cognitive-epistemic dimension, the chemistry textbook addresses two categories only: scientific methods and scientific knowledge. Scientific methods are addressed in three out of eight chapters: Unit 1, Chapter 2 in the process of discussing the periodic table and how is it organized; Unit 4, Chapter 3 when discussing the fractional distillation of petroleum, petroleum refinement, cracking; and Unit 5, Chapter 1 where addressing methods for reducing water pollution or solid waste. The coverage level in these instances is at the level of 1 because the presentation is not detailed enough or does not show scientists or engineers as active agents. The following excerpt, ranked at level 1, refers to the role of scientists in organizing information about the elements but does not provide details regarding how this knowledge builds on previous knowledge or helps predict new knowledge:

> The distribution of electrons allowed scientists to arrange the elements in a chart that organizes information about the elements. This chart is known as periodic table, which is composed of vertical columns (groups), and horizontal rows (periods).
>
> (Chapter 2, pp. 32)

On the other hand, the scientific knowledge category is noted on two occasions, in Unit 1, Chapter 1 in the course of discussing the history of the atomic model and the tentative nature of scientific knowledge (level 2); and in Unit 2, Chapter 1 which notes briefly what scientists used to think about electrons and what they think about them now (level 1). The following two excerpts illustrate the difference in ranking:

Excerpt 1, Level 2, Chapter 1

A model can be a scale model such as a model of rail road, or an architectural model of a house. Sometimes, computer models are used instead of physical models. A model can be a theory or a mental picture, too.

Scientists have developed a mental picture or model of the atom that allows us to explain how the real atom behaves.

Models like the atomic model are subject to change as new evidence is collected.

(CERD, 2000a, p. 17)

This introduction to the development of the atomic model continues on for three additional pages of text, starting with Democritus, proceeding to Dalton's, Thomson's, and Rutherford's models, building the case for each of them and noting the growth of scientific knowledge.

In contrast, note how the next excerpt makes brief reference to some aspect of growth in scientific knowledge, without elaboration:

Level 1, Chapter 2

According to Bohr's model scientists thought that electrons circled the nucleus of an atom in much the same way as planets orbit the sun. However, scientists now know that it is not possible to predict the exact location and speed of an electron at the same time.

(CERD, 2000a, p. 33)

Under the social-institutional dimension, the only category (out of 7) addressed consistently across the chapters is that of social values. The book does a good job of discussing applications that show the utility of scientific knowledge typically in the special sections of each chapter titled '*Insights*, and '*Science and Society*'. There is one instance in which scientific ethos is addressed. The level of coverage is mostly at the level of 1 with few exceptions. The discussed applications range from radioisotopes and their use in medicine to help physicians locate areas that explain certain disorders are discussed in Unit 1, Chapter 1 (level 1) to where petroleum and pollution are discussed in greater detail (level 2) (Unit 4, Chapter 2).

In summary, the chemistry textbook provides sufficient detail in terms of conceptual knowledge as determined by the Lebanese curriculum objectives, but misses the opportunity to introduce students to the epistemological and social aspects of science, even though such opportunities could be easily seized upon as shown in the following example.

Unit 1, Chapter 1: Structure of the Atom

The chapter describes the historical development of the atomic model from the Greeks to the modern atomic model. In addition, it discusses the fundamental particles of the atom, atomic number, atomic mass, isotopes, and the mole. However, the information is presented as 'scientific truth' with no prospect for students to think about the aims and values of science even though there was an opportunity to discuss empirical adequacy, for example, in the context of the many experiments that were conducted during the development of the different atomic models. Moreover, even though modeling was discussed, it was not introduced as a fundamental scientific practice and models were not discussed as significant forms of scientific knowledge. Yet again, discussing modeling and the nature of scientific models was missed. Similarly, there was no discussion of the methods used in science and the human nature of the scientific endeavor even though such a possibility existed in the context of the many scientists who were mentioned in the chapter. Finally, the social–institutional aspects of science were not mentioned. The only idea mentioned in passing is that theories are modified by other scientists through testing or introducing new ideas. Scientists were presented as individuals who worked in isolation of the scientific, social, and political community around them. Discussing the social context in which the scientists' work has contributed to the development of the modern atomic model could be used to highlight several epistemic and cognitive aspects of this domain.

Life and Earth Science Textbook

Under the cognitive-epistemic dimension, the life and earth science textbook addresses few categories to varying extents. The scientific aims and values category is not addressed. The category of scientific practices is addressed in seven of 10 chapters—all at level 1 because reference is limited to either getting students to formulate hypotheses (6 out of 7 chapters) or manipulate information (1 chapter) but there is no discussion or consideration of the significance of those activities as scientific practices. The scientific methods category is superficially addressed at level 1 in six of the 10 chapters. For example, in one activity in Chapter 5, students are instructed to collect data and then "formulate a hypothesis explaining the uneven distribution of tactile sensation of the skin" (CERD, 2000b, p. 113). The modest attempt to link observation and hypothesis testing is a good start that could be used to pose questions regarding the significance of additional tests/observations, or reflect on the different methods used across investigations.

Scientific knowledge is addressed twice minimally as in the course of reporting on scientists' work in Chapters 1 and 7, in relation to scientists' discovery of the ulcer bacteria and Mendel's experiments, respectively. The quality of the coverage of all these instances is at level 1. The following excerpt illustrates one of these episodes:

> In 1989, two Australian researchers discovered the presence of bacterium *Helicobacter pylori*, at the surface of the stomach lining. Nowadays, it is proven that this micro-organism plays a role in the development of ulcer and even cancer of the stomach.
>
> (CERD, 2000b, p. 32)

While the excerpt, which briefly refers to the scientists that discovered the bacterium, followed by the idea that this knowledge has been validated over time, points to the idea of the growth of scientific knowledge, it does not go into much detail and is categorized as level 1 coverage.

Under the social-institutional dimension, the only category out of seven addressed is that of social values noted in seven out of 10 chapters, all concentrated in the special section titled *Info Plus*. Even when addressing this category, the book focuses almost exclusively on the utility of scientific knowledge to improving human lives through basic discovery (such as bacteria causing ulcer) or technological development from a practical perspective (such as artificial kidney to help patients, or genetic fingerprints to identify criminals). Because these references are mainly informational and do not invite reflection, most of this coverage is categorized at level 1.

Unit 1, Chapter 3: Transport and Distribution of Nutrients

The *Info Plus* section discusses advancement of the medical sciences in the treatment of cardiovascular diseases. This section of the chapter explains how artificial hearts work. The social utility of research in basic science leading to development of devices that extend human life is apparent. The quality of coverage of the category of social values would be considered at level 1 because it provides the information in a purely factual way and does not invite further reflection on the topic or its significance.

The information contained in this section reflects the date of the book's publication which stands out in this excerpt:

> As a total, more than 600 patients in the world were equipped with [artificial ventricles] ... The question still remains whether it is possible to make a complete artificial heart, and if yes, when? Specialists would say not before year 2000 for a permanent artificial ventricle and 2010 for a complete artificial heart.
>
> (CERD, 2000b, p. 74)

The apparent drawback of having dated information, however, can be transformed into a learning opportunity to research the current state of artificial heart technology and compare it to the predictions about it in the textbook from 15 years ago.

It is worthwhile to consider how this topic can be used to address a number of other NOS categories that are currently lacking. The discussion of these medical advancements could allude to scientific aims and values by stressing novelty, accuracy, and empirical adequacy. It can address scientific and engineering practices used to improve medical devices, the variety of methods medical researchers use with patients to determine failed and successful interventions, and how various models and theories about the circulatory and immune systems have evolved over time to reach the current level of understanding. Additional categories could be addressed regarding scientific ethos and the importance of respecting human subjects, integrity, carefulness, the establishment of procedures through clinical trials and social certification, and the role of professional activities in the process. In addition, the role of funding and its sources (governments, private foundations, industry) affecting the pace and direction of research in this area, who benefits from the breakthroughs (besides the patients), and matters of competition and cooperation among various organizational structures can be also addressed.

Physics Textbook

Of the three textbooks, the physics textbook was by far the poorest in terms of its coverage of all 11 NOS categories. A thorough analysis of this textbook showed no explicit mention of aims or values. Exercises themselves are formulaic and provide step-by-step guidance from beginning to end with no opportunities for meaning making/inferencing, or metacognitive reflection.

Furthermore, the activities and beginning of chapter objectives are very content-focused and totally decontextualized. There is no sense of building towards a model or conceptual understanding through the exercises and no 'real world' investigations, but rather demonstration-type descriptions of how things work. Finally, there appears to be no connection between methods used in the field and those described in the book. There is, for example, a brief discussion on fiber optics and how it is commonly used, but no exercises or activities inviting any engagement with its principles.

The structure of the chapters may give a clue but not totally explain why the book fails to incorporate NOS ideas. Typically, they start out with a picture of an everyday phenomena or familiar object that provides a quick orientation to the topic, followed by a definition, a set of activities and questions related to it, another concept and definition, followed by activities and questions, then at the end of the chapter a set of exercises and a brief subsection titled "Further Study" in which a principle addressed in the chapter is connected to a common application.

Unlike the other two textbooks, not all chapters in this book include a section inviting further study, and when it is included, it is focused on explaining how the object or tool featured in it works, sometimes with, and sometimes without, a nod to social utility. Furthermore, the physics textbook contains 15 chapters, which is significantly more topics than chemistry (8) and life and earth science textbooks (10) even though the textbooks are about the same length—possibly constraining opportunities to include NOS content. The objectives stated at the beginning of each chapter clearly set the tone for what is to follow. For example, the objectives stated for Chapter 1 (CERD, 2000c, p. 11), refraction of light, are squarely focused on science concepts. They include 1) define refraction, 2) define the index of refraction of a transparent medium, 3) represent by a diagram the deviation of a luminous ray when it passes from air to water or to glass and when it passes from water to air or from glass to air, and 4) define total internal refraction.

The content of the chapter attends to these objectives, using a number of activities and questions about them that guide students (or the teachers) to elaborate on the concepts. While the section at the end of this first chapter deals with fiber optics, the focus of the exposition is to explain how it works, mentioning in passing that it is used in endoscopes, telecommunications, and telephone cables. Thus, it is not surprising that even when applications of concepts are included, the primary focus is set on technical aspects.

Conclusion and Implications

We conclude from this analysis that the three official Lebanese ninth grade science textbooks do not address NOS concepts systematically or adequately to support students' development of scientific literacy in its broader sense. The textbook authors clearly attempt to bring in connections with science and society perhaps as part of the mandate to meet the Lebanese curriculum goal of supporting understanding "the nature of science and technology, their development across history, and their impact on human thought" (CERD, 1997). These connections, however, need to first be systematically included in all Lebanese science textbooks (which is not the case in the physics textbook), and need to be further developed in line with the suggestions proposed in the previous section for the chemistry, and life and earth science textbooks, to support this goal. Most comments for improving connections to NOS are focused on those sections at the end of the chapters that dealt with social connections. This is intended to show how it is possible to capitalize on existing opportunities to enrich the curriculum with NOS discussions. Ideally, however, this type of reflection on NOS-related categories should be embedded throughout the textbook narrative and whenever opportunities to do so could be identified.

Despite the fact that we employed a new analytical framework that, at the time of preparing this study, has not been used in other textbook studies, the results broadly parallel other observations about NOS coverage in textbooks.

Our findings are in agreement with Lumpe and Beck's (1996) in that most of the textbooks they analyzed in the United States focused mainly on the knowledge of science and did not integrate the four aspects of scientific literacy to portray the holistic nature of science. The findings of this study are also consistent with Harbali's (2000), who studied a larger set of middle school Lebanese textbooks, including the ninth grade textbooks analyzed here, albeit using a different framework, in that the textbooks place emphasis on science as a body of knowledge and as a way of investigation, but do not adequately attend to science as way of thinking, and to the interactions among science, technology, and society despite the chapter subsections dedicated to this theme. Finally, the results are consistent with the findings of Abd-El-Khalick and colleagues (2008) who showed that NOS aspects are almost absent from chemistry textbooks published in the United States in the past 40 years.

However, the analysis also indicates some trends not otherwise noted by other studies, possibly because their analytical frameworks did not cast a wide enough net to capture them. For example, there are some allusions to scientific ethos that we found to be encouraging. There are also some references to social values related to the science concepts and their application more so in the chemistry and life and earth science, than in the physics book. By the same token, we note total avoidance of five categories belonging to the social–institutional dimension: social certification, professional activities, financial systems, political power structures, and social organizations and interactions. We would not have noticed the absence of these themes, if the analytical framework we used excluded them. In this sense, application of the Expanded FRA to the textbook storyline, allows researchers to: 1) identify a broad range of NOS ideas, 2) detect oversights, 3) evaluate depth of treatment of these ideas, and 4) use the gained knowledge to improve weak connections and build neglected ones.

While proposed improvements from analyses of the type attempted in this study provide a constructive way forward, we recognize that lasting improvements cannot be done effectively by patching in missing ideas that address one category here, and another there. Rather, it demands a systemic process in which the Expanded FRA framework is taken into consideration when embedding NOS content in a revised set of Lebanese science education goals and objectives. Once this is established, these objectives can be used to better inform science textbook development, as well as instruction and assessment.

The findings call for improving NOS coverage in Lebanese ninth grade textbooks and provide recommendations with the goal of effecting a change in science instruction. Having presented our analysis and suggested ways to improve NOS coverage in these textbooks, we believe that the Expanded FRA analytical framework used in this study provides a useful tool not only for analyzing NOS content, but for identifying specific areas where this content can be elaborated and strengthened.

Note

1 Refer to TIMSS 2003, http://timssandpirls.bc.edu/timss2003.html; TIMSS 2007, http://timssandpirls.bc.edu/TIMSS2007/index.html; TIMSS 2011, http://timssand pirls.bc.edu/timss2011/index.html.

References

Abd-El-Khalick, F., Waters, M., & Le, A-P. (2008). Representations of nature of science in high school chemistry textbooks over the past four decades. *Journal of Research in Science Teaching, 45,* 835–855.

Boutros, T. (1994). *Analyse taxonomique d'un livre de chimie* [Taxonomic analysis of a chemistry textbook]. Unpublished master's thesis, Lebanese University, Beirut, Lebanon.

CERD. (1994). *National educational plan.* Beirut, Lebanon: Author.

CERD. (1995). *New Lebanese educational ladder.* Beirut, Lebanon: Author.

CERD. (1997). *Content of curricula: Science curriculum framework.* Beirut, Lebanon: Author. Retrieved from www.crdp.org/en/desc-evaluation/25299-%20Curriculum%20of%20 Science

CERD. (2000a). *Chemistry: Basic education 9th grade.* Beirut, Lebanon: Lebanese Educational Publishing Company.

CERD. (2000b). *Life and earth science: Basic education 9th grade.* Beirut, Lebanon: Librairie du Liban.

CERD. (2000c). *Physics: Basic education 9th grade.* Beirut, Lebanon: Lebanese Educational Publishing Company.

Chiappetta, E., Sethna, G., & Fillman, D. (1991). A quantitative analysis of high school chemistry textbooks for scientific literacy themes and expository learning aids. *Journal of Research in Science Teaching, 28,* 939–951.

Chiappetta, E., Sethna, G., & Fillman, D. (1993). Do middle school life science textbooks provide a balance of scientific literacy themes? *Journal of Research in Science Teaching, 30,* 787–797.

Chinn, C., & Malhotra, B. (2002). Epistemologically authentic inquiry in schools: A theoretical framework for evaluating inquiry tasks. *Science Education, 86,* 176–218.

Cohen, E., & Dagher, Z. (2005). *An exploratory study of the nature of science in middle school science textbooks.* Paper presented at the International History, Philosophy, and Science Teaching Group Meeting at the University of Leeds, UK.

Dagher, Z. (2009). Epistemology of science in curriculum standards of four Arab countries. In S. BouJaoude & Z. Dagher (Eds.), *The world of science education: Arab states* (pp. 41–60). Rotterdam, the Netherlands: Sense Publishers.

Dagher, Z., BouJaoude, S., & Alameh, S. (2010). *Analysis of nature of science coverage in Egyptian and Lebanese middle school science textbooks.* Paper presented at the Annual meeting of the National Association for Research in Science Teaching, Philadelphia, PA, March 21–24.

de Posada, J. M. (1999). The presentation of metallic bonding in high school science textbooks during three decades: Science education reforms and substantive changes of tendencies. *International Journal of Science Education, 83,* 423–447.

Erduran, S., & Dagher, Z. (2014). *Reconceptualizing the nature of science for science education: Scientific knowledge, practices and other family categories.* Dordrecht, the Netherlands: Springer.

Georg Eckert Institute for International Textbook Research. (2009). *Educational sector, reforms, curricula and textbooks in selected MENA countries: Images of 'self' and 'other' in textbooks of Jordan, Egypt, Lebanon and Oman.* Braunschweig: Germany. Retrieved from www.edumeres.net/uploads/tx_empubdos/MENAreport_-_Educational_Sector_Reforms_Curricula_and_Textbooks.pdf

Gibbs, A., & Lawson, A. (1992). The nature of scientific thinking as reflected by the work of biologists and biology textbooks. *The American Biology Teacher, 54*, 137–152.

Hajj, S. (1997). *Recherche des articuleurs du raisonnement dans le manuel de sciences naturelles: A la découverte du monde vivant et des sciences* [A study of the representation of reasoning skills in biology textbooks]. Unpublished master's thesis, Lebanese University, Beirut, Lebanon.

Harbali, A. (2000). *Content analysis of grades 7 and 10 science textbooks of the new Lebanese science curriculum for scientific literacy themes.* Unpublished master's thesis, American University of Beirut, Beirut, Lebanon.

Hurd, P. (2000). *Transforming middle school science education.* New York: Teachers College Press.

Irez, S. (2009). Nature of science as depicted in Turkish biology textbooks. *Science Education, 93*(3), 422–447.

Irzik, G., & Nola, R. (2014). New directions for nature of science research. In M. Matthews (Ed.), *International handbook of research in history, philosophy and science teaching* (pp. 999–1021). Dordrecht, the Netherlands: Springer.

Khine, M. (Ed.). (2013). *Critical analysis of science textbooks: Evaluating instructional effectiveness.* New York: Springer.

Lumpe, A., & Beck, J. (1996). A profile of high school biology textbooks using scientific literacy recommendations. *The American Biology Teacher, 58*, 147–153.

Muspratt, S., & Freebody, P. (2013). Understanding the disciplines of science: Analysing the language of science textbooks. In M. S. Khine (Ed.), *Critical analysis of science textbooks: Evaluating instructional effectiveness* (pp. 33–60). New York: Springer.

Osborne, J., Collins, S., Ratcliffe, M., Millar, R., & Duschl, R. (2003). What "ideas-about-science" should be taught in school science? A Delphi study of the expert community. *Journal of Research in Science Teaching, 40*, 692–720.

Osborne, J., & Dillon, J. (2008). *Science education in Europe: Critical reflections.* London, England: Nuffield Foundation.

Rodríguez, M., & Niaz, M. (2002). How in spite of the rhetoric, history of science has been ignored in presenting atomic structure in textbooks. *Science Education, 11*, 423–441.

Stern, L., & Roseman, J. (2004). Can middle school science textbooks help students learn important ideas? Findings form project 2061's curriculum evaluation study: Life sciences. *Journal of Research in Science Teaching, 41*, 538–568.

Tai, R., Liu, C., Maltese, A., & Fan, X. (2006). Planning early for careers in science. *Science, 312*(5777), 1143–1144.

Valanides, N., Papageorgiou, M., & Rigas, P. (2013). Science and science teaching. In M. S. Khine (Ed.), *Critical analysis of science textbooks: Evaluating instructional effectiveness* (pp. 259–286). New York: Springer.

5 Exploring Representations of Nature of Science in Australian Junior Secondary School Science Textbooks

A Case Study of Genetics

Christine V. McDonald

The development of scientific literacy is a major goal of school science education throughout the world (e.g., Next Generation Science Standards [NGSS], Australian Curriculum and Reporting Authority [ACARA], 2015; NGSS Lead States, 2013), and a necessary prerequisite to achieving these goals is developing students' understandings of nature of science (NOS). As textbooks have been shown to be heavily utilized in school science classrooms (e.g., Chiappetta, Ganesh, Lee, & Phillips, 2006), and thus significantly influence student learning, it is critical to examine these resources to explore how they represent NOS. A number of empirical studies are beginning to be reported in the international NOS literature specifically focused on representations of NOS in school science textbooks (e.g., Abd-El-Khalick, Waters, & Le, 2008; Irez, 2009); however, none have been conducted in Australia. This is concerning as Australia has recently implemented a new national curriculum (ACARA, 2015), with an explicit emphasis on developing students' views of NOS. The study reported in this chapter explores NOS representations in Australian junior secondary school science textbooks, within the topic of genetics.

Science Education in Australian Schools

Australia is the sixth largest country in the world by area, with a current population of 24 million people (Australian Bureau of Statistics [ABS], 2016), and is comprised of six states and two mainland territories. School education in Australia is mandatory between the ages of approximately 5–16 years, and generally consists of a primary schooling phase (Kindergarten to Year 6), and a secondary schooling phase (Year 7 to Year 12). The secondary schooling phase is commonly divided into two sections: junior secondary (approximately Year 7–10) and senior secondary (approximately Year 11–12), with Year 10 typically considered the final year of compulsory schooling.

Due to Australia's colonial legacy, the school education system was traditionally based on the British curricula model emphasizing behaviorist objectives and teacher-centered pedagogies (Tao, Oliver, & Venville, 2013). Curriculum documents in the 1970s and 1980s were strongly shaped by transmissive models of learning. During the 1990s a significant shift in the educational landscape occurred with the implementation of constructivist-based theories emphasizing student-centered pedagogies and the social construction of knowledge (Tytler, 2007). This shift was not isolated to Australia but underpinned curriculum development across many Western countries, including the United States and the United Kingdom. Within science education, the goal of school science shifted from the acquisition of knowledge and tertiary preparation, to the broader goal of developing scientific literacy for all students. These changes were evidenced in re-developed curriculum documents emphasizing inquiry-based, student-centered learning in Australian schools (Coll & Taylor, 2012).

The first phase of a new national curriculum—*The Australian Curriculum* (ACARA, 2010) was developed in 2009, with implementation commencing in many states and territories in 2011. This marked an important time in Australian education as curriculum development moved from a state/territory responsibility, to a national concern. The Australian Curriculum: Science F-10 (ACARA, 2015) views science as an empirical, dynamic, collaborative, and creative endeavor that enables citizens to answer questions about the world and produce reliable knowledge. It recognizes that scientific knowledge is subject to change, and is revised, refined, and extended over time. The Australian Curriculum: Science F-10 is structured around three interrelated strands: *Science understanding* (focusing on key conceptual knowledge), *Science as a human endeavor* (focusing on science as a unique way of knowing and doing, contemporary decision-making and problem-solving), and *Science inquiry skills* (focusing on evaluating claims, investigating ideas, and developing evidence-based arguments). Within the *Science as a human endeavor* strand, explicit references to NOS content descriptions are included.

Unfortunately, although curriculum documents in Australia are underpinned by contemporary views of NOS and scientific inquiry, research indicates many Australian science classes are still dominated by traditional 'chalk-and-talk' teacher exposition, 'recipe-style' practical activities, and copying notes (Tytler, 2007), even though both teachers and students cite preferences for practical activities, real-world examples, and student-guided research in the classroom (Office of the Chief Scientist, 2012). The reality of time and resource constraints, and the inadequate qualifications of many Australian science teachers (McKenzie, Kos, Walker, & Hong, 2008), have hampered teachers' abilities to implement inquiry-based pedagogies in the science classroom. As a consequence, many Australian science teachers lack the necessary conceptual knowledge to effectively teach science classes, and rely on textbooks to develop their own scientific knowledge, in addition to organizing their teaching of scientific concepts.

This situation is not confined to Australian schools, with international studies continuing to show the dominant and pervasive use of textbooks as a key curricular resource in school science classrooms (e.g., Banilower et al., 2013; Roseman, Stern, & Koppal, 2010). One recent, large-scale Australian study (McDonald, 2016) evaluated the usage of junior secondary science textbooks in Australian schools, with results indicating that a large majority (87 percent) of Australian schools currently use science textbooks in the junior secondary years, and over half of schools surveyed indicated textbooks were used in the majority of science lessons.

A literature search conducted on Australian science textbook research revealed a handful of empirical studies primarily conducted in the late 1980s and early 1990s. Early studies examined the stylistic character of physics textbooks (Strube, 1989), and learning difficulties associated with physical and chemical concepts in science textbooks (de Berg, 1989). A later study by de Berg and Treagust (1993) investigated the presentation of gas properties in chemistry textbooks. Tulip and Cook (1991) sought to compare textbook author intentions with student perceptions of textbook elements, and in a related set of later studies (Cook & Tulip, 1992; Tulip & Cook, 1993) explored teachers' and students' perceptions of junior secondary textbook features and usage in science classrooms. In the mid-1990s Thiele, Venville, and Treagust (1995) analyzed analogies in secondary biology and chemistry textbooks, and Daniels (1996) investigated science textbook readability.

Although a growing body of research is beginning to emerge in the international NOS literature specifically focused on representations of NOS in school science textbooks (refer to Chapter 1 for a discussion), no Australian studies have been identified that have specifically examined the quality of NOS representations in textbooks. A review of the literature revealed three studies that broadly addressed themes related to scientific literacy and indigenous perspectives in Australian textbooks. Wilkinson (1999) examined 20 high school physics textbooks over a three-decade period (1967–1997) for curriculum balance and scientific literacy themes. Results indicated that the majority of examined texts stressed science as a body of knowledge, with little emphasis on science as a way of thinking. More modern texts (post-1990) were found to place an increased emphasis on science, technology, and society, and a decrease in emphasis on science as a way of thinking. Ninnes (2000) analyzed seven junior secondary science textbooks published in Australia and Canada for indigenous knowledge themes. Using discourse analysis techniques, results indicated that some texts represented indigenous knowledge themes more effectively than others, with smaller author teams producing more consistent themes. In a related study, Ninnes (2001) explored representations of ways of knowing in five sets of junior secondary science textbooks published in Australia. Two discourse analysis methodologies were used, and results indicated textbooks did not provide opportunities to examine alternative perspectives, or question scientific knowledge.

As NOS is explicitly addressed in the new national curriculum, it is timely to examine Australian school science textbooks for alignment with stated curricula goals. The study outlined in this chapter utilized a new analytical framework underpinned by the central tenets of the Family Resemblance Approach (FRA) to explore representations of NOS in junior secondary school textbooks.

The Family Resemblance Approach

The Family Resemblance Approach was originally proposed by philosopher Ludwig Wittgenstein (1958), further developed by Irzik and Nola (2011, 2014), and recently expanded and reconceptualized by Erduran and Dagher (2014). In this chapter, Erduran and Dagher's expanded version of the Family Resemblance Approach (herein referred to as the FRA) will be used as the theoretical grounding for the analytical framework used in this study. The idea of a family resemblance with respect to science is based on an understanding that many disciplines of science share certain characteristics; however, none of these characteristics are inherent in all disciplines, and an individual discipline may not share any of them (van Dijk, 2011). As such, this approach highlights both the similarities and differences between scientific disciplines. Dagher and Erduran (2016) assert that the FRA provides a coherent approach whereby domain-general and domain-specific aspects of NOS can coexist, acknowledging the characteristics that disciplines share, and also those that make them unique.

Erduran and Dagher (2014) state the purpose of the FRA is not to teach students individual NOS aspects, but instead to present NOS holistically in a contextualized manner. The framework allows teachers to highlight particular NOS aspects that are already part of the content under study, and does not require coverage of all NOS aspects in all contexts. The suggestive, rather than prescriptive nature of the approach enables teachers to make choices regarding how they would like to embed the NOS ideas present in science content in the curriculum.

The FRA views science as a cognitive-epistemic system and a social-institutional system. Within the cognitive-epistemic system, the following four components are identified: aims and values, scientific practices, methods and methodological rules, and scientific knowledge. Seven components within the social-institutional system are identified, and these include: professional activities, scientific ethos, social certification and dissemination, social values of science, social organizations and interactions, political power struggles, and financial systems. A detailed description of each of these components is provided in the Analytical Framework section later in this chapter.

The 11 components of the FRA are represented by the FRA Wheel presented in Figure 5.1. The FRA Wheel provides an image of science as a holistic and dynamic system, and visually represents the interactions between the components of the cognitive-epistemic and social-institutional systems.

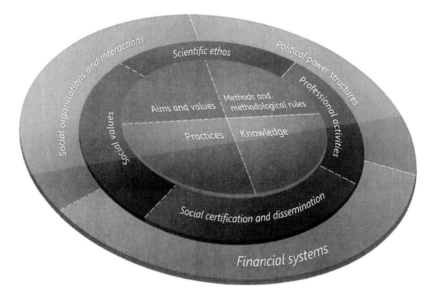

Figure 5.1 FRA Wheel: Science as a Cognitive-Epistemic and Social-Institutional System (Reprinted from Erduran & Dagher, 2014, p. 28)

Methods

Textbook Selection

Representations of NOS were explored in four junior secondary textbooks suitable for Year 10 students. These textbooks were selected based on the findings of a recent large-scale Australian study (McDonald, 2016) indicating the top three textbooks currently being used by Australian schools were Pearson Science (Linstead, et al., 2012), ScienceWorld (Williamson & Stannard, 2012), and Science Quest (Lofts & Evergreen, 2012). These three textbooks were selected for analysis, with an additional textbook Oxford Big Ideas Science (Cash, Quinton, Tilley, & Silvester, 2012) also chosen as it was the next highest ranked textbook produced by publishers other than Pearson, Macmillan, and Wiley/Jacaranda. Each of the four Year 10 textbooks was the final textbook in connected textbook series (each series comprised four textbooks, one for each year level from Year 7 to Year 10). All of the examined textbooks were the student editions and were the first editions published to align with the new Australian Curriculum.

Junior secondary textbooks for Year 10 students were selected for use in the current study as research suggests students' experiences in these years are pivotal in influencing their decisions to continue studying science in the post-compulsory years of schooling (Lyons & Quinn, 2010; Tytler & Osborne, 2012). As Year 10 is the final year of junior secondary in the majority of Australian schools, and subsequently the year when students decide whether they will continue studying science in the post-compulsory years, this year level was deemed the most appropriate for the present study.

Topic Selection

The topic of genetics was chosen for examination in this study. The decision to limit the exploration of NOS representations to a single topic was made for the following reasons. First, the analysis undertaken in the study seeks to identify NOS aspects that emerge from a particular context, in this case—genetics. This case-based analysis will provide a sample of relevant NOS aspects in this context, which may be supplemented with future analyses of other topic areas. Second, by exploring a single topic in depth, a holistic analysis can be conducted to discover which NOS aspects are highlighted, which NOS aspects are left out, and how the NOS aspects are represented. Finally, the presentation of NOS is typically concentrated in the introductory 'What is science?' chapter of school science textbooks. This is a particular concern in connected textbook series such as those utilized in junior secondary (Years 7–10), as this chapter may only be included in the Year 7 textbook, and absent in subsequent texts. Thus, it is critical to examine how NOS is represented in individual chapters/topics within science textbooks.

Importantly, any of the Year 10 science topics could have been chosen for analysis in this study. Genetics was selected as the context for analysis as a number of recent studies have examined how genetics can be used as a platform for teaching NOS (e.g., McComas & Kampourakis, 2015; Smith & Gericke, 2015; Williams & Rudge, 2016), with one identified study assessing representations of NOS in genetics sections of high school biology textbooks (Campanile, Lederman, & Kampourakis, 2015). Genetics comprises one of two core biological science topics in the Year 10 curriculum (ACARA, 2015). Along with evolution, these two topics occupy one-quarter of the Year 10 science curriculum and are typically taught over a single term (approximately 10 weeks).

All four textbooks were guided by these content descriptors and addressed the topic of genetics in a single chapter within each textbook. The chapters varied in length from 30 pages (ScienceWorld) to 66 pages (Science Quest) and presented the topic of genetics across a number of units, which included a variety of figures, diagrams, photos, activity boxes, online/digital activities, question sets, links to curriculum standards, inquiry-based activities, skill development activities, definitions, and reviews—in addition to the main text narrative predominantly focused on the presentation of key science concepts. Other narrative sections included historical vignettes and contemporary issues vignettes.

Analytical Framework

The following categories of NOS formed the basis of the analytical framework in this study based on the expanded FRA outlined by Erduran and Dagher (2014). A brief description of the 11 categories is provided in Table 5.1.

Table 5.1 Cognitive-Epistemic and Social-Institutional NOS Categories

Cognitive-epistemic system dimensions	
Aims and values	The scientific enterprise is underpinned by adherence to a set of values that guide scientific practices. These aims and values are often implicit and they may include accuracy, objectivity, consistency, skepticism, rationality, simplicity, empirical adequacy, prediction, testability, novelty, fruitfulness, commitment to logic, viability, and explanatory power.
Scientific practices	The scientific enterprise encompasses a wide range of cognitive, epistemic and discursive practices. Scientific practices such as observation, classification, and experimentation utilize a variety of methods to gather observational, historical, or experimental data. Cognitive practices such as explaining, modeling, and predicting are closely linked to discursive practices involving argumentation and reasoning.
Methods and methodological rules	Scientists engage in disciplined inquiry by utilizing a variety of observational, investigative, and analytical methods to generate reliable evidence and construct theories, laws, and models in a given science discipline, which are guided by particular methodological rules. Scientific methods are revisionary in nature, with different methods producing different forms of evidence, leading to clearer understandings and more coherent explanations of scientific phenomena.
Scientific knowledge	Theories, laws and models (TLM) are interrelated products of the scientific enterprise that generate and/or validate scientific knowledge, and provide logical and consistent explanations to develop scientific understanding. Scientific knowledge is holistic and relational, and TLM are conceptualized as a coherent network, not as discrete and disconnected fragments of knowledge.
Social-institutional system dimensions	
Professional activities	Scientists engage in a number of professional activities to enable them to communicate their research, including conference attendance and presentation, writing manuscripts for peer-reviewed journals, reviewing papers, developing grant proposals, and securing funding.
Scientific ethos	Scientists are expected to abide by a set of norms both within their own work, and during their interactions with colleagues and scientists from other institutions. These norms may include organized skepticism, universalism, communalism and disinterestedness, freedom and openness, intellectual honesty, respect for research subjects, and respect for the environment.

Social certification and dissemination	By presenting their work at conferences, and writing manuscripts for peer-reviewed journals, scientists' work is reviewed and critically evaluated by their peers. This form of social quality control aids in the validation of new scientific knowledge by the broader scientific community.
Social values of science	The scientific enterprise embodies various social values including social utility, respecting the environment, freedom, decentralizing power, honesty, addressing human needs, and equality of intellectual authority.
Social organizations and interactions	Science is socially organized in various institutions including universities and research centers. The nature of social interactions among members of a research team working on different projects is governed by an organizational hierarchy. In a wider organizational context, the institute of science has been linked to industry and the defense force.
Political power structures	The scientific enterprise operates within a political environment that imposes its own values and interests. Science is not universal, and the outcomes of science are not always beneficial for individuals, groups, communities, or cultures.
Financial systems	The scientific enterprise is mediated by economic factors. Scientists require funding in order to carry out their work, and state and national level governing bodies provide significant levels of funding to universities and research centers. As such, these organizations have an influence on the types of scientific research funded, and ultimately conducted.

Note: Adapted from Erduran & Dagher, (2014).

Analytical Procedure

A qualitative content analysis approach was used to explore the NOS representations in the examined chapters. Underpinned by the guiding principles of ethnographic content analysis (Altheide, 1996), this approach is oriented to documenting and understanding meaning by implementing a systematic, yet flexible analytical approach. The analysis was conducted in three phases. In the first phase of analysis, the textbook chapters focused on the topic of genetics were identified in each textbook. Each chapter was examined holistically, with all narrative and text-based questions and activities carefully read, and all figures, diagrams, and photos viewed. Chapters were then individually examined for evidence of representation of the NOS categories of the analytical framework. In this study, the unit of analysis was defined as an individual curriculum outcome, sentence, paragraph, figure, diagram, photo, or question.

In the second phase of analysis, the four genetics chapters were carefully examined to determine the key concept organizers guiding the structure of the chapters. As the analysis undertaken utilized a case-based approach, it was deemed more appropriate to identify NOS aspects in particular conceptual areas of genetics, rather than provide an analysis of individual NOS aspects across all four chapters. Five key organizing sections were identified in the four chapters: 1) DNA, Chromosomes, and Genes, 2) The Discovery of DNA, 3) Inheritance, 4) The History of Genetics, and 5) Gene Technology and Human Applications. Each of these organizing sections was further examined to determine the location of representation, with five possibilities identified: (a) science content (main narrative), (b) science inquiry activity, (c) historical vignette, (d) contemporary issues vignette, and (e) question set. Each of the identified NOS units were then collated into a key organizing section and location, and then grouped into a NOS category.

In the final phase of analysis, each unit was then coded as an explicit or implicit representation of NOS, and examples of both types of representations are presented in the next section. Following Abd-El-Khalick et al. (2017, p. 91):

> an explicit representation of a NOS aspect entailed the identification of some textual elements (statements, figure captions, etc.), or reflective prompts (questions, etc.), which convey messages that are epistemological in nature, or that invite students to think about the text in ways that help them draw some conclusions about the NOS aspect in question. An implicit representation of this NOS aspect, in comparison, was noted when relevant epistemological ideas could be *inferred* from textual materials.

The following procedures were implemented to establish inter-rater reliability in this study. First, two researchers independently analyzed the marked units of analysis in each of the four chapters for representations of NOS across all 11 categories. The researchers also independently assessed the nature of NOS representation in each marked unit to determine whether the representation was explicit or implicit. The researchers compared their analyses and any differences were discussed, negotiated, and resolved. After this process, agreement was reached on all units of analysis. Second, findings from the analysis were supported by representative quotes and descriptions directly from the textbooks, further adding to the reliability of the study.

Results and Discussion

Results from this exploratory study indicated NOS is not explicitly addressed in genetics chapters in Australian junior secondary school textbooks, with only three explicit NOS examples identified in the examined chapters. These findings align with results reported in international contexts examining NOS representations in school science textbooks (e.g., Abd-El-Khalick et al., 2008; Irez, 2009; Wei, Li, & Chen, 2013). Similar findings were also recently reported by Campanile et al. (2015) who examined representations of NOS and scientific inquiry in the Mendelian genetics sections of U.S. high school biology textbooks. Other findings indicated numerous implicit representations of NOS were present throughout the chapters, providing opportunities to discuss NOS content. However, without prompts or guiding questions and statements highlighting links to explicit representations, it is highly unlikely that these opportunities will be capitalized upon, as research has consistently shown that NOS needs to be addressed explicitly to facilitate the development of students' views of NOS (e.g., Abd-El-Khalick & Lederman, 2000; Khishfe & Abd-El-Khalick, 2002).

Analysis of the representations of NOS across the 11 categories of the FRA analytical framework indicated that all three explicit NOS references were coded as *scientific knowledge*, with a variety of other NOS categories represented implicitly across the five key organizing sections. Opportunities to consider cognitive-epistemic system dimension NOS categories were present throughout the five sections, with many opportunities to implicitly consider *scientific knowledge*, and to a lesser degree *scientific practices* and *methods and methodological rules*. One cognitive-epistemic category, *aims and values*, was not addressed in any of the sections. Social-institutional system dimension NOS categories were represented implicitly in the 'The Discovery of DNA' and 'Gene Technology and Human Applications' sections, and to a lesser extent in 'The History of Genetics' sections. All seven NOS categories within this dimension were represented; however, the categories of *professional activities, social values of science, social certification and dissemination*, and *social organizations and interactions* were more frequently evidenced in these sections.

To illustrate the manner in which the NOS aspects were represented in the examined chapters, two of the five cases developed during the data analysis phase (corresponding to the key organizing sections) will be presented. These two cases were selected to provide contrasting examples of how NOS was represented in different sections of the chapters. The first case 'The Discovery of DNA' was underpinned by a historical focus, whereas the second case 'Gene Technology and Human Applications' presented a contemporary focus.

Case 1—The Discovery of DNA

This key organizing section focused on the development of the double helix model of the structure of DNA. It includes a consideration of the numerous scientists who contributed to this discovery including Miescher, Levene, Avery, Chargaff, Pauling, Franklin, Watson, Crick, and Wilkins. A concerning finding indicated none of the four chapters made explicit references to any of the examined categories of NOS; however, two of the four texts (Pearson and Oxford) provided extended narratives outlining the historical development of the model of DNA, with numerous implicit NOS references. Interestingly, the ScienceWorld text only included a single paragraph on the development of the DNA model within a science content section on the structure of DNA (citing Miescher, and Watson, Crick and Wilkins only), and a small text-box activity asking students to search the internet to find out more about Rosalind Franklin. The Science Quest text did not outline the historical development of DNA at all within the chapter, with one question identified asking students to consult a digital activity about the ownership of scientific discoveries. It is important to note the Science Quest textbook contained an introductory chapter addressing many historical aspects of science, including a three-page unit on the discovery of DNA. However, as this study sought to explore NOS representations *within* the topic chapters, information in the introductory chapter was not analyzed.

The Pearson text contained a two-page historical vignette addressing the discovery of DNA, whereas the Oxford text outlined the discovery of DNA within a science content section. No references to *aims and values* were identified; however, implicit references to *scientific practices, methods and methodological rules, scientific knowledge*, and numerous NOS categories within the social-institutional system dimension were identified within both texts. For example, the construction, extension, and revision of scientific knowledge was evident throughout the Pearson vignette, with the key contributions of the various scientists involved outlined in detail. The vignette commenced with an implicit reference "James Watson and Francis Crick are often credited with the discovery of DNA in 1953, but the history of the molecule extends further back in time" (Pearson, Historical vignette, p. 5); however, no explicit statements regarding the developmental nature of historical knowledge were included to highlight this important NOS aspect.

Scientific practices and *methods and methodological rules* were also implicitly represented in the two texts, with details of the various methods employed (e.g., X-ray crystallography, protein isolation techniques) and scientific practices utilized (e.g., modeling, predicting, explaining) outlined in detail in the Pearson text, and to a lesser degree in the Oxford text. Unfortunately, opportunities to explicitly represent these NOS categories were not taken up, with short statements or questions guiding the student to consider the role of different methods and practices in the development of the model, absent from these sections.

Numerous implicit references to social-institutional system dimensions were also evident in both texts. *Professional activities* and *social certification and dissemination* were highlighted with references to conference attendance: "In 1951, American molecular biologist James Watson (1928-) attended a lecture in which Franklin presented her research" (Pearson, Historical vignette, p. 6), and publication "Watson and Crick wrote a one-pager on their model of DNA that was published in the journal *Nature*." (Oxford, Science content, p. 132). Opportunities to consider the *social values of science* were also highlighted in the Pearson vignette with references regarding the contribution of Franklin's X-ray images to Watson and Crick's model. Importantly, none of these implicit references were supplemented with additional statements or questions highlighting explicit links to NOS.

The Oxford text also provided a separate one-page historical vignette focused on the contribution of Rosalind Franklin to the development of the model of DNA. Although this vignette did not provide explicit references to the examined NOS categories, the implicit references contained in the section were highly effective examples. The vignette provided a historical overview of Franklin's personal and professional life, and highlighted a number of social-institutional system dimensions. For example, references to *political power structures* were evident with a discussion of Franklin's father's disapproval of women in higher education, and the treatment of Franklin in Randall's laboratory "Only males were allowed in the university dining rooms, and after hours Franklin's colleagues went to men-only pubs" (Oxford, Historical vignette, p. 135). *Social organizations and interactions* were also highlighted whilst discussing how the research team was organized, with Franklin being treated as a technical assistant, instead of a research associate. In addition, references to *scientific ethos* and *social values of science* were identified, particularly with regard to the lack of credit attributed to Franklin from her contributions, and the actions of Watson and Crick regarding the use of her images. Finally, *professional activities* and *social certification and dissemination* were also highlighted in the following vignette:

> Between 1951 and 1953 Rosalind Franklin came very close to solving the DNA structure. She was beaten to publication by Crick and Watson in part because of the friction between Wilkins and herself. At one point, Wilkins showed Watson one of Franklin's crystallographic portraits of DNA. When he saw the picture, the solution became apparent to him, and the results went into an article in *Nature* almost immediately. Franklin's work did appear as a supporting article in the same issue of the journal.
>
> (Oxford, Historical vignette, p. 135)

Case 2—Gene Technology and Human Applications

This key organizing section focused on gene technology and engineering, including the Human Genome Project, gene testing, genetically modified organisms, gene therapy, biotechnology, stem cells, cloning, and issues and implications arising from these technologies. Three of the four texts contained contemporary issue vignettes outlining stem cells (Pearson), cystic fibrosis (Oxford), and genetic counseling and DNA testing (ScienceWorld). Interestingly, these vignettes did not provide many opportunities to consider NOS content, with the majority of NOS representations located in science content sections and question sets. No explicit references to any of the examined categories of NOS were identified in the chapters. However, numerous opportunities to consider relevant NOS content were identified throughout the chapters, particularly with regard to *methods and methodological rules, scientific knowledge, social values of science, social organizations and interactions* and *financial systems.* Examples of some of these implicit representations will be outlined in the following paragraphs.

Methods and methodological rules were represented in all examined chapters, with detailed descriptions of the variety of methods utilized in gene technology and engineering provided, including methods associated with recombinant DNA technology and gene sequencing, and their associated techniques. Providing details of gene splicing, techniques for genetic modification and harvesting of stem cells, and processes of DNA profiling and reproductive technologies allows students to appreciate that science does not follow a strict scientific method dominated by hypothesis-driven experimentation. An effective example highlighting the diversity of methods utilized in genetics is the Human Genome Project (HGP), which utilizes data-driven methods to generate evidence. The examined texts varied in the manner in which they represented the HGP with the majority of chapters emphasizing the important role of fast computers as a central component of the project.

The HGP also provided an effective context for considering the NOS categories—*social organizations and interactions* and *financial systems.* Many examined chapters made reference to the international nature of the project "This massive task was co-ordinated by the United States National Institutes of Health and involved hundreds of scientists from at least 18 countries, including Australia" (ScienceWorld, Science content, p. 69). Importantly, some of the implications of the project were also considered, including economic considerations:

> Although the HGP was coordinated by government departments, one of the project's aims was to transfer all the technologies to private companies. Now much of the HGP follow-up research is being done by private commercial companies, particularly multi-national US-based companies, who expect to earn billions of dollars through sales of new drugs, equipment, technologies and information.
>
> (ScienceWorld, Science content, p. 69)

Unfortunately, none of the texts utilized these examples to explicitly highlight the nature and relationship of social organizations and their interactions with government and private business interests, or the key role of financial considerations in directing research.

Social values of science were highlighted throughout the examined chapters, particularly when discussing stem cells, cloning, genetically modified organisms (GMOs), and genetic screening:

> The discovery of DNA and the development of various gene technologies have enabled us to manipulate organisms even further. But along with all the great spin-offs there are ethical issues. How much is human

interference affecting human welfare and the welfare of other species both positively and negatively?

(Oxford, Science content, p. 168)

Numerous examples were provided in science content sections highlighting the need to consider values such as respecting the environment (GMOs), freedom (genetic screening), addressing human needs (reproductive technologies), and social utility (development of new gene technologies). Many of these values were also implicitly highlighted in question sets in the chapters, with examples including "Suggest ways in which information from genetic tests may be used by organisations such as insurance companies, medical facilities and workplaces" (Science Quest, Question set, p. 99), and "Investigate the arguments used against the introduction of genetically modified plants such as Golden rice-2" (Pearson, Question set, p. 32). However, explicit links to social values were not included in the science content sections or question sets.

Finally, implicit references to *scientific knowledge* were also identified in the examined chapters. For example, an understanding of the role of scientists working together, in addition to technological advances, was evident in some chapters "More equipment and dramatic developments in technology have had a major impact. There is also the cumulative effect of scientists working to decipher the events that occur" (Oxford, Science content, p. 157). The contribution of scientific evidence to 'finding the answer' was also highlighted whilst discussing the HGP:

It was anticipated that once we had the human genome sequenced, many mysteries would be unfolded, answers to ancient riddles would be unlocked and a new understanding of who we are would be unwrapped. Unfortunately, rather than an explosion of wonder and explanation, the sequencing only promoted more questions. Just like knowing the ingredients for a cake or the components that make up a car, we had the list, but not the delicious cake or the speeding racing car.

(Science Quest, Science content, p. 62)

These examples provided opportunities to discuss the role of evidence in the construction of scientific knowledge, but did not make explicit connections to these critical NOS aspects.

Location of NOS Representations

In this study it was deemed important to examine the location of NOS representations in the examined textbooks for a number of reasons. First, Sharma (2013) recently reported middle-school science teachers pay more attention to the main narrative in science textbooks than other features of the text. Second, Allchin (2014) proposes that NOS is ideally contextualized through the complementary approaches of utilizing science inquiry activities, contemporary cases, and historical cases. Finally, Overman, Vermunt, Meijer, Bulte, and Brekelmans (2013) state that student learning is activated and directed by textbook questions. Thus, in this study a close examination of the science content (main narrative), science inquiry activities, historical vignettes, contemporary issues vignettes, and question sets was undertaken.

Data analysis indicated the majority of implicit NOS representations were located in the science content sections of the examined chapters, with two of the three explicit NOS representations also located in these sections. Both of these explicit NOS representations were primarily categorized as *scientific knowledge*:

> New technologies and new knowledge can modify how we see, understand and communicate our knowledge. This eventually results in the creation, modification or replacement of terminology and theories that are used by a majority or enforced by those with the highest authority or persuasion.
> (Science Quest, Science content, Inheritance section, p. 75)

> So, what has changed? More equipment and dramatic developments in technology have had a major impact. There is also the cumulative effect of scientists working to decipher the events that occur at the microscopic level in living cells. Scientists build on the work that has been done by those before them and eventually the 'jigsaw' begins to make sense.
> (Oxford, Science content, The history of genetics section, p. 157)

Opportunities to consider the NOS categories of *scientific practices* and *methods and methodological rules* were primarily provided whilst examining science inquiry activities. Unfortunately, scientific practices were generally portrayed as isolated activities, and many student investigations included in the chapters followed a recipe-style format. Although the methods included did not reinforce the 'myth of the scientific method', and a variety of methods were often presented to students, no explicit consideration of how these methods contribute to knowledge in the field was considered. Allchin (2014) proposes that students need to reflect on the quality of evidence, consensus on alternative models, and differing interpretations of data to capitalize on NOS considerations whilst engaged in scientific inquiry.

The historical vignettes contained in 'The Discovery of DNA' sections provided rich opportunities to consider many NOS categories, particularly those included in the social-institutional system dimension, and the cognitive-epistemic NOS category *scientific knowledge*. These sections were effective in providing opportunities to discuss the construction, extension, and revision of scientific knowledge, in addition to considering the role of professional activities such as conference attendance and publication in socially certifying scientific knowledge. The vignette focused on the life of Rosalind Franklin (Oxford) was particularly effective in providing a platform for discussion of many social-institutional issues set in the prevailing cultural context of the time. However, the absence of explicit statements linking the issues identified to relevant NOS categories failed to capitalize on these opportunities.

Interestingly, few NOS categories were considered in the contemporary issues vignettes included in the 'Gene Technology and Human Applications' sections. These sections tended to focus on the science content underpinning the topics, and failed to critically evaluate the debates associated with the topics. As such, these vignettes missed important opportunities to highlight the relevance of NOS categories such as the *social values of science* in their presentation.

References to some NOS categories were also identified in question sets throughout the examined chapters, with one of the three explicit NOS references located in a question set, and categorized as *scientific knowledge:*

> Q13. With increased knowledge and understanding, previous metaphors used to describe DNA are increasingly appearing to be less accurate in describing its complexities. The double helix, for example, describes its shape but not its function.
>
> a. Find out more about two of the metaphors below and suggest reasons why each is becoming less useful.
>
> Double helix, Chemical building block, Alphabet of life, Book of life, Computer code of life, Symphony of life, Blueprint
>
> (Science Quest, Question set, DNA, chromosomes and genes section; p. 61)

As textbook questions are considered to be effective tools for directing student attention to relevant content, opportunities to focus student attention on related NOS aspects in these question sets were also missed.

Conclusion and Recommendations

This exploratory study of NOS representations in junior secondary school science textbooks revealed multiple opportunities to consider relevant NOS aspects embedded within the topic of genetics, although these opportunities were almost exclusively implicit in nature. It was not a focus of this study to evaluate or score the individual textbooks for their NOS representations, with data analysis indicating the four textbooks presented NOS ideas in a variety of organizing sections and formats, with some textbooks providing more opportunities for NOS discussion (e.g., Oxford, Science Quest,

Pearson), than others (e.g., ScienceWorld). Importantly, the examined chapters varied in length, with the shortest chapter (ScienceWorld) providing more limited opportunities to consider NOS. In addition, although some studies have highlighted the inaccurate presentation of some NOS aspects within historical contexts, such as Mendelian genetics (e.g., Campanile et al., 2015), this study did not seek to evaluate the accuracy of the historical vignettes in the examined textbooks. From a pragmatic perspective, the goal was to explore *how* NOS ideas were presented, as empirical research continues to show that the NOS content of school science textbooks has not significantly changed, and in some cases, regressed, over nearly half a century (e.g., Abd-El-Khalick et al., 2017). Similar to findings reported by Fuselier, Jackson, and Stoiko (2016) in an evolutionary context, results from this study show school science textbooks are not capitalizing on opportunities to explicitly highlight relevant NOS aspects within content already included. These changes could be made with only minor modification to existing materials, by simply including reflective statements, prompts, or questions to explicitly focus students' attention on relevant NOS aspects.

The application of a new analytical framework based on Erduran and Dagher's (2014) reconceptualized and expanded FRA enabled an in-depth, holistic exploration of how NOS was represented in the topic, and identified aspects of NOS highlighted in the various key organizing sections (subtopics), science content (main narrative), historical and contemporary vignettes, science inquiry activities, and question sets. As stated earlier, the FRA allows particular NOS aspects that are already part of the content under study to be highlighted, and does not require that all NOS aspects are included in all contexts. Importantly, the FRA may be applied to other conceptual areas from the biological sciences domain, such as evolution, in addition to topics from the physical, chemical, and earth and space sciences. Findings from research conducted in these areas will provide new perspectives on relevant NOS aspects highlighted in different disciplines, and contribute to scholarship utilizing both domain-general and domain-specific approaches to NOS.

To conclude, the selection of a classroom textbook is a complex decision and must take into account a variety of factors. A recent, large-scale study conducted in the Australian context (McDonald, 2016) reported the most important factor guiding the selection of junior secondary science textbooks by schools was layout/color/illustrations, followed by emphasis on science content, readability, and alignment with the curriculum, with an emphasis on NOS not considered to be an important factor. This is a concerning finding as NOS is explicitly addressed in the new national science curriculum in Australian schools. For example, by the end of Year 10, students are required to achieve a number of NOS-related objectives, including examples such as: "Scientific understanding, including models and theories, is contestable and is refined over time through a process of review by the scientific community (ACSHE191)" (ACARA, 2015). Findings from this study suggest that current representations of NOS in junior secondary school textbooks may not be sufficient to facilitate the achievement of NOS-related curricula objectives, particularly in the absence of a suitably qualified science teacher, with a robust understanding of NOS.

References

Abd-El-Khalick, F., & Lederman, N. G. (2000). The influence of history of science courses on students' views of nature of science. *Journal of Research in Science Teaching*, *37*(10), 1057–1095.

Abd-El-Khalick, F., Myers, J. Y., Summers, R., Brunner, J., Waight, N., Wahbeh, N., . . . Belarmino, J. (2017). A longitudinal analysis of the extent and manner of representations of nature of science in U.S. high school biology and physics textbooks. *Journal of Research in Science Teaching*, *54*(1), 82–120.

Abd-El-Khalick, F., Waters, M., & Le, A-P. (2008). Representations of nature of science in high school chemistry textbooks over the past four decades. *Journal of Research in Science Teaching*, *45*(7), 835–855.

Allchin, D. (2014). From science studies to scientific literacy: A view from the classroom. *Science & Education*, *23*, 1911–1932.

Altheide, D. L. (1996). *Qualitative media analysis*. Thousand Oaks, CA: Sage.

Australian Bureau of Statistics [ABS]. (2016). *Population clock*. Retrieved March 28, 2016, from www.abs.gov.au/ausstats/abs@.nsf/94713ad445ff1425ca25682000192af2/1647 509ef7e25faaca2568a900154b63?OpenDocument

Australian Curriculum and Reporting Authority [ACARA]. (2010). *Australian curriculum: Science F-10*. Sydney: Commonwealth of Australia.

Australian Curriculum and Reporting Authority [ACARA]. (2015). *Australian curriculum: Science F-10*. Sydney: Commonwealth of Australia.

Banilower, E. R., Smith, P. S., Weiss, I. R., Malzahn, K. A., Campbell, K. M., & Weis, A. M. (2013). *Report of the 2012 national survey of science and mathematics education*. Chapel Hill, NC: Horizon Research.

Campanile, M. F., Lederman, N. G., & Kampourakis, K. (2015). Mendelian genetics as a platform for teaching about nature of science and scientific inquiry. *Science & Education*, *24*, 205–225.

Cash, S., Quinton, G., Tilley, C., & Silvester, H. (2012). *Oxford big ideas Science 10: Australian Curriculum*. South Melbourne: Oxford University Press.

Chiappetta, E. L., Ganesh, T. G., Lee, Y. H., & Phillips, M. C. (2006). *Examination of science textbook analysis research conducted on textbooks published over the past 100 years in the United States*. Paper presented at the annual meeting of the National Association for Research in Science Teaching, San Francisco, CA.

Coll, R. K., & Taylor, N. (2012). An international perspective on science curriculum development and implementation. In B. J. Fraser, K. G. Tobin, & C. J. McRobbie (Eds.), *Second international handbook of science education* (Vol. II, pp. 771–782). Dordrecht, the Netherlands: Springer.

Cook, A., & Tulip, D. (1992). The importance of selected textbook features to science teachers. *Research in Science Education*, *22*, 91–100.

Dagher, Z. R., & Erduran, S. (2016). Reconceptualising the nature of science for science education—Why does it matter? *Science & Education*, *25*(1), 147–164.

Daniels, D. (1996). A study of science textbook readability. *Australian Science Teachers Journal*, *42*(3), 61–65.

de Berg, K. C. (1989). The emergence of quantification in the pressure-volume relationship for gases: A textbook analysis. *Science Education, 73*(2), 115–134.

de Berg, K. C., & Treagust, D. F. (1993). The presentations of gas properties in chemistry textbooks and as reported by science teachers. *Journal of Research in Science Teaching, 30*(8), 871–882.

Erduran, S., & Dagher, Z. (2014). *Reconceptualising the nature of science in science education.* Dordrecht, the Netherlands: Springer.

Fuselier, L. C., Jackson, J. K., & Stoiko, R. (2016). Social and rational: The presentation of nature of science and the uptake of change in evolution textbooks. *Science Education, 100*(2), 239–265.

Irez, S. (2009). Nature of science as depicted in Turkish biology textbooks. *Science Education, 93*(3), 422–447.

Irzik, G., & Nola, R. (2011). A family resemblance approach to the nature of science for science education. *Science & Education, 20*(7–8), 591–607.

Irzik, G., & Nola, R. (2014). New directions for nature of science research. In M. Matthews (Ed.), *International handbook of research in history, philosophy and science teaching* (pp. 999–1021). Dordrecht, the Netherlands: Springer.

Khishfe, R., & Abd-El-Khalick, F. (2002). Influence of explicit and reflective versus implicit inquiry-oriented instruction on sixth graders' views of nature of science. *Journal of Research in Science Teaching, 39*, 551–578.

Linstead, G., et al. (2012). *Pearson science 10 student book.* Melbourne: Pearson.

Lofts, G., & Evergreen, M. J. (2012). *Science quest 10.* Milton: Wiley.

Lyons, T., & Quinn, F. (2010). *Choosing science: Understanding the declines in senior high school science enrolments.* Armidale: National Centre of Science, ICT and Mathematics Education for Rural and Regional Australia, University of New England.

McComas, W. F., & Kampourakis, K. (2015). Using the history of biology, chemistry, geology, and physics to illustrate general aspects of nature of science. *Review of Science, Mathematics and ICT Education, 9*(1), 47–76.

McDonald, C.V. (2016). Evaluating junior secondary science textbook usage in Australian schools. *Research in Science Education, 46*, 481–509.

McKenzie, P., Kos, J., Walker, M., & Hong, J. (2008). *Staff in Australia's schools 2007.* Canberra: DEEWR.

NGSS Lead States. (2013). *Next generation science standards: For states, by states.* Washington, DC: The National Academies Press.

Ninnes, P. (2000). Representations of indigenous knowledges in secondary school science textbooks in Australia and Canada. *International Journal of Science Education, 22*(6), 603–617.

Ninnes, P. (2001). Representations of ways of knowing in junior high school science texts used in Australia. *Discourse: Studies in the Cultural Politics of Education, 22*(1), 81–94.

Office of the Chief Scientist. (2012). *Health of Australian science.* Canberra: Australian Government.

Overman, M., Vermunt, J. D., Meijer, P. C., Bulte, A. M. W., & Brekelmans, M. (2013). Textbook questions in context-based and traditional chemistry curricula analyzed from a content perspective and a learning activities perspective. *International Journal of Science Education, 35*(17), 2954–2978.

Roseman, J. E., Stern, L., & Koppal, M. (2010). A method for analysing the coherence of high school biology textbooks. *Journal of Research in Science Teaching, 47*(1), 47–70.

Sharma, A. (2013, April). *Where are the people? Understanding representations of society-nature relationships in a middle grade science classroom.* Paper presented at the annual meeting of American Educational Research Association, San Francisco, CA.

Smith, M. U., & Gericke, N. M. (2015). Mendel in the modern classroom. *Science and Education, 24*, 151–172.

Strube, P. (1989). The notion of style in physics textbooks. *Journal of Research in Science Teaching, 26*, 291–299.

Tao, Y., Oliver, M., & Venville, G. (2013). A comparison of approaches to the teaching and learning of science in Chinese and Australian elementary classrooms: Cultural and socioeconomic complexities. *Journal of Research in Science Teaching, 50*(1), 33–61.

Thiele, R. B., Venville, G. J., & Treagust, D. F. (1995). A comparative analysis of analogies in secondary biology and chemistry textbooks used in Australian schools. *Research in Science Education, 25*(2), 221–230.

Tulip, D., & Cook, A. (1991). A comparison of author intentions and student perceptions about textbook characteristics. *Research in Science Education, 21*(1), 313–319.

Tulip, D., & Cook, A. (1993). Teacher and student usage of science textbooks. *Research in Science Education, 23*, 302–307.

Tytler, R. (2007). *Re-imagining science education: Engaging students in science for Australia's future*. Camberwell: Australian Council for Educational Research.

Tytler, R., & Osborne, J. (2012). Student attitudes and aspirations toward science. In B. J. Fraser, K. G. Tobin, & C. J. McRobbie (Eds.), *Second international handbook of science education* (pp. 597–626). Dordrecht, the Netherlands: Springer.

van Dijk, E. (2011). Portraying real science in science communication. *Science Education, 95*, 1086–1100.

Wei, B., Li, Y., & Chen, B. (2013). Representations of nature of science in selected histories of science in the integrated science textbooks in China. *School Science and Mathematics, 113*, 170–179.

Wilkinson, J. (1999). A quantitative analysis of physics textbooks for scientific literacy themes. *Research in Science Education, 29*(3), 385–399.

Williams, C. T., & Rudge, D. W. (2016). Emphasizing the history of genetics in an explicit and reflective approach to teaching the nature of science—a pilot study. *Science & Education, 25*(3), 407–427.

Williamson, K., & Stannard, P. (2012). *ScienceWorld 10: Australian curriculum edition*. South Yarra: Macmillan.

Wittgenstein, L. (1958). *Philosophical investigations*. Oxford: Wiley.

6 Nature of Science Representations in Greek Secondary School Biology Textbooks

Kostas Kampourakis

Introduction

Science education researchers and teacher educators generally agree that students should be taught about nature of science (NOS) along with science content (e.g., Abd-El-Khalick, 2012; Lederman, 2007; McComas, Clough, & Almazroa, 1998; Rudolph, 2000), although there has been some debate about what exactly should be taught (see Kampourakis, 2016 for an overview). Interestingly, NOS has been a consistent focus in reform documents, and is given increasingly more attention in recent science standards and curricula (e.g., IBO, 2014; NGSS Lead States, 2013). Nevertheless, research indicates that teachers face difficulties in effectively teaching about NOS. Even well-qualified and highly motivated teachers may think that they are teaching science as inquiry or NOS, when they are actually not (Bartos & Lederman, 2014; Capps & Crawford, 2013). It seems that teachers need to complete intensive secondary science education programs with a strong focus on NOS, in order for them to eventually be able to teach NOS effectively (Herman, Clough, & Olson, 2013). At the same time teachers seem to rely heavily on textbooks for their teaching. For example, in the United States, the 2012 National Survey of Science and Mathematics Education (Banilower et al., 2013, p. 92) found that 52 percent of secondary science teachers use a single textbook for their teaching. However, textbook studies show that they represent narrow and inconsistent images of how science is done (e.g., Binns & Bell, 2015), as well as a lack of explicit messages about NOS (e.g., Campanile, Lederman, & Kampourakis, 2015).

Several conceptualizations of NOS have been proposed but the most widely used one is the 'general aspects' conceptualization of NOS (Kampourakis, 2016). According to this, there are some general aspects of NOS which can effectively be taught in the context of science courses. These include aspects of the nature of scientific knowledge (NOSK), and the inquiry methods and processes by which this knowledge is produced (NOSI). The aim of this conceptualization is not to exhaustively cover all aspects of NOS, rather it is to address students' usual preconceptions about NOS and introduce them to teaching and learning about this topic. For example, if students think that scientific knowledge is certain, that scientists are always objective, that they work in isolation from their social context, or that there is a single scientific method that all scientists use, then teaching about NOS should challenge these conceptions and help students understand, through explicit and reflective teaching, that scientific knowledge can be subject to change, that scientists can be subjective, that they can be influenced by their social context, and that they may use a variety of methods and approaches.

The aim of this chapter is to explore the representations of NOS in the biology curriculum in Greece and in the respective textbooks.[1] But before turning to this aim, it is useful to provide some information about the Greek science education context. Surprisingly, there are still no education programs for pre-service or in-service Greek secondary science teachers. This means that someone with a degree in science, who went through the process of selection of personnel, could end up working as a science teacher in a public or a private school, without undergoing any training or gaining teacher certification. For the past twenty years or so, the major component of this selection process was written exams during which elements of pedagogical content knowledge were assessed. Nevertheless, teachers did not go through the very valuable experience of teacher preparation programs, and the respective theoretical and practical courses. Some universities offer the opportunity for teachers to obtain a Master's degree in education, or a relevant teaching certificate. These are useful, but they are not a requirement for all science teachers in Greece, and in those university departments that offer biology education courses, these courses are usually provided by external collaborators. Thus, it is a significant problem that there are no faculty members with Ph.D.'s and research in science education, as well as experience as secondary science teachers, who could develop appropriate teacher preparation courses.

At the same time, the Ministry of Education imposes the use of a single textbook for each grade, which forms the basis for the exams at the end of the year and eventually replaces the curriculum, and becomes the single resource for teaching. It must be noted that most of the time, the topics that are to be assessed at the final exams are prescribed by the Ministry of Education, in terms of page numbers from the respective textbook that correspond to the topics. As teachers are not trained how to teach, and as a single textbook forms the basis for the exams, eventually many teachers draw exclusively on these textbooks for their teaching. This means that more often than not Greek biology teachers have not received the necessary training to look for or develop appropriate teaching tools, and the means to evaluate their teaching. Given these constraints and time limitations, as teachers have to teach more than 20 hours per week, relying on the textbook becomes the easiest solution. Of course, outstanding teachers exist who develop other resources to complement those that the Ministry of Education provides. But these could have been more if there was a systematic attempt to support and guide teachers to do this. Under these conditions, one should not expect

Greek secondary teachers to be prepared to teach NOS. Nevertheless, and most interestingly, the curriculum expects them to do so, and the respective curriculum documents include statements and objectives that explicitly refer to NOS aspects that should be taught. Therefore, before examining Greek secondary biology textbooks, it is important to consider the respective curriculum.

Nature of Science Representations in the Greek Biology Curriculum

In Greece, biology is taught in most secondary grades (the equivalent of Grades 7 to 12 in the United States). There is an explicit distinction between middle school and high school, each of which comprises three distinct grades (officially, middle school is compulsory whereas high school is not). For convenience, I will refer to these grades as M1-M3 (middle school, Grades 1–3) and H1-H3 (high school, Grades 1–3), and to the respective biology textbooks as M1 Biology, H1 Biology, etc. A single textbook is available for each grade for a biology course that all students take. In H3 there is an additional biology course that only students intending to study medicine, sciences, or engineering also take. I will refer to these textbooks as HE3 Biology (E stands for elective) to distinguish from the compulsory H3 Biology course. All textbooks and the curriculum for biology for all grades are available here: http://ebooks. edu.gr/new/ps.php and have been used in Greece for past 15 years or so.[2]

The documents about the Greek biology curriculum are explicit in stating that NOS is a main objective. For instance, in the first paragraph of the document (FEK 304, 2003), it is stated that the large growth of the science of biology poses the demand of making students familiar with the scientific method of approaching knowledge (p. 4171). In the next section, in which the general objectives of the biology curriculum are presented, there are several explicit objectives that refer to NOS aspects, such as studying a topic by following the principles of the scientific method (p. 4171), or relating the main milestones in the evolution of the science of biology to the social and the scientific context of their time (p. 4172). Therefore, understanding how and in what contexts science is done are central objectives of the Greek biology curriculum. These objectives are repeated and further described in the guidelines of each of the grades. In the description of the program for M1 Biology, the first objective stated is that students should be able to relate the scientific method to the study of the processes of life (p. 4176). Similarly, in the description of the program for M3 Biology, the first objective is that students are able to apply the scientific method in resolving a simple problem (p. 4176). The recommendations for teaching M1–3 Biology further note the tentative nature of biological knowledge and recognize the difficulties that this poses to teaching. Additionally, more detailed list of objectives for M1 and M3 Biology are provided in this document, including the recognition of the importance of the scientific method for the study of the processes of life (M1, p. 4178) and the description of the scientific method and its application in resolving a simple problem (M3, p. 4186). Understanding and using the 'scientific method' is considered as an important objective for Greek middle school biology.

However, the document is not explicit about what the scientific method is, but leaves readers to infer this from implicit statements such as, observation and simple and precise experimentation are the main tools for the study of the structures and the functions of organisms, which give to students the opportunity to be initiated in the principles of the scientific method (p. 4175); or that the teaching of biology has to make students familiar with the method with which this knowledge was produced, and so develop their skills in observing and describing, comparing and classifying, proposing hypotheses and conclusions (p. 4177). From these statements one can infer that the scientific method comprises a variety of activities such as observing, experimenting, describing, comparing, classifying, proposing hypotheses and conclusions. However, nowhere in this curriculum document can one find suggestions about *how* this can be taught in the classroom. The only exception is some vague statements about the proposed laboratory work, which may help students acquire a first taste of scientific method if they actively participate (p. 4194).

A similar case exists for high school. In the description of the objectives for H2 Biology, it is stated that students should know that the scientific interpretations for the phenomena of life should fulfill specific criteria in order to be accepted (ΦΕΚ 366, 1999, p. 4840). Then, in the objectives of the course we also read that students should know the basic scientific methods (note the plural) that were used in the study of biological phenomena (p. 4841). In contrast, the curriculum about H3 Biology includes no objectives relative to NOS or the scientific method. Things become even more interesting in HE3 Biology, a course that as mentioned only certain students intending to study medicine, sciences, or engineering take, where it is stated that students should be able to apply the basic principles of the scientific method in order to design and implement simple experimental studies for testing hypotheses (p. 4852).

Based on all the above, it becomes clear that the Greek Biology curriculum documents consider understanding the scientific method as a central objective. However, neither what this is, nor how it should be taught is explicitly stated in these documents. Of course, several inferences can be made, but a lot is left open to interpretation. This is not necessarily negative, as it allows for flexibility in the selection of what could be taught to students. However, at the same time one might infer that all that is given is a widely used term that could be devoid of meaning. Let us now see whether textbook authors have addressed this issue and, more broadly, how NOS aspects are presented in Greek secondary biology textbooks.

Nature of Science Representations in Greek Biology Textbooks

Previous studies have shown that textbooks convey distorted or implicit messages about NOS (e.g., Abd-El-Khalick et al., 2008; Binns & Bell, 2015; Blachowicz, 2009; Campanile et al., 2015; Niaz, 2016; Niaz & Maza, 2011). This chapter provides an overview of how Greek secondary biology textbooks present NOS aspects. Five biology textbooks, out of the six that are currently taught at Greek secondary schools, were selected for the study. These are labeled on the basis of the respective grade in which they are used as M1 Biology (Μαυρικάκη, Γκούβρα, & Καμπούρη, 2013a), M3 Biology (Μαυρικάκη, Γκούβρα, & Καμπούρη, 2013b), H2 Biology (Καψάλης, Μπουρμπουχάκης, Περάκη, & Σαλαμαστράκης, 2012), H3 Biology (Αδαμαντιάδου et al., 2012), and HE3 Biology (Αλεπόρου-Μαρίνου, Αργυροκαστρίτης, Κομητοπούλου, Πιαλόγλου, & Σγουρίτσα, 1999).[3]

Importantly, this is not an exhaustive study, rather it aims at providing a general picture. In order to allow for comparisons, the following chapters were analyzed: 1) the introductory chapters of all textbooks in which certain NOS aspects are explicitly discussed (M1 Biology, M3 Biology, H2 Biology, H3 Biology, and HE3 Biology); 2) the chapters on evolution (M3 Biology, and H3 Biology); and 3) the chapters on Mendelian genetics (M3 Biology, and HE3 Biology). The chapters on evolution and genetics were selected because they include references to history of science, and to historical figures like Darwin and Mendel, and so NOS aspects are expected to be found therein (see Campanile et al., 2015; Kampourakis & McComas, 2010).

For the analysis, the method described in Campanile et al., 2015, (content analysis method) was used. I read the whole chapters mentioned above and I identified statements that described or corresponded to NOS aspects, implicitly or explicitly. Statements that were presented in a manner that would not require further explanation from the teacher were considered to be explicit, whereas those that did not make any explicit reference to NOS but could be used by teachers to teach about NOS were labeled as implicit. The aspects of the nature of scientific inquiry (NOSI) and the nature of scientific knowledge (NOSK) used were those described in Kampourakis (2016). However, I did not use a fixed list of NOS aspects. Research has shown that particular NOSK and NOSI aspects can be effectively taught and learned (e.g., Lederman, 2007; Lederman & Lederman, 2012). In certain cases, aspects of the nature of scientific explanation (NOSE) were also identified.[4] For the analysis, I took note of every statement that implicitly or explicitly corresponded to a NOSI, NOSK, or NOSE aspect, insofar as it fulfilled the following criteria:

1) NOSI: Statements that refer to the inquiry processes that scientists use, such as state a hypothesis, ask a research questions, conduct an experiment, collect data, confirm hypothesis on the basis of evidence, etc.

2) NOSK: Statements that refer to the characteristics of scientific knowledge, such as that it is subject to change, the product of empirical investigations, often stems from human imagination and creativity, can be independently tested, can be refuted or confirmed, etc.
3) NOSE: Statements that refer to the development of explanations on the basis of scientific inquiry processes and the knowledge thus produced.

These criteria were used to analyze the NOS representations in the introductory chapters and the evolution and Mendelian genetics chapters of Greek secondary school biology textbooks.

Nature of Science Representations in Introductory Chapters of Biology Textbooks

The introductory chapters of four textbooks in this study were the only chapters that explicitly referred to NOS aspects. Overall, the authors of the examined textbooks present an explicit view of how science is done, and even provide problems to test students' understandings of this view. However, these chapters are generally not included in the topics studied for the final exams for each grade, and thus are not usually taught. They rather appear as encyclopedic chapters that students might read on their own, and which some teachers might find worthwhile discussing in the classroom. Therefore, this is a lost opportunity to begin the respective biology courses with some explicit discussion and reflection about NOS. However, when one looks in more detail about what comprises the content of these chapters, one finds that more often than not they include explicit statements about NOS aspects that convey a distorted view of NOS.

For example, the M1 Biology textbook includes a section titled "Introduction to the scientific method" (pp. 11–12) in its introductory chapter "The science of biology". The text describes the scientific method with a concrete example. This description is similar to the one usually found in textbooks: propose hypotheses and conduct experiments to test them (both typical NOSI aspects). A box (p. 12) also includes further considerations about factors that might influence the experimental results. Similarly, the introductory chapter "The science of biology" of the M3 Biology textbook begins with the section "Principles of biological sciences—The scientific method". The description of the scientific method in this textbook greatly resembles that of the M1 book, which is not a surprise as the books were written by the same authors. However, the descriptions of the scientific method, and the relevant NOSI aspects, in this textbook are more elaborated and more detailed. Overall, the presentation of the scientific method in these two textbooks follows the ideas included in the respective curriculum, as described in the previous section. A very interesting statement in the M3 book is this: "This procedure is the scientific method . . . Even though the name makes this method sound glorious, however this is exactly the process

that everybody follows when one wants to find a solution to a simple problem." It is argued that this procedure is implemented by the physician who
wants to diagnose a disease, a mechanic who wants to identify the malfunc-
tion in an engine, or a police officer who wants to solve a crime. "Therefore,
in reality the scientific method is just common sense" (p. 10). This statement
raises many questions: is common sense similar to the scientific habit of
mind, or is the latter different than everyday human thinking? Certain NOS
aspects can indeed also be found in other kinds of human knowledge. For
example, that knowledge is subject to change, or that it is produced by systematic investigation, or that multiple competing explanations may coexist
are aspects that may characterize both the work of a scientist and the work
of a detective. However, at the same time, there exist particular NOS aspects
that make science distinct, such as the use of experimentation. It is this point
that I think this statement is trying to make, but I am not sure that it suc-
ceeds in achieving this aim.

Turning to high school textbooks, the H2 Biology text also includes a
chapter that focuses on the scientific method. The last section has the heading: "The scientific method as a tool for the development of Biology" (p.
10). Then the typical presentation of the scientific method follows, accompanied by a relevant diagram. This chapter also includes a list of questions
that could provide the basis for some useful reflection on NOS. In contrast,
the H3 Biology textbook includes no introductory chapter on the scientific
method. So, for the majority of high school students the final opportunity to
read anything about NOS is the second grade of high school, as the last textbook, for HE3 Biology, is used for an elective course that only those students
intending to study medicine, sciences, or engineering take. The title of the
introductory chapter of this textbook is "Biology as all sciences uses the scientific method." This chapter includes many explicit statements about NOS.
Things become more interesting in the section under the heading: "Chance
favors the prepared mind" where the story of how Alexander Fleming "discovered" penicillin is described (pp. 11–12). The chapter concludes with
how the development of molecular biology, the focus of the textbook, is
changing biology and society. It is also noted that this development depends
on other disciplines such as Chemistry, Physics, and Mathematics, as well as
on the interaction between science and technology (p. 12).

The NOS aspects in the introductory textbooks and the respective page
numbers are presented in Table 6.1. Overall, the introductory chapters of
the examined biology textbooks include explicit NOS statements (mostly
NOSI) that nevertheless advance the view that there is a single scientific
method that all scientists use. This is a kind of implicit essentialism about
NOS that deprives students of the opportunity to consider the variety of
methods that scientists working in the various scientific disciplines use. But
even in this form, teachers with a good understanding of NOS could use
these chapters to initiate reflection about various NOS aspects and motivate
students to challenge the statements included in the textbooks. But as these

Table 6.1 Explicit NOS Aspects in the Introductory Chapters of Greek Biology Textbooks

Textbook	Page	NOS aspects
M1 Biology	11	• Answer questions about the world (NOSI)
	11–12	• Rely on observations (NOSI), propose hypotheses (NOSI), conduct experiments to test hypotheses (NOSI), draw conclusions from data (NOSI), propose general rules (NOSI)
		• Attempt to explain (NOSE)
	13	• Appropriate experimental design ensures valid and reliable results (NOSI), test hypotheses (NOSI), conduct experiments (NOSI), replications of results (NOSI), define variables and manipulate only one of them (NOSI)
M3 Biology	10	• Collect information (NOSI), make hypotheses (NOSI), design and conduct experiments, and evaluate their results (NOSI), the scientific method is common sense (NOSI)
	10–11	• Observation (NOSI), make hypotheses and predictions (NOSI), conduct experiments (NOSI), test hypotheses (NOSI), draw conclusions from results (NOSI), the experiments should be appropriately designed (NOSI), confirm or reject the initial hypothesis (NOSI)
		• Provide explanations (NOSE)
H2 Biology	10	• Collection and evaluation of information (NOSI), interpret phenomena or processes (NOSI)
	11	• Make observations (NOSI), formulate questions and choose those that can be answered (NOSI), collect information (NOSI), exchange views with others (NOSI), ensure that we can test it (NOSI), design an experiment (NOSI), use control group (NOSI), collect experimental data (NOSI), analyze and interpret data (NOSI), take earlier knowledge into account (NOSI), arrive at conclusions (NOSI)
		• Propose a hypothetic answer (explanation) (NOSE)
		• When the same conclusions are independently reached, a theory can emerge (NOSK)
H3E Biology	12	• Science is a way of thinking and of systematic investigation of the world (NOSI), the observations made, the questions asked and the design of experiments depend on the creativity of the scientist (NOSI), the scientific method consists of hierarchical steps and is used by all scientists (NOSI)
		• The scientific habit of mind is creative and dynamic, changes over time and is influenced by the socio–historical context (NOSK)
	12	Steps to propose a law in biology:
		• Observation (NOSI), identify the problem (NOSI), ask a question (NOSI), collect and evaluate older data (NOSI), propose a hypothesis (NOSI), conduct an experiment (NOSI), analyze data (NOSI), interpret results (NOSI)
		• Develop theory and subject to peer review (NOSK), propose a specific law (NOSK)

chapters are not included in the topics that will be examined at the end of the year, they only serve encyclopedic purposes as they are usually not taught or discussed in classrooms.

Nature of Science Representations in Evolution and Mendelian Genetics Chapters

Several scholars have argued that the history of science is a useful tool to effectively teach about NOS (e.g., Abd-El-Khalick & Lederman, 2000; Allchin, 2013; Clough, 2011; McComas & Kampourakis, 2015; Niaz, 2016). In particular, the history of evolution and the history of genetics provide various opportunities for discussing NOS aspects (e.g., Kampourakis, 2013; Kampourakis & McComas, 2010). However, at least in the latter case most NOS aspects in textbooks appear to be implicit (Campanile et al., 2015). Chapters on evolution are included in the M3 Biology (Chapter 7) and the H3 Biology (Chapter 3) textbooks, whereas chapters on Mendelian genetics are included in the M3 Biology (Chapter 5) and the HE3 Biology (Chapter 5) textbooks. In this section I present some NOS aspects included in these chapters that could be potentially used by teachers.

One major problem is that there are several historical inaccuracies in these textbooks. For example, the Mendelian genetics chapter of the HE3 Biology textbook presents Mendel as a lonely pioneer of genetics, although he was working on hybridization and he was not trying to develop a theory of heredity as Darwin and others were at the same time. Or, the evolution chapter of the H3 Biology textbook compares Darwin's and Lamarck's theory (p. 131), noting that Lamarck believed in the inheritance of acquired characters whereas Darwin provided an alternative explanation. However, what is not mentioned is that Darwin also accepted the inheritance of acquired characters and that, in a sense, he was more Lamarckian than Lamarck himself. In the same textbook, it is also stated that although Darwin had developed his theory already in 1839, he was afraid to proceed to publication and he did not do so until 1858 (p. 125). However, the theory published in 1859 was in important respects different from Darwin's initial ideas of 1839 (see Burkhardt, 2015; Kampourakis, 2014, 2015; Richards, 2015, for an overview).

If we can overlook these problems, implicit messages about NOS can be found in these chapters that students could discuss in the classroom. But this is rarely the case because relevant questions are not asked in tests and exams, because teachers are not trained to discuss topics like these. For example, in the evolution chapter of the M3 Biology textbook, it is stated that Darwin made observations (p. 132), that scientists cannot observe evolution and so have to find other ways to study the evolution of life on Earth (p. 133), that scientists study data from fossils, genetics, and ecology (pp. 133–134), and that from the study of fossils, stone tools, and DNA, scientists have concluded that human evolution started four million years ago (p. 136). All these are implicit references to important NOSI aspects such as scientists make observations, rely on indirect means of study, collect data, and make conclusions on the basis of the collected data. This would be an effective opportunity for 14–15-year-old students to reflect on the inquiry process of evolutionary science, and perhaps even reflect on how this mostly historical approach differs from the experimental approach of other fields such as genetics, or even physics and chemistry.

More opportunities are provided by the implicit statements in the evolution chapter of the H3 Biology textbook, where many NOSI and some NOSK aspects are implicitly mentioned. For example, it is stated that Darwin was the first to propose a theory of evolution in scientific terms and who also pointed to a mechanism by which it occurs (p. 119), that Lamarck was the first to support with arguments that species transform and to present a complete theory for the evolution of plants and animals (p. 123), that although Darwin had the main principles of his theory already in 1839, he was concerned about the reactions it might cause and so he wanted to collect additional evidence (p. 125), that Darwin's theory was not accepted immediately because evolution cannot be directly observed by humans (p. 119), that Darwin's theory did not become completely accepted because it lacked a convincing theory of heredity (p. 132), that Darwin's theory was reformulated in a modern theory of evolution, the synthetic theory (p. 132), that organisms are classified on the basis of the typological criterion, which was an invention made by Linnaeus (p. 122), or that different pieces of evidence are combined together like the pieces of a jigsaw puzzle to construct phylogenetic trees (p. 135). These are implicit references to important NOSK aspects such as that scientists propose theories, that scientists are influenced by their social contexts, that empirical data are necessary for the acceptance of a theory, that scientific theories are subject to change, and that scientific work can be quite creative. But, once again, all these references to NOSK aspects are implicit. The only explicit reference to NOSK found was that biology, as any science, is based on some fundamental generalizations, or general principles (pp. 119–120).

The case for the NOSI aspects is similar, with these again implicit in this chapter. For example, there are many statements about the collection, analysis, and use of data such as that the study of organisms would be impossible without their collection, their classification, and their comparison (p. 121), that during the Beagle voyage Darwin was able to collect animals, plants, and fossils, and to make geological, climatological, and anthropological observations (p. 124), that Darwin's theory was based on his personal observations as well as on the studies of other scientists (p. 128), or that the comparison of fossils with others, as well as with extant species provides information about evolution (p. 137). In other cases, it is stated that the data are incomplete. In particular, it is stated that as the fossil record is incomplete, because both fossilization and the discovery of fossils are chance processes, phylogenetic trees lack some information (p. 138). However, the available data are sufficient to draw important conclusions: The evidence for the phylogenetic relationship between the gorilla, the chimpanzee and man is abundant (p. 146).[5]

Similar implicit references to NOS aspects were also found in the Mendelian genetics chapters of the M3 and HE3 Biology textbooks, but these were less frequent than those identified in the evolution chapters. Ignoring the historical and philosophical problems here (see Kampourakis, 2015), this could provide opportunities to discuss experimentation and the development of laws and theories, with 14–15 year-old students. On page 109 of the M3 Biology textbook, it is stated that Mendel studied the inheritance of characters, as well as that he used peas for his experiment but his laws work for all diploid organisms. Further opportunities are provided in the Mendelian genetics chapter of the HE3 Biology textbook, where it is stated that the first scientific study of heredity was made by Mendel who selected peas for his experiments (p. 73), that Mendel proposed the laws of heredity on the basis of his experiments (p. 74), that from his results Mendel suggested that each character is controlled by two factors (p. 74), and that Mendel presented his results in 1865 but they were ignored and his work was appreciated in 1900 when other scientists arrived independently at the same results (p. 78). These are all implicit references to NOSK aspects, such as that science is based on empirical data, that inferences and conclusions can be drawn from the collected data, and that the work of a scientist is affected by its social context (in this case, the acceptance of one's conclusions).

Conclusions and Implications for Science Education

Most secondary Greek biology textbooks include an introductory chapter on the scientific method; however, these chapters are usually not taught. Although these chapters explicitly present a distorted image of how science is done, as they all describe 'the scientific method' without any further reference to NOS, they could nevertheless provide opportunities to discuss NOS in the classroom. At the same time, in the evolution and genetics chapters of the analyzed textbooks there are several statements that refer to NOS aspects, usually in an implicit manner, which might nevertheless again provide the opportunity for NOS reflection. This is especially the case in the discussion of the work of historical figures such as Lamarck, Darwin, and Mendel.

However, as there is still no compulsory pre-service teacher training for science teachers in Greece, and the opportunities for in-service training are rare, teachers lack the necessary pedagogical content knowledge (PCK) to teach many topics, including NOS. This presents a major problem. When science teachers have not been through any teacher training before going to teach at schools, and more often than not reach retirement without any additional training, it is hardly surprising they are not able to teach about NOS, correct the distorted images of the introductory chapters of textbooks, and explicitly teach NOS using the implicit messages in the other chapters. Furthermore, textbook authors—who in the case of the textbooks discussed in this chapter are either biology teachers or teacher educators who do not necessarily have a Ph.D. in science education—may also lack the necessary expertise for writing appropriate textbooks. An additional issue is the exam-centered educational system in Greece. What determines the topics taught is the content that is going to be tested in the exams. The rest of the textbook (and the curriculum) is simply ignored. Therefore, we have a situation where teachers lack the necessary pedagogical content knowledge to teach about NOS, and who have to consider science content only as important factor. In addition, science content is also relatively easy to assess in examinations, whereas NOS is not; thus, it is no surprise that NOS has not been explicitly taught in Greek secondary schools, except for some rare cases in very specific settings (e.g., Καμπουράκης et al., 2004).

However, even if the introductory chapters were included in the subject matter tested in examinations, the image of science presented in Greek secondary biology textbooks is not an authentic one, but rather a distorted one. The notion of scientific method may seem simple, clear and straightforward, but it is not. There is no single method, or collection of methods, that all scientists use. Historically, there have been a variety of approaches to address problems and to answer questions about nature that cannot be considered to form 'the' scientific method (Thurs, 2015). However, there are certain habits of mind that are common in all science disciplines, such as asking questions, proposing and testing hypotheses, developing explanations, and understanding phenomena. It must be noted that some of these are not exclusive features of science; for example, a detective can also propose and test hypotheses (McCain, 2015; Sober, 2015). Therefore, if with the idea of scientific method one wanted to demarcate science from other human activities, this is not possible when certain general NOS aspects are considered. Most interestingly, it has been historically and philosophically challenging to demarcate science from non-science (Gordin, 2015). Therefore, what is the scientific method? Does the term refer to the aspects that are common in all sciences? This would be difficult to accept because it would not include some specific methods of particular disciplines. Could the term then refer to the distinctive characteristics of science? This would also be difficult to accept, because there are important NOS aspects that are not exclusive to science. In short, the notion of scientific method fails to describe science comprehensively, as well as to demarcate it from non-science. Therefore, it becomes devoid of meaning.

Beyond that, the Greek case effectively illustrates an unfortunate global problem in science education research and practice. Teaching about scientific theories and models is at the core of science teaching all over the world, and students learn about scientific theories and their respective models in some detail. They are often able to describe these theories and models, and even to use them to predict and explain. But do all students understand what a scientific model is, and which are its features? I think not. For example, do we explain to students that there is no point in calling a model true or false? That a model simply fits to a system, so that it makes no sense to say that a model is true of a particular system? Or that it makes more sense to talk about similarity between the model and the system because this fit is not expected to be perfect? Probably not. For example, we often imply that the model of the double helix of DNA that every biology teacher teaches is true. We do not explain why this model is not true, that it only exhibits similarities with the actual molecule of DNA, and that it does not portray how the molecule of DNA actually is.

An effective example that can be used in order to clearly show the properties of a scientific model is a map. Maps, like models, are representational tools with specific features: They exhibit similarities with aspects of real systems; they do not represent whole systems, neither are they true of them; they are neither entirely precise, nor entirely accurate; and they are used by scientists for a particular purpose in a specific context. In my view, science courses at every grade of secondary school should start with a discussion of the nature of scientific theories and models, and maps would be an excellent example (Giere, 2006, pp. 72–80). Nevertheless, not only this is not done, but also teachers often fail to explain important aspects of the nature of models, which in turn are related to aspects of NOS. Whereas students will most likely forget the details of the models of the atom, of the solar system, or of the DNA molecule, they could end up understanding the general features of a scientific model. This would enable them to understand later as scientifically literate citizens why, for example, weather forecasts are not always confirmed, as they would have understood what to expect, and what not to expect, from a scientific model.

For these reasons, NOS should be a core component of science curricula and textbooks. The relevant documents should be explicit about which NOS aspects should be taught along with the associated content throughout the curriculum. NOS aspects can emerge in every subject and they should be explicitly and reflectively discussed; introductory chapters on NOS are not sufficient. It appears that currently science teachers do not teach their students about the nature and structure of scientific models, explanations, predictions, etc., and many other relevant aspects of NOS. To achieve this, a major restructuring of the goals of science education is required, including changes in the objectives, the textbooks used, and the assessments. The recent changes in the International Baccalaureate Diploma Program are a possible step forward (see Chapter 9). Although the implementation will be difficult and time-consuming, there is a simple question we need to answer: Do we want our students to simply learn the details of a few maps, or more generally learn how to use them?

Assuming that most would agree that a robust understanding of science concepts and NOS is the aim of science teaching, rather than the meaningless transmission of information, the Greek educational system still has a long way to go. There are many problems that governments in recent years have attempted to address but the lack of teacher training programs is a major problem. When I started working as a biology teacher in 2001 (in a private school), I had degrees in biology and no studies or training in science education; I did not even know that research in science education existed.

I was lucky enough to join a creative group of teachers at Geitonas School, and in two years I had advanced so much that I started my Ph.D. But these opportunities are rare. What is necessary is for the Ministry of Education to establish compulsory pre-service and in-service teacher training programs, and motivate teachers to participate. The current fiscal problems make this difficult, but I believe that many colleagues in Greece and abroad would volunteer to offer their services for this purpose. There is no lack of competent trainers in Greece. What we have always lacked is organizing education in a systematic way, with a long term perspective and goals. Let us hope that, one day, this might eventually be achieved.

Acknowledgments

I am indebted to Panagiotis Stasinakis for providing me with updated material on Greek secondary biology curriculum and textbooks, as well as for his comments and suggestions on an earlier version of this chapter. I am also grateful to the editors for their comments and suggestions, as well as for the invitation to contribute to this book.

Notes

1 All these documents are written in Greek, so I have made all translations from Greek to English of all the excerpts included or described in this chapter.
2 I should note that I have worked as a secondary biology teacher in Greece between 2001 and 2011 and taught all biology courses using these books, before moving to the International Baccalaureate Diploma Program in 2011 and to the University of Geneva in 2013.
3 H1 Biology has been introduced in recent years and does not include an introductory chapter about how science is done; therefore, it was not considered for the present analysis.
4 Although students and teachers discuss scientific explanations, more often than not they do not have the opportunity of reflecting on their nature. Thus, students end up learning scientific explanations without any consideration about the inquiry processes and the scientific knowledge that underlie these explanations, as well as about the respective scientific theories and models from which these explanations are derived. Therefore, in this chapter, I also suggest that NOSE is an additional dimension of NOS that we should aim at teaching at schools, along with NOSI and NOSK. However, developing this in detail falls outside of the scope of this chapter. For some ideas in a recent research project with biology teachers, see Kampourakis, Silveira, and Strasser (2016).
5 The Greek word for 'proof' is used in several cases instead of evidence, but this might have been used inadvertently. Nevertheless, whether science proves anything at all could be a nice NOS topic to discuss.

References

Abd-El-Khalick, F. (2012). Examining the sources for our understandings about science: Enduring conflations and critical issues in research on nature of science in science education. *International Journal of Science Education, 34*(3), 353–374.

Abd-El-Khalick, F., & Lederman, N. G. (2000). The influence of history of science courses on students' views of nature of science. *Journal of Research in Science Teaching, 37*(10), 1057–1095.

Abd-El-Khalick, F., Waters, M., & Le, A. P. (2008). Representations of nature of science in high school chemistry textbooks over the past four decades. *Journal of Research in Science Teaching, 45*(7), 835–855.

Allchin, D. (2013). *Teaching the nature of science: Perspectives and resources.* Saint Paul, MN: SHiPS Education Press.

Αδαμαντιάδου, Σ. Μ., Γεωργάτου, Μ., Γιαπιτζάκης, Χ., Νοταράς, Δ., Φλωρεντίν, Ν., Χατζηγεωργίου, Γ., Καλαϊτζιδάκη, Μ., & Πανταζίδης, Γ. (2012). *Βιολογία Γενικής Παιδείας Γ' Λυκείου.* Αθήνα: ΟΕΔΒ.

Αλεπόρου-Μαρίνου, Β., Αργυροκαστρίτης, Α., Κομητοπούλου, Α., Πιαλόγλου, Π., & Σγουρίτσα, Β. (1999). *Βιολογία Θετικής Κατεύθυνσης Γ' Τάξης Γενικού Λυκείου.* Αθήνα, ΟΕΔΒ.

Banilower, E. R., Smith, P. S., Weiss, I. R., Malzahn, K. A., Campbell, K. M., & Weis, A. M. (2013). *Report of the 2012 national survey of science and mathematics education.* Chapel Hill, NC: Horizon Research.

Bartos, S. A., & Lederman, N. G. (2014). Teachers' knowledge structures for nature of science and scientific inquiry: Conceptions and classroom practice. *Journal of Research in Science Teaching, 51*(9), 1150–1184.

Binns, I. C., & Bell, R. L. (2015). Representation of scientific methodology in secondary science textbooks. *Science & Education, 24*(7–8), 913–936.

Blachowicz, J. (2009). How science textbooks treat scientific method: A philosopher's perspective. *British Journal for the Philosophy of Science, 60*, 303–344.

Burkhardt, R. W. (2015). Myth 10: That Lamarckian evolution relied largely on use and disuse and that Darwin rejected Lamarckian mechanisms. In R. N. Numbers & K. Kampourakis (Eds.), *Newton's apple and other myths about science* (pp. 80–87). Cambridge, MA: Harvard University Press.

Campanile, M. F., Lederman, N. G., & Kampourakis, K. (2015). Mendelian genetics as a platform for teaching about nature of science and scientific inquiry: The value of textbooks. *Science & Education, 24*(1–2), 205–225.

Capps, D. K., & Crawford, B. A. (2013). Inquiry-based instruction and teaching about nature of science: Are they happening? *Journal of Science Teacher Education, 24*(3), 497–526.

Clough, M. P. (2011). The story behind the science: Bringing science and scientists to life in post-secondary science education. *Science & Education, 20*(7–8), 701–717.

FEK 304 (Φύλλο της Εφημερίδος της Κυβερνήσεως 304). (2003). Διαθεματικό Ενιαίο Πλαίσιο Προγραμμάτων Σπουδών (Δ.Ε.Π.Π.Σ.) και Αναλυτικά Προγράμματα Σπουδών (Α.Π.Σ.) Δημοτικού Γυμνασίου.

FEK 366 (Φύλλο της Εφημερίδος της Κυβερνήσεως 366) (1999). Πρόγραμμα Σπουδών Βιολογίας Ενιαίου Λυκείου.

Giere, R. N. (2006). *Scientific perspectivism.* Chicago: University of Chicago Press.

Gordin, M. D. (2015). Myth 27: That a clear line of demarcation has separated science from pseudoscience. In R. L Numbers & K. Kampourakis (Eds.), *Newton's apple and other myths about science* (pp. 219–225). Cambridge, MA: Harvard University Press.

Herman, B. C., Clough, M. P., & Olson, J. K. (2013). Teachers' nature of science implementation practices 2–5 years after having completed an intensive science education program. *Science Education, 97*, 271–309.

IBO. (2014). *Biology guide*. Retrieved from https://ibpublishing.ibo.org/server2/rest/app/tsm.xql?doc=d4biologui14021e&part=1&chapter=1

Kampourakis, K. (2013). Mendel and the path to genetics: Portraying science as a social process. *Science & Education, 22*(2), 293–324.

Kampourakis, K. (2014). *Understanding evolution*. Cambridge: Cambridge University Press.

Kampourakis, K. (2015). Myth 16: That Gregor Mendel was a lonely pioneer of genetics, being ahead of his time. In R. L. Numbers & K. Kampourakis (Eds.), *Newton's apple and other myths about science* (pp. 129–138). Cambridge, MA: Harvard University Press.

Kampourakis, K. (2016). The "general aspects" conceptualization as a pragmatic and effective means to introducing students to nature of science. *Journal of Research in Science Teaching, 53*(5), 667–682.

Kampourakis, K., & McComas, W. F. (2010). Charles Darwin and evolution: Illustrating human aspects of science. *Science & Education, 19*(6–8), 637–654.

Kampourakis, K., Silveira, P., & Strasser, B. J. (2016). How do pre-service biology teachers explain the origin of traits? A philosophical analysis. *Science Education, 100*(6), 1124–1149.

Καμπουράκης, Κ., Νοταράς, Δ., Αποστόλου, Α., Κουβάτσος, Χ., Γιαλούμης, Σ., & Πούλη, Α. (2004). Άμεση και έμμεση διδασκαλία για τη φύση της επιστήμης: αποτελέσματα μιας εμπειρικής μελέτης στο πλαίσιο της βιοτεχνολογίας. *Διδασκαλία των Φυσικών Επιστημών—Έρευνα και Πράξη, 8–9*, 60–68.

Καψάλης, Α., Μπουρμπουχάκης, Ι. Ε., Περάκη, Β., & Σαλαμαστράκης, Σ. (2012). *Βιολογία Γενικής Παιδείας Β΄ Γενικού Λυκείου*. Αθήνα: ΙΤΥΕ—ΔΙΟΦΑΝΤΟΣ.

Lederman, N. G. (2007). Nature of science: Past, present, and future. In S. K. Abell & N. G. Lederman (Eds.), *Handbook of research on science education* (pp. 831–879). Mahwah, NJ: Lawrence Erlbaum.

Lederman, N. G., & Lederman, J. S. (2012). Nature of scientific knowledge and scientific inquiry: Building instructional capacity through professional development. In B. J. Fraser, K. Tobin, & C. J. McRobbie (Eds.), *Second international handbook of science education* (pp. 335–359). Dordrecht, the Netherlands: Springer.

Μαυρικάκη, Ε., Γκούβρα, Μ., & Καμπούρη, Α. (2013a) *Βιολογία Α΄ Γυμνασίου*. Αθήνα: Εκδόσεις Πατάκη.

Μαυρικάκη, Ε., Γκούβρα, Μ., & Καμπούρη, Α. (2013b) *Βιολογία Γ΄ Γυμνασίου*. Αθήνα: Εκδόσεις Πατάκη.

McCain, K. (2015). Explanation and the nature of scientific knowledge. *Science & Education, 24*(7–8), 827–854.

McComas, W. F., Clough, M. P., & Almazroa, H. (1998). The role and character of the nature of science in science education. In W. F. McComas (Ed.), *The nature of science in science education: Rationales and strategies* (pp. 3–39). Dordrecht, the Netherlands: Springer.

McComas, W. F., & Kampourakis, K. (2015). Using the history of biology, chemistry, geology, and physics to illustrate general aspects of nature of science. *Review of Science, Mathematics and ICT Education, 9*(1), 47–76.

NGSS Lead States. (2013). *Next generation science standards: For states, by states*. Washington, DC: The National Academies Press.

Niaz, M. (2016). *Chemistry education and contributions from history and philosophy of science*. Dordrecht, the Netherlands: Springer.

Niaz, M., & Maza, A. (2011). *Nature of science in general chemistry textbooks*. Dordrecht, the Netherlands: Springer.

Richards, R. J. (2015). Myth 11: That Darwin worked on his theory in secret for twenty years, his fears causing him to delay publication. In R. N. Numbers & K. Kampourakis (Eds.), *Newton's apple and other myths about science* (pp. 88–95). Cambridge, MA: Harvard University Press.

Rudolph, J. L. (2000). Reconsidering the "nature of science" as a curriculum component. *Journal of Curriculum Studies, 32*(3), 403–419.

Sober, E. (2015). Is the scientific method a myth? *Metode, 5*, 195–199.

Thurs, D. P. (2015). Myth 26: That the scientific method accurately reflects what scientists actually do. In R. L. Numbers & K. Kampourakis (Eds.), *Newton's apple and other myths about science* (pp. 210–218). Cambridge, MA: Harvard University Press.

7 Representations of Nature of Science in U.S. Elementary Science Trade Books

Jeanne L. Brunner and Fouad Abd-El-Khalick

Having adequate resources is one major mediating factor that impedes teachers in effectively teaching nature of science (NOS) (Wahbeh & Abd-El-Khalick, 2014). As such, recent interest has focused on the representations of NOS in textbooks. However, most elementary science instruction in the United States does not rely on one textbook. In a recent survey, only 31 percent of elementary teachers indicated that they relied mainly on commercially published textbooks (Banilower et al., 2013), while the rest relied on a combination of textbooks from multiple publishers or non-commercially published resources—including teacher-made materials and trade books (i.e., books that are marketed to the general public). Additionally, the use of trade books in elementary science instruction is advocated due to their many instructional benefits, such as being more current, containing colorful illustrations or photographs, and being written at a variety of reading levels that allows teachers to choose books appropriate for a diverse group of students (see Halliday [1993] for an extended discussion). Finally, utilizing trade books draws on the strengths of elementary teachers, who tend to be specialists in language arts and not science (Akerson, 2007). Therefore, to obtain a comprehensive view of representations of NOS in U.S. science education, it is important to have an understanding of the types of references to NOS present in trade books that may be used in elementary science instruction.

Although there is substantial variability in the structure of elementary classes, the recent *Horizon Report* (Banilower et al., 2013) described the general context of elementary science instruction in the United States. Elementary students are typically taught by a generalist. In fact, only 5 percent of elementary teachers have a degree in science, engineering, or science education. Elementary teachers tend to schedule science instruction flexibly, so that science is not taught every day. A majority of elementary teachers reported teaching science three times or fewer per week. This translated to an average of 24 minutes per day or less. Interestingly, reading plays a prominent role in elementary science instruction, with 48 percent of elementary teachers reporting that students read at least once a week during science, and as many stating that they explicitly focus on literacy skills while teaching science. This integration of science and reading instruction provides further support for focusing on the use of trade books in NOS instruction, as teachers are likely to use such materials in their instruction.

Inclusion of NOS has been advocated for in U.S. reform documents for several decades (e.g., *Science for All Americans* [AAAS, 1990], *Benchmarks for Science Literacy* [AAAS, 1993], and *A Framework for K-12 Science Education: Practices, Crosscutting Concepts, and Core Ideas* [NRC, 2011], on which the Next Generation Science Standards [NGSS; NGSS Lead States, 2013] were based). The description of NOS put forth by these documents aligns closely with the "shared-wisdom view" of NOS described by Abd-El-Khalick (2012), as it relies on the aspects of NOS for which there is general agreement among philosophers and researchers of science—at least at the precollege level of understanding (Lederman, Abd-El-Khalick, Bell, & Schwartz, 2002). The NOS aspects advocated for inclusion in K-12 science education include the empirical, creative, inferential, theory-laden, tentative, social, and sociocultural nature of scientific knowledge, as well as the difference between theories and laws, and the 'myth of the scientific method' (i.e., the myth that there is one method all scientists follow that leads to the uncontested production of scientific knowledge).

To date, very few studies have focused on the representations of NOS in science trade books. Abd-El-Khalick (2002) noted very little attention had been devoted to understanding the quality of the science content of trade books, and in particular identified the need to investigate representation of NOS in these books. In addition to citing the use of trade books in formal instruction, he pointed out that students were developing naïve views of NOS outside of instruction. They were encountering these views as they read the trade books on their own. Abd-El-Khalick investigated representations of NOS in four middle-grade trade books. These books were award-winning books, randomly selected from the National Science Teacher's Association's (NSTA) Outstanding Trade Book list (OSTB; www.nsta. org/publications/ostb/). Each book was read through and the NOS ideas that were presented, both implicitly and explicitly, were coded and grouped into themes in line with representations of NOS emphasized in the *National Science Education Standards* (NRC, 1996). He found that none of the books addressed NOS in an explicit manner. Rather, the books represented science as a body of knowledge or a collection of facts. The books did this generally while distancing the body of knowledge from those who created the knowledge—the scientists.

Similarly, Ford (2006) analyzed the representation of science in 44 children's books. Her study was motivated by the need for books that could be used in inquiry-based science learning. As such, she analyzed the explicit and implicit representations of NOS in books found in a public library, a source on which teachers are likely to rely. Specifically, explicit representations had to meet one of three criteria: 1) they referred to science, scientists, scientific knowledge, or a scientific thinker; 2) they addressed a specific scientist or scientific specialty; or 3) they described a science activity. Ford found that

33 of the books contained some explicit mention of NOS. However, her framework allowed for a simple mention of science to count as an explicit reference and as such the depth of the references to NOS varied substantially across the books. They rarely described how scientific knowledge was developed or the role of the scientific community. In contrast, the main focus of the books seemed to be to transmit science facts to the reader. This finding is in line with that of Abd-El-Khalick's earlier study. She concluded that it would be difficult for teachers to use individual trade books to teach NOS in a meaningful way.

In a more recent study, Zarnowski and Turkel (2013) analyzed references to NOS in trade books that focused on the literature of inquiry. This type of nonfiction book aims to make the processes of science visible, including contexts in which people are engaged in scientific problem solving, and may be fruitful for addressing NOS through a focus on science as a human endeavor (NGSS Lead States, 2013). Following a similar line of reasoning, other researchers have investigated representations of scientists in trade books (e.g., Dagher & Ford, 2005; Sharkawy, 2009, 2013). Indeed, the use of stories from the history of science as a venue for addressing NOS is advocated for and supported by research (Abd-El-Khalick & Lederman, 2000a). Zarnowski and Turkel specifically described how each book addressed science as problem solving, the development of new scientific knowledge, and collaboration in science. Although these themes are present in each of the books, unlike Abd-El-Khalick's and Ford's earlier analyses, Zarnowski and Turkel did not identify the manner in which these references address NOS—that is, if they were implicit or explicit messages.

The distinction between implicit or explicit references to NOS is an important one. Empirical evidence shows that learning of NOS occurs through explicit and planned consideration of these ideas (Khishfe & Abd-El-Khalick, 2002). When texts refer to NOS ideas in an implicit manner, it is up to the reader to make the connections on his or her own. This is unlikely to happen if the reader does not have a mastery of the content. Indeed, Zarnowski and Turkel addressed this issue by providing a set of questions that teachers might use to more explicitly target the NOS content in the books. However, their conclusion that books that include the identified themes would allow NOS to "naturally emerge" (p. 308) from the text must be considered with caution, as it is possible that teachers with less than informed views of NOS would not be able to effectively use these questions to lead discussions around NOS content. Instead, it is much more likely that the desired learning will happen when trade books include explicit references.

In this chapter, we examine the representation of NOS in 50 elementary science trade books. We focus on trade books due to their prevalent use in elementary science instruction. We examine the books within a framework that aligns with a view of NOS advocated for in the U.S. reform documents and identify instances of both explicit and implicit references. After presenting our analysis and results, we provide research-based recommendations for improving the use of science trade books for effective NOS instruction.

Methods

Sample Book Selection

To identify trade books for the study, we turned to the list of Outstanding Science Trade Books put forth by the National Science Teachers Association (NSTA) and Children's Book Council (CBC). Because choosing appropriate science texts may be difficult for elementary teachers (Donovan & Smolkin, 2001), the use of lists that identify quality trade books is recommended (Broemmel & Rearden, 2006). By using a list that was created by the CBC in tandem with NSTA, we attempted to select from high-quality books that teachers were likely to use in their own classroom instruction. It is important to note that, while all the books would be considered informational texts, they represent a variety of genres including non-narrative, narrative, and poetry. Teachers may use books of different genres in varying ways. For example, a teacher may put a non-narrative book such as *Ultimate Bodypedia* (Daniels, Wilsdon, & Agresta, 2014) in a science resource center as a reference while she may read aloud a narrative book such as *Ferdinand Fox's First Summer* (Holland, 2013). We included all genres of books in our selection as students may interact with all types of books in a general elementary classroom.

We focused on lists created in the past five years (i.e., OSTB lists published between 2011 and 2015). Because one of the benefits of using trade books is they allow for inclusion and discussion of current topics in science, it makes sense to focus on books published most recently. We chose to look at the past five years, as this provided a large enough sample that patterns could be identified. Additionally, it also increased the chance that these books have made their way into classrooms, as it may be unlikely that teachers would have access to books as soon as they are published.

The number of trade books included in the OSTB list varied from year to year from a low of 43 to a high of 58, for a total of 253 books. Of these, we only included elementary-level books in our analysis (i.e., they were identified as being appropriate for grades K-5, ages up to 11, or "children"). This only removed four books from consideration, resulting in a sample of 239 books. After identifying the relevant books for the study, we sorted them into categories based on topic: Life Science, Earth and Space Science, Physical Science, and Other. The Other category contains books that do not fit clearly into the first three categories. For example, *Extreme Laboratories* (Squire, 2014) describes scientific laboratories in unusual places, such as the International Space Station. It is important to note that the OSTB lists for 2011 and 2012 were already sorted into categories. These lists included the previously stated categories, as well as *Unifying Concepts and Processes in Science* (in 2011), *History and Nature of Science* (in 2012) and *Science as Inquiry* (in 2011 and 2012). However, as books in these three categories could almost always be placed into one of the previously-described categories, we chose the simpler of the systems.

We included 50 trade books, 10 from each year's list, for an in-depth analysis. We chose 50 trade books, or 21 percent of the total books identified, because this number allowed for the inclusion of a diverse selection of books, but also allowed for in-depth analysis of each book. The vast majority of trade books in the lists were categorized as Life Science books (ranging from 67 percent to 87 percent across years, with an aggregate of 73 percent), with substantially fewer categorized as Earth and Space Science (ranging from 5 percent to 19 percent across years, with an aggregate of 26 percent), Physical Science (ranging from 2 percent to 23 percent across years, with an aggregate of 9 percent) and Other (ranging from 4 percent to 11 percent across years, with an aggregate of 7 percent). We aimed for a representative sample of books based on the identified categories, in addition to the years selected. As such, we analyzed 39 books from the Life Science category, three books from the Earth and Space Science category, four books from the Physical Science category, and four books from the Other category.

Analysis

The analysis procedure was similar to that of Abd-El-Khalick (2002). We first read through the trade books in their entirety, identifying statements and passages that included references to NOS. We used a framework that was in line with U.S. reform documents. Specifically, we coded for passages that described the following: scientific knowledge is empirically based; scientists must use inferences to draw conclusions about phenomenon about which they cannot directly observe; scientific knowledge is durable, but subject to change with new developments or reinterpretation of evidence; the development of scientific knowledge requires creativity; the use of multiple methods in developing scientific knowledge (i.e., there is no one 'Scientific Method'); science is a social process; scientific progress is guided by sociocultural factors; and there is a difference between scientific theories and laws (i.e., theories do not become laws once they have been 'proven'). For example, *Scaly Spotted Feathered Frilled* (Thimmesh, 2013) stated, "Greg Paul based his restoration [of dinosaurs and their habitat] on several known fossil skeletons and skulls from each of these dinosaurs, as well as skin impressions" (p. 4). This was coded as a reference to the empirical NOS. This passage relates that scientists had observable evidence (i.e., the fossils and skin impressions) on which they based their knowledge (i.e., the restoration of dinosaurs).

Additionally, we coded these passages as being explicit or implicit. We define implicit references as opportunities that allow for the discussion of NOS content, but do not direct or require such discussion of readers. By way of example, *The Case of the Vanishing Golden Frogs: A Scientific Mystery* (Markle, 2011) describes how pathologists could not determine the cause of the frogs' death based on skin samples but an aquatic fungi specialist could. This is an implicit reference to the theory-laden NOS because scientists of different backgrounds look at evidence in different ways. However, because the author did not follow up with a discussion of why a pathologist and an aquatic fungi specialist would 'see' different things in the skin sample, the reference remains implicit. Explicit references are those that directly relate to NOS content. In *Scaly, Spotted, Feathered, Frilled* (Thimmesh, 2013), the author contrasts the purposes of illustration for entertainment with those of paleoartists, many of whom are trained scientists: "Whereas many illustrators depict dinosaurs for entertainment and draw from their imagination, paleoartists draw first from scientific evidence. Their goal is to create the most accurate representation possible, not the most dramatic" (p. 7). This contrast explicitly connects the creative work of the paleoartists with the underlying evidence.

We then used results from the first read-through to group ideas into broader themes. The analysis of books that contained either implicit or explicit references to NOS was grouped into themes based on the framework described above. Books that did not contain references to NOS or contained references that were inconsistent with those of reform documents were analyzed with respect to the misconceptions or alternative views of NOS that they supported. For example, *S is for Scientists: A Discovery Alphabet* (Verstraete, 2010) referenced the 'Scientific Method' as the way in which scientific knowledge is developed. This is not in line with the view of NOS presented in the reform documents, and thus was considered a naïve representation. Another theme consisted of presenting science as a series of facts about a topic, without contextualizing the development of these ideas in the work of scientists. Finally, we looked for possible relations between the category of the book and the representations of NOS, as it is possible that some categories lend themselves more naturally to discussion of NOS concepts. We paid particular attention to those books selected from the 2012 list that were categorized as History and Nature of Science, and from both the 2012 and 2011 lists that were categorized as Science as Inquiry. Although these books were listed as addressing NOS, there was no description as to the manner in which this was done; thus, it was important to determine if the references were explicit or implicit. A second rater read through 20 percent of the selected books to establish reliability. A high level of agreement was reached on all codes (87 percent).

Results

The vast majority of trade books analyzed did not contain any informed references to NOS (62 percent). Substantially more books contained implicit informed references (34 percent), while very few contained explicit informed references (4 percent). Table 7.1 provides a distribution of types of

Table 7.1 Number of Science Trade Books with References to One or More Target Aspect of NOS

Reference to NOS	Life science		Earth and space science		Physical science		Other		Total books	
	n	%	n	%	N	%	n	%	n	%
Explicit	1	3	0	0	0	0	1	25	2	4
Implicit	13	33	2	67	1	20	1	25	17	34
None	25	64	1	33	3	75	2	50	31	62
Total	39	100	3	100	4	100	4	100	50	100

references across topics of analyzed trade books. In the following sections we will describe first the character of the NOS references made in the explicit and implicit references, and then the alternative conceptions of science represented in the books without references to NOS.

Explicit References to NOS

We found explicit and informed references to NOS in only two analyzed trade books. The first, *Scaly Spotted Feathered Frilled* (Thimmesh, 2013), is a discussion of the work paleoartists—often scientists themselves—who reconstruct images of dinosaurs. This book was placed in the Other category, as it deals with the process of reconstructing dinosaurs and not primarily with information about the dinosaurs themselves. This book explicitly explores the empirical, inferential, creative, tentative, and social nature of science in an informed manner. One example of the inferential nature of science comes when the author writes, "Working from what is known of the scales [semi-hexagonal in shape, rosette pattern] toward what is unknown [how the scales were distributed over the entire body], the paleoartists often make comparisons to modern analogs—that is, to living animals such as a Jackson's chameleon or a Komodo dragon" (p. 38). This text describes how scientists take what is known, the color of living animals, and make inferences about what they cannot know, the color of extinct dinosaurs. The book also implicitly addresses the 'myth of the scientific method.' The book remains silent on the sociocultural and theory-laden NOS, as well as the difference between laws and theories.

The second, *Alien Deep* (Hague, 2012), follows "biologist Tim Shank and the crew of the *Okeanos Explorer*, America's first research ship dedicated solely to exploration, on their expedition along the Galapagos Rift in the Pacific" (p. 7). This book was placed into the Other category, as it dealt mainly with the process of exploration, rather than focusing primarily on the life or earth features found in the deep ocean. This book explicitly addressed the empirical, inferential, theory-laden, and tentative nature of science. For example, the tentative nature of science is addressed with the description of changing views of life in the deep ocean: "No photosynthesis, scientists thought, meant no great concentrations of life. With the discovery of the amazing creatures at the vents, scientists had to toss out the assumed limits of life. Here were creatures that could withstand conditions previously thought impossible" (p. 15). Additionally, the text implicitly addressed the 'myth of the scientific method.' The book remains silent on the creative, social, and sociocultural nature of science, as well as the distinction between laws and theories.

Although these books explicitly address the specified aspects of NOS, it is important to note that they do not *fully* address all of these aspects. For example, the tentative NOS refers both to changes in scientific knowledge based on availability of new evidence and the reinterpretation of existing evidence. Only the former interpretation of the tentative NOS was included in either book. One illustration comes from *Scaly Spotted Feathered Frilled*: The author only discusses how the discovery of new bones allowed for more complete representations of dinosaurs to be developed. Similarly, the theory-laden NOS includes both scientists' beliefs and expectations influencing their work, and the idea that observations are guided by theoretical perspectives. In *Alien Deep*, the author only discusses the latter, stating, "Scientific revolutions happen when we stop seeing the world we expect and start seeing the world as it is" (p. 12).

Implicit References to NOS

Seventeen books in our sample contained implicit references to NOS. These books were distributed across all categories and contained content specific to multiple aspects of NOS, including the tentative, sociocultural, theory-laden, creative, inferential, empirical, and social NOS as well as the 'myth of the scientific method.' Three common themes relating to implicit references were identified.

One common theme among many of the trade books was describing the development of new knowledge (i.e., the tentative NOS). One example of an implicit reference is in *Rachel Carson and Her Book that Changed the World* (Lawlor, 2012). One page is devoted to Carson's research for her book *Silent Spring*:

> As early as 1945, Rachel had read about studies of declining bird populations across the country. Each year researchers reported fewer nesting and migrating birds. The more she investigated, the more alarmed she became. Insecticides were deadly to birds, insects, fish and other animals. What about people? No one had taken a stand against big business, federal agencies that approved chemical uses, or universities that performed shoddy research about the effects of chemicals. She knew she was walking into dangerous territory. However, because she had no connection with industry, government, or any university, she felt she could gather facts more freely. People would read what she wrote and fight to demand clean air, clean water.
>
> (p. 26)

The text of the book does not explicitly state the additions Carson made to scientific knowledge or the ways in which she performed her research; however, it provides a ripe foundation for knowledgeable teachers to help students make the connections.

Another common theme in the trade books was the implicit reference to the sociocultural NOS. This was especially present in books that dealt with environmental issues. Both *Eco Dogs* (Stamper, 2011) and *Super Sniffers* (Patent, 2014) describe how dogs' sensitive noses can be used to identify items such as invasive species. Similarly, *Saving Animals from Oilspills* (Person, 2012) describes how researchers identified new ways to clean animals after oil spills in the environment. All of these books implicitly relate to the sociocultural NOS by demonstrating a connection between a problem in society and the need for new science to address this problem. As with the explicit references, the implicit references do not *fully* address the NOS aspects. In the case of the sociocultural NOS, the influence of cultural values related to environmentalism was present, but other values, such as political or religious values, were absent.

The third common theme relates to the abundance of implicit references to the empirical NOS. Several of the books listed evidence that scientists gathered. However, the connection between scientific claims necessarily being reliant on this evidence was not made explicit. For example, *The Case of the Vanishing Golden Frogs: A Scientific Mystery* (Markle, 2011) contained five passages that described gathering evidence, but did not clarify that evidence was necessary for the development of scientific knowledge. Thus, these remained implicit references to the empirical NOS. To illustrate, one passage describes change in a climate as a possible reason for frogs dying. The book states, "Lips [a scientist] measured the temperature and humidity. Conditions in the forest were exactly the same as when the frogs were alive and healthy. She ruled out climate change as the problem." This passage illustrates that in this instance the scientist used evidence to reach a scientific conclusion. However, based solely on reading this passage, it is unlikely that teachers or students would reach the generalized conclusion that all scientific claims rely on empirical evidence.

Our investigation into the relation between the context of the book and quality of references to NOS found that all of the books that addressed NOS, either implicitly or explicitly, addressed some component of human activity in science. Interestingly, one of the analyzed books included an implicit reference to NOS only in the author's note. The main text of *Ubiquitous: Celebrating Nature's Survivors* (Sidman, 2010) presents facts about evolutionary 'successes' along a timeline. However, it is not until the author's note that any reference to NOS, or human activity in science, is found. Sidman addresses the tentative NOS by describing how, as scientists gather more 'clues' to the past, they revise their estimates of the evolutionary timeline. Within the main text of the book there is no discussion of revision and instead the evolutionary timeline is presented as fixed—a 'fact' of science.

Alternative Conceptions

We also explored the degree to which texts aligned with representations of NOS in current U.S. reform documents. The vast majority of either implicit or explicit references to NOS were adequately aligned with desired conceptions of NOS, although one book did present mixed messages regarding NOS. *S is for Scientists: A Discovery Alphabet* (Verstraete, 2010) contains one page with an illustrated caption relating to science for each letter of the alphabet, along with a more extensive description relating to the concept. On the page "M is for measure" (p. 15), the author describes how Galileo observed a chandelier swinging in a cathedral, leading to his investigations of pendulums. The page ends by stating, "Galileo not only discovered the principle of the pendulum, he also showed that measurement and experimentation could be used to prove natural laws—the basis of the scientific method." Within this one page, the author addressed the tentative NOS in an informed way by describing how Galileo created new knowledge of pendulums, but also reinforced the 'myth' that there is one scientific method that scientists use to develop scientific knowledge.

We also explored how the trade books presented science content knowledge. In line with Abd-El-Khalick's (2002) findings, we found the majority of books presented science as a listing of facts, with very little, or no representation of the processes underlying the development of scientific knowledge. For example, *The Beetle Book* (Jenkins, 2012) combines colorful illustrations of beetles with captions containing a plethora of facts, from descriptions of body parts, the growing cycle, or different species of beetles. Some books, especially those aimed at very young students, do not even list these facts in full sentences but instead just have words or phrases listed on the page. One of this is *Full Speed Ahead!* (Cruschiform, 2014), which simply pairs illustrations of animals or vehicles and their speeds.

It is also important to attend to the way NOS content is contextualized within the science topic (Clough, 2006), beyond a simple listing of facts. As such, we investigated the manner in which the two trade books that explicitly addressed NOS contextualized the content. Both books included substantial amounts of content related to the science topics (i.e., dinosaur physiology in *Scaly Spotted Feathered Frilled* [Thimmesh, 2013] and deep sea vent habitats in *Alien Deep* [Hague, 2012]). In *Scaly Spotted Feathered Frilled* much of this content was interwoven within the main text. This was also the case in *Alien Deep*; however, there was also substantial content found in captions or sidebars. As such, these two books demonstrate that it is possible to explicitly address NOS in a contextualized manner in elementary science trade books.

Discussion

Having access to high-quality trade books that can be used to teach NOS in an informed manner is essential for elementary teachers. Teachers who are motivated to teach NOS and have informed views of NOS cite a lack of resources as one of the main drawbacks to their effective teaching (Wahbeh & Abd-El-Khalick, 2014). However, despite the widespread use of trade books in science education, there have been very few studies that have investigated the character of NOS references in trade books (Abd-El-Khalick, 2002; Ford, 2006; Zarnowski & Turkel, 2013). In the following sections we explore the nature of effective texts for teaching NOS and describe implications for teaching NOS with trade books.

Teaching NOS With Trade Books

This study points out several findings related to teaching NOS with trade books. First, unlike Abd-El-Khalick's previous study (2002) in which no references to NOS were found in science trade books, we found two books that explicitly addressed NOS in an informed manner. These books addressed multiple aspects of NOS throughout their text. It would be reasonable to assume that, while utilizing these texts in science instruction, a teacher would convey the desired views of the relevant NOS aspects to her students. However, the explicit NOS references in the analyzed books were generally not complete representations and thus require the teacher to supplement with additional content to adequately address NOS. Moreover, we found several books that addressed NOS in an implicit and informed manner. The implicit nature of the references provides teachers with the opportunity to address NOS in their instruction, although it requires more effort and knowledge on the teacher's part to do so.

For a teacher to effectively utilize trade books with implicit references to NOS, the teacher must be able to first identify the connections with NOS and then understand how to capitalize on these connections in their instructional practice. Although it is possible, it is unlikely teachers would do this for several reasons. Overwhelmingly research on teachers' views of NOS has indicated that teachers have naïve conceptions of NOS (Abd-El-Khalick & Lederman, 2000b; Lederman, 1992). It is unlikely these teachers would be able to identify the implicit NOS references in trade books. Additionally, even teachers who have informed views of NOS struggle translating these views into practice (Abd-El-Khalick et al., 1998; Akerson & Abd-El-Khalick, 2003; Lederman, 1999) and would benefit from scaffolds. Thus, although it is possible for teachers to use trade books with implicit references to teach NOS, it is improbable that teachers will do so in an effective manner.

Of more concern are the texts that remain silent on aspects of NOS, or address NOS in naïve ways. Including naïve representations will teach students undesirable conceptions of NOS, which must then be overcome before desired conceptions are learned. Similarly, by remaining silent on aspects of NOS, science is presented to students in a manner devoid of any human component. Instead, science is mainly presented as a listing of facts, and thus misrepresents the nature of the scientific endeavor.

Effective Texts for Teaching NOS

We found that books that included a discussion of human activity in science allowed for the inclusion of NOS concepts, while those that removed the human aspect did not. This is not a new insight, as Zarnowski and Turkel (2013) previously investigated the representations of NOS in non-fiction books that focus on 'literature of inquiry.' In an alternative view, Abd-El-Khalick (2002) pointed out the lack of references to scientists in his initial study on science trade books, which contained no references to NOS. Indeed, support for discussing human activity in the development of scientific knowledge is found in the NGSS, which lists "science as a human endeavor" in the description of NOS. However, we caution against readers drawing the conclusion that the inclusion of a discussion of people engaged in scientific activity automatically ensures sufficient references to NOS. One of the books identified by Zarnowski and Turkel was also included in this study: *The Case of the Vanishing Golden Frogs: A Scientific Mystery* (Markle, 2011), and will be used to illustrate the problems with this assumption.

Zarnowski and Turkel identified this book as addressing the development of new knowledge. The text describes how researchers first identify a new type of fungus that kills frogs and then attempt to stop the fungal infections by asking how frogs could survive long enough for treatment, and how a treatment could be implemented. Based on these issues, Zarnowski and Turkel concluded that, "Readers see quite clearly that new knowledge—while making a major contribution towards solving this problem—raises even further questions" (p. 301), implying that the book explicitly addresses NOS. We argue that this is not a clear conclusion and that in fact it requires much of the reader to draw these ideas together, leading us to describe this book as implicitly addressing NOS.

The ability to draw this conclusion requires the reader to first identify the relevant distinct ideas in the book, connect the ideas together, and then critically consider their relationship. The ideas are spatially separated in the book, and interwoven with a wealth of other information. Additionally, the reader must understand how the ideas relate to each other and to NOS content to fully understand the implications of the text. Therefore, we conclude that although books that situate NOS within the literature of inquiry provide one method for addressing NOS, we maintain that it is more effective to be done in an explicit manner rather than an implicit manner.

In summary, the majority of science trade books do not explicitly address NOS in an informed manner. However, these resources are needed to support effective NOS teaching (Wahbeh & Abd-El-Khalick, 2014), and therefore the creation of trade books that explicitly attend to NOS is necessary. Additionally, although explicit and informed references to NOS in trade books may be used in NOS instruction, the effectiveness of the instruction relies on the teacher's interpretation of the text, which itself is dependent on the teachers' understanding of NOS. As such, it is desirable, and perhaps necessary to support teachers in teaching NOS with trade books by providing alternative scaffolds that help highlight the NOS content and guide teachers' pedagogical decisions. Specific recommendations for effective scaffolds are discussed in the following section.

Recommendations for Supporting NOS Instruction With Trade Books

Science trade books remain a widely used resource in elementary science instruction and have several benefits over traditional textbooks. However, when it comes to NOS instruction, there remains much room for improvement. Although trade books that represent NOS in an explicit and informed manner, such as *Alien Deep* or *Scaly Spotted Feathered Frilled* exist and, if used by teachers in science instruction, can be assumed to foster desired views of NOS in students, these books are not the norm. Many more books that include implicit references to NOS, or remain silent about NOS, exist that do not directly support the effective teaching of NOS in elementary science classrooms.

To this end, we make two recommendations for improving teaching of NOS with trade books in elementary science classrooms. The first is that additional trade books with explicit references to multiple aspects of NOS be developed. This study uncovered two such books, demonstrating that it is possible to create such books in a manner that is considered to be generally of high quality (as demonstrated by being listed on the OSTB). Like others before us, we found that books that dealt with the human aspect of NOS (similar to the previously identified literature of inquiry by Zarnowski and Turkel [2013]) included references to NOS, while those devoid of the human aspect did not. Although we do not deny the opportunity to address NOS in books devoid of references to human activity, we believe the inclusion of content around human activity aids the discussion of NOS as it contextualizes the development of knowledge within the activity of scientific problem-solving.

Our second recommendation is that trade books include an educative component to assist teachers in developing more informed conceptions of NOS, and guide their pedagogical decision-making. It is unlikely that teachers will teach effectively content that they do not understand. And, as a wealth of studies indicate that teachers generally hold naïve views of NOS (e.g., Abd-El-Khalick & Lederman, 2000b; Lederman, 1992), it stands to reason that teachers will not effectively teach NOS without first changing their naïve views. Additionally, teachers with informed conceptions of NOS still struggle to translate their views of NOS into instructional practice (Abd-El-Khalick, Bell, & Lederman, 1998; Abd-El-Khalick & Lederman, 2000b; Lederman, 1999) without guidance. There is some evidence to suggest that an educative component improves teacher understanding of, and instruction in, NOS when coupled with a textbook (Lin, Lieu, Chen,

Huang, & Chang, 2012). As such, trade books that include an educative component also can be designed to address both of these issues.

One such method for supporting teachers that we are currently exploring is the use of an educative teacher's guide that accompanies trade books (Brunner, 2016). Similar to a traditional teacher's guide, an educative teacher's guide aims to improve student learning through guiding teachers' pedagogical decisions, but it also has the specific goal of supporting *teacher* learning (Ball & Cohen, 1996; Davis & Krajcik, 2005). In this way, the use of educative teacher's guides addresses both teachers' understanding of NOS as well as strategies for translating the views into practice. Additionally, educative teacher's guides provide explanations of the importance of teaching the specific NOS content, which may help teachers to understand the role of the content within the larger unit.

Furthermore, including educative teacher's guides with trade books builds on the benefits of having explicit references to NOS in trade books, by also including a reflective component to NOS instruction. It has been well documented that the most effective method of instruction is an explicit and reflective method (Khishfe & Abd-El-Khalick, 2002). The reflective component of this instruction is frequently enacted in elementary science through journaling or class discussions (e.g., Akerson & Donnelly, 2010; Akerson & Volrich, 2006; Quigley, Pongsanon, & Akerson, 2011). None of the books examined contained any reflective component. Therefore, in our work, we have included reflective questions in the sidebars of the text that encourage the reader to make connections between the material in the book, the relevant NOS concepts, and his or her own experiences. Additionally, we have supported teacher use of these questions in the teacher's guide by providing desirable responses, possible student misconceptions, and a rationale for the importance of the question.

Importantly, these educative curriculum materials can be made easily accessible and do not rely on researcher-led professional development activities. As previous research on improving NOS instruction has depended on intensive and lengthy professional development activities that are difficult to replicate on a large scale (e.g., Akerson & Hanuscin, 2007; Lederman & Lederman, 2004), the use of educative teacher's guides may be a more effective method of reaching a large number of teachers. Indeed, the development of educative curriculum materials can even be done ad-hoc to book publication, to support teachers in using already-published books with which they are familiar.

In conclusion, the current state of trade books available for use in elementary science instruction does not support the effective teaching of NOS. Most books in publication remain silent regarding NOS and those that do address NOS overwhelmingly do so in an implicit manner. As such, it is highly unlikely that these books will be used by teachers to teach the conceptions of NOS put forth by U.S. reform documents (e.g., AAAS, 1990,

1993; NRC, 2011) and the NGSS (NGSS Lead States, 2013). However, we discovered two books that explicitly addressed NOS in an informed manner, which provide an excellent foundation on which teachers can begin their NOS instruction. Despite this foundation, there is a lack of these books available and so it is important that more books be developed in the future that contain explicit references to NOS. Moreover, it is necessary to support teachers more substantially both in developing their own informed views of NOS and in guiding their pedagogical decisions. In addition to the development of trade books that explicitly address NOS in the future, the use of educative teacher's guides is one promising method that may be an effective way to do so.

References

Abd-El-Khalick, F. (2002). Images of nature of science in middle grade science trade books. *New Advocate, 15*(2), 121–127.

Abd-El-Khalick, F. (2012). Nature of science in science education: Toward a coherent framework for synergistic research and development. In B. J. Fraser, K. Tobin, & C. J. McRobbie (Eds.), *Second international handbook of science education* (Vol. 24, pp. 1041–1060). Dordrecht, the Netherlands: Springer.

Abd-El-Khalick, F., Bell, R. L., & Lederman, N. G. (1998). The nature of science and instructional practice: Making the unnatural natural. *Science Education, 82,* 417–436.

Abd-El-Khalick, F., & Lederman, N. G. (2000a). The influence of history of science courses on students' views of nature of science. *Journal of Research in Science Teaching, 37,* 1057–1095.

Abd-El-Khalick, F., & Lederman, N. G. (2000b). Improving science teachers' conceptions of nature of science: A critical review of the literature. *International Journal of Science Education, 22,* 665–701.

Akerson, V. L. (2007). *Interdisciplinary language arts and science instruction in elementary classrooms: Applying research to practice.* New York: Routledge.

Akerson, V. L., & Abd-El-Khalick, F. (2003). Teaching elements of nature of science: A yearlong case study of a fourth-grade teacher. *Journal of Research in Science Teaching, 40*(10), 1025–1049.

Akerson, V. L., & Donnelly, L. A. (2010). Teaching nature of science to K-2 students: What understandings can they attain? *International Journal of Science Education, 32,* 97–124.

Akerson, V. L., & Hanuscin, D. L. (2007). Teaching nature of science through inquiry: Results of a 3-year professional development program. *Journal of Research in Science Teaching, 44,* 653–680.

Akerson, V. L., & Volrich, M. L. (2006). Teaching nature of science explicitly in a first-grade internship setting. *Journal of Research in Science Teaching, 43,* 377–394.

American Association for the Advancement of Science. (1990). *Science for all Americans.* New York: Oxford University Press.

American Association for the Advancement of Science. (1993). *Benchmarks for science literacy.* New York: Oxford University Press.

Ball, D. L., & Cohen, D. K. (1996). Reform by the book: What is—or might be—the role of curriculum materials in teacher learning and instructional reform? *Educational Researcher, 25,* 6–14.

Banilower, E. R., Smith, P. S.,Weiss, I. R., Malzahn, K. A., Campbell, K. M., & Weis, A. M. (2013). *Report of the 2012 national survey of science and mathematics education*. Chapel Hill, NC: Horizon Research.

Broemmel, A. D., & Rearden, K. T. (2006). Should teachers use the teachers' choices books in science classes? *The Reading Teacher, 60*, 254–265.

Brunner, J. L. (2016). *Enriching science trade books with explicit-reflective nature of science instruction: Impacting elementary teachers' practice and improving students' learning*. Unpublished doctoral dissertation, University of Illinois, Urbana-Champaign, IL.

Clough, M. P. (2006). Learners' responses to demands of conceptual change: Considerations for effective nature of science instruction. *Science Education, 15*, 463–494.

Cruschiform. (2014). *Full speed ahead*. New York: Abrams.

Dagher, Z. R., & Ford, D. J. (2005). How are scientists portrayed in children's science biographies? *Science & Education, 14*, 377–393.

Daniels, P.,Wilsdon, C., & Agresta, J. (2014). *Ultimate bodypedia*.Washington, DC: National Geographic Society.

Davis, E. A., & Krajcik, J. S. (2005). Designing educative curriculum materials to promote teacher learning. *Educational Researcher, 34*, 3–14.

Donovan, C. A., & Smolkin, L. B. (2001). Genre and other factors influencing teachers' book selections for science instruction. *Reading Research Quarterly, 36*, 412–440.

Ford, D. J. (2006). Representations of science within children's trade books. *Journal of Research in Science Teaching, 43*, 214–235.

Hague, B. (2012). *Alien deep*. Des Moines, IA: National Geographic Children's Books.

Halliday, M. A. K. (1993). Some grammatical problems in scientific English. In M. A. K. Halliday & J. R. Martin (Eds.), *Writing science: Literacy and discursive power* (pp. 69–85). Pittsburgh, PA: University of Pittsburgh Press.

Holland, M. (2013). *Ferdinand fox's first summer*. Mount Pleasant, SC: Sylvan Dell.

Jenkins, S. (2012). *The beetle book*. Boston, MA: Houghton Mifflin Harcourt.

Khishfe, R., & Abd-El-Khalick, F. (2002). Influence of explicit and reflective versus implicitly inquiry-oriented instruction on sixth-graders' views of nature of science. *Journal of Research in Science Teaching, 39*, 551–578.

Lawlor, L. (2012). *Rachel Carson and her book that changed the world*. New York: Holiday House.

Lederman, J. S., & Lederman, N. G. (2004, April). *Early elementary students' and teacher's understandings of nature of science and scientific inquiry: Lessons learned from Project ICAN*. Paper presented at the annual meeting of the National Association for Research in Science Teaching,Vancouver, BC.

Lederman, N. G. (1992). Students' and teachers' conceptions of the nature of science: A review of the research. *Journal of Research in Science Teaching, 29*, 331–359.

Lederman, N. G. (1999). Teachers' understanding of the nature of science and classroom practice: Factors that facilitate or impede the relationship. *Journal of Research in Science Teaching, 36*, 916–929.

Lederman, N. G., Abd-El-Khalick, F., Bell, R. L., & Schwartz, R. S. (2002). Views of nature of science questionnaire: Toward valid and meaningful assessment of learners' conceptions of nature of science. *Journal of Research in Science Teaching, 39*(6), 497–521.

Lin, S-F., Lieu, S-C., Chen, S., Huang, M-T., & Chang,W-H. (2012). Affording explicit-reflective science teaching by using an educative teachers' guide. *International Journal of Science Education, 34*, 999–1026.

Markle, S. (2011). *The case of the vanishing golden frogs: A scientific mystery*. Minneapolis, MN: Millbrook.

National Research Council. (1996). *National science education standards.* Washington, DC: The National Academic Press.

National Research Council. (2011). *A framework for K-12 science education: Practices, crosscutting concepts, and core ideas.* Washington, DC: The National Academy Press.

NGSS Lead States. (2013). *The next generation science standards.* Washington, DC: The National Academy Press.

Patent, D. H. (2014). *Super sniffers.* New York: Bloomsbury.

Person, S. (2012). *Saving animals from oil spills.* New York: Bearport Publishing.

Quigley, C., Pongsanon, K., & Akerson, V. L. (2011). If we teach them, they can learn: Young students views of nature of science during an informal science education program. *Journal of Science Teacher Education, 22,* 129–149.

Sharkawy, A. (2009). Moving beyond the lone scientist: Helping 1st grade students appreciate the social context of scientific work using stories about scientists. *Journal of Elementary Science Education, 21,* 67–78.

Sharkawy, A. (2013, April). *How are the intelligence/scientific ability of scientists portrayed in biographies of scientists written for elementary students?* Paper presented at the annual meeting of the American Education Research Association, San Francisco, CA.

Sidman, J. (2010). *Ubiquitous: Celebrating nature's survivors.* Boston, MA: Houghton Mifflin Harcourt.

Squire, A. O. (2014). *Extreme laboratories.* New York: Scholastic.

Stamper, J. B. (2011). *Eco dogs.* New York: Bearport Publishing.

Thimmesh, C. (2013). *Scaly spotted feathered frilled.* Boston, MA: Houghton Mifflin Harcourt.

Verstraete, L. (2010). *S is for scientists: A discovery alphabet.* Ann Arbor, MI: Sleeping Bear.

Wahbeh, N., & Abd-El-Khalick, F. (2014). Revisiting the translation of nature of science understandings into instructional practice: Teachers' nature of science pedagogical content knowledge. *International Journal of Science Education, 36,* 425–466.

Zarnowski, M., & Turkel, S. (2013). How nonfiction reveals the nature of science. *Children's Literature in Education, 44,* 295–310.

8 Improving Representation of Nature of Science in Textbooks Through Action Research

A Canadian Perspective

Maurice DiGiuseppe

Introduction and Background

Commercial science textbooks play a significant role in K–12 science education. Textbooks assist teachers in lesson planning, and provide students and teachers with curricular content and useful assessment exercises (Chiappetta, Ganesh, Lee, & Phillips, 2006; Miller & Krumhansl, 2009). However, despite their many benefits, science textbooks have been roundly criticized for being poorly organized, difficult to read, and overstuffed with information (Chambliss & Calfee, 1998; McTigue & Slough, 2010). They have also been criticized for promulgating misconceptions about science and the nature of science (NOS)—the methods used to generate, validate, and legitimize scientific knowledge (Abd-El-Khalick, Waters, & Le, 2008; Stansfield, 2006). Propagating incorrect ideas about NOS runs counter to current calls for students and teachers to develop more informed views of this important aspect of science (McComas, 2000; National Research Council, 2012; NGSS Lead States, 2013). Thus, many educators believe publishers should do what they can to improve commercial science textbooks. For example, Guzzetti, Hynd, Skeels, and Williams (1995) note that since "science textbooks are likely to remain in science classrooms, making . . . [them] more effective should be a primary goal" (p. 662), and, in terms of NOS, Abd-El-Khalick et al. (2008) recommend that publishers "direct serious attention to the representation and treatment of NOS in textbooks" (p. 851).

Views of NOS

Numerous research studies have been conducted on the views held by teachers and students about NOS and on the ways in which NOS is represented in learning materials such as textbooks. These have included studies on professional development activities involving pre-service and in-service teachers (e.g., Akerson, Abd-El-Khalick, & Lederman, 2000), classroom strategies for addressing NOS more explicitly in teaching and learning (e.g., Morrison, Raab, & Ingram, 2009; Osborne, 2010), content analyses of representations of NOS (RNOS) in science textbooks (Abd-El-Khalick et al., 2008; Brito, Rodriguez, & Niaz, 2005; Chiappetta et al., 2006); and case studies of the development of RNOS in science textbooks (e.g., DiGiuseppe, 2014). Many of these studies have indicated that students and teachers hold deep-seated, uninformed views about NOS that are resistant to change. They have also indicated that NOS ideas need to be taught more deliberately and explicitly for positive change to occur.

Science Textbook Content

Science textbooks are not simply compendiums of neutral science facts. Like all teaching-learning materials, they convey particular views, values, and beliefs. According to Gardner (1993), "the text . . . is a representation of the voice, the ideological position, the construction of reality . . . of the author" (p. 87). Apple and Christian-Smith (1991) concur, stating that textbooks communicate "particular constructions of reality . . . [and] . . . someone's vision of legitimate knowledge" (p. 1). Moreover, commercial textbook publishing operates at the intersection of education and big business, an endeavor where:

> human subjects are engaged actively in the process of conceiving, designing and authoring texts, within the economic constraints of the commerce of text publishing and the politics of text adoption . . . the textbook is an artefact of human expression *and* an economic commodity.
> (Luke, 1988, p. 28, emphasis in original)

Given that the RNOS in textbooks convey powerful messages about NOS, textbook developers should do what they can to become familiar with current understandings of NOS, and represent NOS in the most appropriate ways possible.

Textbook Development

Commercial textbooks are typically developed by authors, editors, and publishers who commonly work for large, often multi-national, publishing companies. These individuals influence the textbook development process and shape textbook content according to their particular views, values, interests, and beliefs (Mikk, 2000). The study on which this chapter is based focused on the work of one group of textbook developers in the process of producing a Grade 12 chemistry textbook, *Chemistry Today 12* (pseudonym) for use in Canada. In the study, it was assumed that authors, editors, and publishers share responsibility for the RNOS contained in their textbooks since they jointly create the representations and decide whether or not to incorporate them into their books.

Thus, a major component of the study involved analysis of the multiple discourses that arose as the developers reflected on, reviewed, and revised their personal and shared understandings of NOS; squared these understandings with the requirements of mandated curricula, the educational needs of twelfth grade chemistry students and teachers, and the demands of large-scale commercial publishing; and made decisions about how to represent the NOS in the words and inscriptions (pictures, graphs, diagrams, mathematical formulas) of their textbook.

The developers of the *Chemistry Today 12* textbook were veteran textbook developers who had developed other textbooks and teacher guides before being commissioned to produce *Chemistry Today 12*. Through my previous textbook development work with the *Chemistry Today 12* authors, and information gleaned from interviews conducted within the AR project discussed in this chapter, it became evident that these authors, especially the principal author, had, over the years, developed a keen interest in improving the NOS content of their science textbooks. However, they had largely abandoned this goal because of conventional publishing practices they believed severely restricted their ability to 1) engage in professional development aimed at improving their understanding of the NOS, 2) focus attention specifically on the NOS content of the textbooks they were commissioned to develop, and 3) hold sway in cases where their suggested RNOS were at odds with the views of textbook reviewers (including teacher reviewers), editors, and publishers. As a result, they agreed to develop the *Chemistry Today 12* textbook in the context of a collaborative action research (CAR) project focused on improving the textbook's NOS content, believing that CAR may help address some of the issues that had vexed them in the past.

Action Research

In general, action research (AR) is a form of disciplined research that professionals may engage in to examine and improve their practice. AR typically occurs through linked cycles involving critical examination of current practices, reflection, research, generation of strategies for improving practice, planning action, taking action, examining modified practices, and reflecting on and evaluating the decisions and actions taken. Carr and Kemmis (1986) conceptualize AR as "a form of self-reflective enquiry undertaken by participants in social situations in order to improve the rationality and justice of their own practices, their understanding of these practices, and the situations in which the practices are carried out" (p. 162). Though primarily a research approach in the naturalistic tradition, AR is by nature a fluid and flexible research paradigm allowing for methods applicable to the practice under study and the emergent situations that arise as practice and research unfold.

AR may involve an individual or groups of individuals. When conducted by groups of collaborating individuals, all group members actively contribute to all aspects of the inquiry process (Oates, 2002). According to Kemmis and Wilkinson (1998), collaborative action research is "a social process of learning, realized by groups of people who join together in changing the practices through which they interact in a shared social world" (p. 23).

AR in a Business/Corporate Setting

As mentioned earlier, textbook publishing operates at the intersection of business and education (Westbury, 1990). The activities and products of the textbook industry are of vital interest to many in the education community, including textbook users (students, teachers, administrators) and textbook analysts (researchers, scholars). As such, AR in this field ought to address both corporate/business and educational/academic interests. In 2004, computer science professors Stefan Cronholm and Göran Goldkuhl proposed an AR model that addresses corporate/business and academic/research components of AR in a corporate setting. Cronholm and Goldkuhl's (2004) model follows from Checkland's (1991) single cycle AR process and McKay and Marshall's (2001) dual-cycle framework (all developed in the context of Information Systems research). A simple version of Cronholm and Gold-kuhl's (2004) AR model is depicted in Figure 8.1.

The 'research practice' illustrated in Stages 1 and 2 of Figure 8.1 commonly represents the work of academic researchers who, with pure and

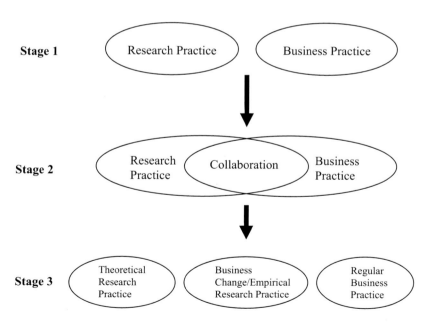

Figure 8.1 Development of Three Practices in Action Research (adapted from Cronholm & Goldkuhl, 2004, pp. 49–50)

applied research interests, collaborate with business practitioners, forming a *business change/empirical research practice* (variously called the BCERP, the AR project, the change practice, or the intersected practice). Cronholm and Goldkuhl (2004) resolve the *research practice* in Stages 1 and 2 into two 'sub-practices'—a *theoretical research practice* in which researchers, through their collaboration with business practitioners in the BCERP, develop concepts, theories, and models about real-world social systems; and a *regular business practice* in which business practitioners, through their collaboration with researchers in the BCERP, develop strategies that may improve their corporate practices and products. Further, Cronholm and Goldkuhl (2004) acknowledge that the three practices illustrated in Stage 3 are highly interrelated, and they treat them separately for analytical purposes only. In the model, the theoretical research practice and the regular business practice have different assignments and clients, and each is related to the BCERP through various inputs and outputs.

Inputs to the BCERP include research themes and questions (research interests), while business change interests (business change requests) emanate from business practitioners. Outputs from the BCERP include empirical data for theoretical research purposes and change results for the business practice. Emphasizing the highly interrelated nature of the three practices, Cronholm and Goldkuhl (2004) characterize the BCERP as "the interaction arena between the research practice and business practice where researcher-supported change work is performed . . . the existence of the change practice [BCERP] is motivated by needs/assignments from both the research practice and the business practice" (p. 54). As a study of academic interest occurring within the context of a corporate-commercial activity, the CAR project of this chapter will be analyzed through the lens of Cronholm and Goldkuhl's (2004) three practices model of AR.

Education in Canada: An Overview

In Canada, elementary and secondary education is a provincial/territorial responsibility administered by ministries or departments of education of the country's 10 provinces and two territories—essentially resulting in 12 distinctive school systems. The following is a brief overview of the Canadian education system garnered from sources such as *Council of Ministers of Education, Canada* (CMEC) (CMEC, n.d.) and the *Canadian Association of Public Schools-International* (CAPS-I, 2016).

Education in Canada is compulsory to age 18 in three provinces (Manitoba, Ontario, New Brunswick), and to age 16 in all other provinces and territories. In general, public elementary and secondary education is provided free of charge to all Canadians who meet necessary age and residency requirements, and although private schools charging tuition are also permitted, they constitute only about 6 percent of all elementary and secondary schools in the country. Elementary and secondary education extends from Kindergarten to Grade 12 (K-12) in all jurisdictions except Quebec, where secondary school ends after Grade 11. The grouping of grades in elementary and secondary divisions varies from province to province, with some provinces having a Middle School or Junior High division. In general, elementary school encompasses Kindergarten to Grades 4, 5, 6, 7, or 8, Middle School/Junior High (if present) may include Grades 5–8, 6–8, 6–9, or 7–9, and the secondary division may include Grades 8–12, 9–12 or 10–12 (Grades 7–11 in Quebec).

Canada is a very large North American country with a relatively small population (approximately 36 million) with vast energy resources and other natural resources. Historically, science and technology education was assessed in economic terms, primarily serving to produce a globally competitive workforce through the education of future scientists and engineers (Fawcett, 1991). In this context, science textbooks functioned as elaborate training manuals, filled with facts, figures, laboratory procedures, and copious practice problems; with scant, if any, attention to NOS. Furthermore, teachers across the grades tended to use student textbooks for their own science content learning, with elementary school teachers relying on them more extensively than secondary school teachers partly because, in Canada, elementary teacher certification required less undergraduate science education than secondary science teacher certification (Crocker, 1990), a situation that continues to this day. Through the 1980s and 1990s, the various provincial/territorial jurisdictions began to embrace the 'scientific literacy' movement, with its emphasis on Science-Technology-Society (STS) or Science-Technology-Society-Environment (STSE) curricular emphases (CMEC, 1997; Science Council of Canada, 1984), with relevant adjustments made to mandated science curricula and the science textbooks that followed.

Fully entrenched in today's K-12 science programming, STS/STSE outcomes form a basis for science curricula in Canada, with all students expected to "explore, analyse, evaluate, synthesize, appreciate, and understand the interrelationships among science, technology, society, and the environment that will affect their personal lives, their careers, and their future" (CMEC, 1997, p. 4). More recently, the results of a pan-Canadian 'Delphi' study proposed a new orientation for science education in Canada, suggesting that Canadian K-12 science programs should emphasize science education for sustainability of Earth systems; literacy in socio-scientific issues; relevance of science for students of First Nations, Métis and Inuit cultures; and, contributions to human health and wellbeing (Murray, 2015, p. 20). This vision, with its focus on 'sustainability science' inclusive of Aboriginal perspectives will have significant implications for the development of science learning resources, including textbooks, and the ways in which relevant aspects of NOS (e.g., sociocultural NOS) are represented therein—a development that could benefit considerably from CAR-based science textbook development process.

Science Textbook Development and Use in Canada

In general, textbooks and other basic teaching-learning resources are provided free of charge to students in all publicly funded K-12 schools in Canada. These resources are developed on the basis of subject-specific curricula produced by each provincial ministry of education, and from which local school boards and other resource providers, such as textbook publishers, produce teaching-learning materials for classroom use. Unlike some other countries (e.g., United Kingdom, Australia), Canada does not produce mandated national curricula for use in K-12 schools; however, in 1997, CMEC published the *Common framework of science learning outcomes K to 12: Pan-Canadian protocol for collaboration on school curriculum* (CMEC, 1997)—a curriculum framework that each province may use in developing provincially mandated science curricula. Science textbook development teams and other resource developers employ the Pan-Canadian Framework and, more importantly, mandatory provincial/territorial curricula to guide their resource development work. Owing to their sheer size and complexity, contemporary textbook-based resources are commonly developed by large publishing companies, usually in response to the release of new provincial/territorial curricula. Typically, two or three publishers will produce textbooks (in print and/or digital forms) for particular grades and courses, and compete in selling their textbooks to local boards of education. School boards normally form textbook selection committees that review available textbooks, and make recommendations for their adoption and use in their districts' schools. Once purchased, schools either lend textbooks to individual students for the duration of a course or term, or otherwise make textbooks available for use in the classroom.

Research on Textbook Use and Development in Canada

In general, published research focused on the nature, development, and/or use of textbooks in Canadian K-12 education is relatively limited (e.g., Lebrun et al., 2002; Pinto, 2007; Pinto, McDonough, & Bailin, 2011). Though research on the extent to which textbooks are being currently used in Canadian K-12 classrooms (in general) has not been found, results of the 2011 Trends in Mathematics and Science Study (TIMSS) indicate that while, internationally, an average of 70 percent of 4th Grade 4 and 74 percent of Grade 8 students' teachers used science textbooks as a basis for instruction, in Canada's three most populous provinces (Alberta, Ontario, Quebec), an average of 19 percent of Grade 4 and 47 percent of Grade 8 students' teachers used science textbooks as a basis for instruction (Martin, Mullis, Foy, & Stanco, 2012). These figures seem to show that, on average, a significantly smaller proportion of teachers in Alberta, Ontario, and Quebec (combined) use science textbooks as a basis for instruction than do teachers in other parts of the world. However, like their international counterparts, teachers in these three provinces tend to use science textbooks more heavily in higher grades.

In terms of empirical research on the development, distribution, and use of Canadian science textbooks, only a few studies having been published in the last 30 years. These include a comparative study of representations of Indigenous knowledge in Canadian and Australian science textbooks (Ninnes, 2001); content analysis studies examining 1) representations of science and technology in five Canadian senior high school physics textbooks (Gardner, 1999) and 2) representations of scientists in Canadian high school and college textbooks (van Eijck & Roth, 2008); and an empirical study of the development of representations of NOS in a senior Canadian chemistry textbook (DiGiuseppe, 2014). Clearly, there exists a great need for the Canadian science education research community to add to, and extend, the limited literature base on the development, use, and effectiveness of Canadian science textbooks, in general, and on studies focused specifically on representations of NOS in those books.

Chemistry Today 12 Textbook Development

The *Chemistry Today 12* textbook discussed in this chapter was developed in Western Canada over a 12-month period, and the development process was studied in detail over a period of four months. The development team included three experienced science textbook developers and two manuscript reviewers: Alan (author), Edith (editor), Peter (publisher), Cody and Jamie (external accuracy reviewers), and Nader, a university-based researcher (acting as AR facilitator and critical friend) (all pseudonyms). This AR entailed in-depth analysis of the actions, interactions, negotiation of meanings, and exchange of perspectives among author, editor, publisher, and manuscript reviewers as various RNOS were developed and considered for inclusion in the *Chemistry Today 12* textbook. In particular, the AR project focused on the development of one unit of the four-unit textbook, namely, *Unit 6: Chemical Energy*, encompassing Chapter 11: *Enthalpy Change* and Chapter 12: *Explaining Chemical Changes*. The study focused on the development of a single unit of the *Chemistry Today 12* textbook because a unit was the largest repeating organizational component of the book, and was considered to provide a representative overview of the book's overall development.

Data sources for the AR study included focus group discussions; semi-structured personal interviews and follow-up interviews; Views of Nature of Science-Form C (VNOS-C) questionnaire (Lederman, Abd-El-Khalick, Bell, & Schwartz, 2002); and primary source documents, including textbook development notes, raw textbook manuscripts, manuscript reviewer's reports and jot-notes, e-mail messages, and other documentary artifacts including interoffice memos and provincial curriculum documents.

Action Plan Development and Execution

During the *Chemistry Today 12* textbook development process, personal interviews with the editor, Edith, provided unique insights into the culture of educational publishing, the day-to-day technical aspects of developmental editing, and the constraints and trade-offs caused by tight publication timelines. Edith's views on the potential effects of competing interests among editors, authors, and publishers on the development of textbook contents, including RNOS, were highly relevant and useful. Interviews with the publisher, Peter, provided additional insight into the culture and conventional practices of the commercial textbook publishing world. More importantly, however, Peter's interviews provided detailed information regarding the costs, risks, trade-offs, and constraints associated with commercial textbook production, and how these and other corporate/political considerations affected development of the textbook's content, including its NOS content.

Contrasted with the interviews of development team members were data garnered from interviews of the two manuscript reviewers, Jamie and Cody. From their unique vantage point external to the development process core, Jamie and Cody provided opinions regarding issues arising from the development team's ideas for representing NOS that had implications for the textbook's overall instructional quality and integrity. They also provided useful elaborations of their reviews of manuscript content, especially content involving RNOS. However, focus group discussions involving all development team members were by far the richest sources of data in the study. These discussions were intensive, extensive, meaningful, and enriching. They provided a unique opportunity for participants to exchange views, negotiate meanings, clarify misunderstandings, respond elaborately and passionately to each other's queries and concerns, compare notes, resolve disputes, and review and revise their textbook development work in situated activity. Such meetings were not normally a part of the developers' regular professional activities, and, over time, began to exhibit the characteristics of Cronholm and Goldkuhl's (2004) BCERP. This occurred primarily because the publishing company allowed its employees (the textbook development team) to engage with an academic researcher (the study's principal investigator (PI) and AR (action research) coordinator in a collaborative change process focused on improving/enhancing the chemistry textbook's content (including NOS content), *and* in helping to develop a better theoretical understanding of the ways in which RNOS are developed and implemented in a commercial textbook.

In the normal course of their work, Alan, Edith, and Peter met from time-to-time either face-to-face or via teleconference to discuss broad textbook development issues such as the textbook's overall instructional design and development schedule, but rarely engaged in detailed conversations regarding subject matter such as NOS. AR focus group meetings afforded them this opportunity. The focus group meetings that formed a significant part of the study were in keeping with Powell and Single's (1996) conception of a focus group as "a group of individuals selected and assembled by researchers to discuss and comment on, from personal experience, the topic that is the subject of the research" (p. 499). Focus group discussions often took the form of focused interviews (Merton, Fiske, & Kendall, 1990) in a group setting. In the context of the textbook development activities of this study, focus group meeting discussions often resulted in the development of action plans containing suggestions for modifying RNOS and improving textbook contents. Successive action plans were developed by the focus group and then acted upon by Alan and Edith, and Peter where appropriate, in their roles as textbook author, editor, and publisher. Copies of modified manuscripts were sent to all focus group members upon their completion in preparation for critique and discussion in ensuing meetings.

The focus group activities primarily focused on detailed discussions regarding verbal and pictorial RNOS the authors were suggesting for Chapters 11 and 12. In general, these RNOS corresponded to NOS themes described in recent consolidations of NOS deemed appropriate for use in K-12 science education (e.g., McComas & Olson, 2000; Osborne, Ratcliffe, Collins, Millar, & Duschl, 2003), and included representations regarding 1) the role creativity plays in the development of scientific knowledge; 2) observation and inference; 3) the tentativeness of scientific knowledge; and 4) sociocultural aspects of science.

Results and Discussion

Factors Affecting RNOS Development in a Science Textbook

In general, the AR activities in this study brought to light several factors that influenced the developers' decisions for representing NOS in particular ways. These included 'accuracy' (the extent to which suggested RNOS aligned with accepted views of NOS); 'appropriateness' (the age/grade appropriateness of suggested RNOS); 'consistency' (the extent to which RNOS in different parts of the book aligned with each other): 'curricular alignment' (the extent to which suggested RNOS aligned with mandated curriculum); 'marketability' (the potential impact of suggested RNOS on book sales); and 'resources' (the adequacy of textbook resources, such as space in the textbook, for representing NOS in particular ways).

Though described separately, these factors interacted in complex ways in the RNOS development process. From the very beginning of the AR project, Peter, Alan, and Edith were interested in addressing the accuracy of the RNOS they were developing for the *Chemistry Today 12* textbook, and, as a result, made this a primary focus of their AR. Alan suggested early on that the team take "a very close look" at the NOS language and conceptual development framework used in the textbook, wanting to make sure these conveyed a "modern" view of the NOS throughout.

In the next section, I will briefly detail an RNOS development activity that occurred during the AR-oriented textbook development process.

Empirical NOS and Tentative NOS in Thought Experiments

In science education, it is common for students to conduct scientific investigations according to instructions provided in textbook- or teacher-generated guides. These instructions involve varying degrees of student and teacher control of research questions, materials, methods, procedures, and outcomes. In some cases, investigations are carried out with real materials in the laboratory or field, while in other cases, investigations are performed in computer-based virtual environments involving animations and simulations. When conducted in the laboratory or field, knowledge may be developed empirically. Alternatively, students may be asked to conduct 'thought experiments' in which they think/reason through experiments without actually performing them.

In a thought experiment described in a section of the first draft of the *Chemistry Today 12* textbook, entitled "Empirical Effect of the Nature of Reactants," students were asked to consider a thought experiment "to determine which solid element iron or carbon reacts faster with oxygen" while variables such as temperature, concentration of oxygen, and surface area of iron are controlled. In the description of the thought experiment, the text states:

> When oxygen gas is directed onto the solids and an ignition flame is introduced, the carbon burns while the iron shows evidence of oxidizing slightly. The evidence provided is that carbon reacts faster with oxygen than does iron. Although this thought experiment provides obvious results, what does it mean? Well, with all other variables being controlled, the evidence suggests that the nature of the reactant is an important variable for determining the rate of a chemical reaction.

This is the first time in the book that students are introduced to the idea that the rate of a chemical reaction may be affected by the 'nature' of the reactants. When, in Focus Group Meeting 2, the developers were asked why the text suggests to students that the results of the thought experiment are 'obvious,' Alan stated, "I think we would agree that thought experiments have to be fairly simple and fairly common sense and fairly experience-oriented." In response, Edith added "and perhaps this example of iron and carbon oxidizing is not sufficiently experience-based for the students; not sufficiently common sense." Alan then responded, "I think that the thought experiment ... has to be carefully used in terms of whether this is within the students' experience, and quite frankly, this isn't even within my experience."

In the dialogue described above, Alan and Edith make it clear that, in retrospect, neither of them had ever witnessed the burning of carbon fiber, and could not ascertain whether carbon fiber or iron fiber would oxidize more quickly under controlled conditions. Assuming that, in general, students would likewise not have experienced this phenomenon, the developers unanimously agreed that students should not be forced to rely on authority to justify a knowledge claim. Thus, the team changed the introduction to the thought experiment exercise from "Consider an experiment to determine which solid element iron or carbon reacts faster with oxygen" to "*From your own experience, including the Exploration on Page 51*, you can see that some reactions do not proceed spontaneously at room temperature unless additional energy is added to start them off."

As can be seen, the developers made significant changes to the text, including reference to an "Exploration" that students were supposed to conduct before performing the thought experiment. In this, and other exercises, the developers made a point of employing language highlighting the tentativeness of scientific knowledge and the personal nature of empirical evidence by, for example, referring to the reaction of methane and oxygen as "the predicted reaction," and suggesting that readers "may have noticed" in their everyday lives or other school activities that "different reactants appear to react at different rates." Furthermore, the development team endeavored to transform some of the expository text in the first draft of Chapter 12 to argumentative text—a change that, according to some scholars, may help students improve their understanding of scientific concepts (Osborne, Erduran, & Simon, 2004; Sampson, Grooms, & Walker, 2011).

Jamie, in his review of the first draft of Chapter 12, indicated that he had serious concerns regarding the thought experiment in terms of what the thought experiment implies about theory-generation in science, claiming:

> This . . . indicates a misunderstanding of the nature of scientific thought and the production of new scientific knowledge. To go from two observations to a theory is very difficult. People who do that rely on an extensive background in their field that frames the observations and lets them explain why it happens. Beginner scientists don't have that depth of background.

Jamie's comments sparked an impassioned exchange between Edith, Alan, and the PI in Focus Group Meeting 4:

Nader: What do you think about Jamie's statements regarding the thought experiment?

Edith: I think he's confusing it. There's science and there's science education. Most of science education works by having a theory and fitting observations into it.

Nader: He says, "Students will say to each other, hey this thing runs faster than this other thing, so let's come up with a theory!

Alan: He doesn't recognize that a curriculum goes through these things very, very fast. Whereas in the history of science what might take hundreds of years, we're doing it in a few pages.

Edith: Of necessity, our nature of science is very much simplified and speeded up and it's really . . . a kind of a cartoon of science, a caricature of the nature of science. We're just kind of giving them a taste and trying to show them—show the students a little bit of how science and theories come and go.

Alan: My concern . . . is people who argue "this isn't a good enough representation of the nature of science—it isn't complete enough so we shouldn't be doing it at all . . . Does he really believe that we shouldn't be presenting anything about the nature of science? . . . We're saying that . . . that is appropriate to the age level of the students and is appropriate . . . to the curriculum that we're given.

It is obvious that Alan and Edith agreed with Jamie regarding the development of theories in 'real' (professional) science, but disagreed on how this should be represented in a senior chemistry textbook. Although Jamie believed that thought experiments and lab/field investigations are useful exercises, he believed that students should not be asked to formulate theoretical explanations on the basis of inadequate data as this could create serious misconceptions about this aspect of NOS. However, the textbook developers believed that simplified exercises involving theory development were suitable for a variety of reasons, including limited space in the textbook; students' lack of readiness to generate and/or analyze large amounts of experimental data; and the lack of curricular guidance in dealing with this particular aspect of NOS. As a result, the development team chose not to act on Jamie's recommendations in this case.

The Role of CAR in RNOS Development

The developers of the *Chemistry Today 12* textbook decided to engage in CAR because they were intent on improving the RNOS in their textbook, and also because they believed that the exigencies of conventional textbook development militated against their ability to focus on this aspect of a science textbook. Alan articulated this view in one of the last focus group meetings, stating:

It is critical that NOS be given a place of greater prominence in science curricula and instruction . . . A problem with textbook development is the lack of time to reflect, think, ponder. Being involved in an action research promotes reflection—both personal and group reflection. Reflection is forced upon the participants.

In a journal reflection written near the end of the AR project, Edith warned:

> Nature of science can be implemented only after agreement has been reached on what "NOS" means, and to what extent it is practical to implement it. With agreement on the definition has to come acknowledgement that [in this book] the text is for Grade 12 students. Many of them do not have the maturity to handle the new and sometimes abstract theories presented at the same time as the somewhat convoluted language of NOS. While it is, on occasion, appropriate to talk about NOS directly in the textbook, we have to be wary of turning students and teachers off with too much abstract discussion.

This particular comment indicates that Edith was very concerned about the potential negative effect specialized NOS-related terms and expressions might have on the text's 'readability'—the relative difficulty students might have in accessing information from the text.

Peter, seemingly convinced by the end of the AR project of the value of addressing RNOS more rigorously than usual, stated:

> If we need to address NOS in our textbooks, and I believe we do, then we will have to hire authors and editors who have a strong background in NOS . . . at the very least, authors with an NOS background.

In general, the AR project discussed in this chapter involved collaboration among corporate and academic participants who, with a common interest in improving the RNOS in science textbooks, created a development environment in line with Cronholm and Goldkuhl's (2004) BCERP. In this case, the participants created a BCERP in which assumptions about NOS and RNOS development were discussed and challenged, and in which alternative RNOS were critically examined and evaluated. Evidence from the study indicates that CAR activities strengthened the developers' resolve to make NOS a focus of their textbook development work.

In Focus Group Meeting 4, Edith stated "I think perhaps we would seriously consider having an NOS reviewer next time. What do you think Peter?" In response, Peter stated, "If it was recommended, then yes. I think in this project, it initially just didn't seem to be something that was a recognized need." Alan then added:

> What Peter says is right. I think that there are enough of us around this project who have gone through . . . the awareness–understanding–action component. But I think what really comes out from a study like this is that it kind of shows you that when you are immersed in it, you quite often need some outside eyes at some things. Even if all of us were well versed in nature of science, you still need somebody to kind of hold you to account on it at various points in time.

Implied in this statement is a recommendation for future science textbook development teams to engage in CAR projects in which academic facilitators may act as critical friends who prompt, probe, critique, and question the textbook developers as they immerse themselves in their textbook development work.

Peter summarized his final thoughts as follows:

> To address the nature of science more accurately and thoroughly, we should hire authors and editors who have a strong background in NOS, and who care about infusing NOS in the textbook. We should also include a NOS framework into the writing guide created at the beginning of a project.

Following publication of a draft version of the *Chemistry Today 12* textbook, Alan, Peter, and Edith made journal entries that included their recommendations for improving science education in general, and the development of more suitable/appropriate RNOS in science textbooks, including 1) incorporating a full range of NOS ideas in the textbook's laboratory program; 2) allowing for falsification during laboratory work in order for students to replace an existing concept with the next concept in the curriculum; 3) using the terms hypothesis, prediction, data, and evidence correctly and appropriately; 4) making NOS part of the content in the textbook to be learned by students and assessed by teachers; and 5) modeling language (and overall communication) that portrays more informed views of NOS.

In their concluding remarks, Alan and Peter acknowledged CAR as a promising methodology for helping to enhance the science textbook development process, especially in terms of enabling poorly understood or traditionally marginalized aspects of science, such as NOS, to be addressed with greater care and attention. In their comments, both developers stated that action-oriented collaboration within a BCERP (Cronholm & Goldkuhl, 2004) would benefit the process. Edith's comments, however, imply that no matter what development process is used, it is essential that NOS (or any other aspect of science) is represented in ways that are easily accessible by students and teachers.

Conclusion

Representing NOS more suitably in science learning materials, including textbooks, partially addresses the goal of enhancing the scientific literacy of all students. The CAR study discussed in this chapter focused on the work of a Canadian textbook development team that developed RNOS for their senior chemistry textbook that they believed were sufficiently accurate, consistent, appropriate, and aligned with mandated curricula.

This study represents a milestone in empirical research focused directly on the situated development of RNOS in a Canadian science textbook, with implications for RNOS development in textbooks in general. Needless to say, incorporating more informed RNOS in science textbooks remains an important issue requiring further investigation. And, as the current study shows, CAR projects involving textbook developers and academics, including NOS experts, and possibly, also science curriculum developers and district textbook selection committees, may further inform us of ways in which more informed RNOS may be incorporated into textbooks and related resources.

References

Abd-El-Khalick, F., Waters, M., & Le, A-P. (2008). Representations of the nature of science in high school chemistry textbooks over the past four decades. *Journal of Research in Science Teaching, 45*(7), 835–855.

Akerson, V., Abd-El-Khalick, F., & Lederman, N. (2000). Influence of a reflective explicit activity-based approach on elementary teachers' conceptions of nature of science. *Research in Science Teaching, 37*(4), 295–317.

Apple, M., & Christian-Smith, L. (1991). The politics of the textbook. In M. Apple & L. Christian-Smith (Eds.), *The politics of the textbook* (pp. 1–21). London: Routledge.

Brito, A., Rodriguez, M. A., & Niaz, M. (2005). A reconstruction of the development of the periodic table based on history and philosophy of science and its implications for general chemistry textbooks. *Journal of Research in Science Teaching, 42*(1), 84–111.

Canadian Association of Public Schools-International (2016). *Education in Canada.* Retrieved from www.caps-i.ca/education-in-canada/

Carr, W., & Kemmis, S. (1986). *Becoming critical: Education, knowledge and action research.* Philadelphia, PA: Falmer.

Chambliss, M. J., & Calfee, R. C. (1998). *Textbooks for learning: Nurturing children's minds.* Malden, MA: Wiley.

Checkland, P. (1991). From framework through experience to learning: The essential nature of action research. In E. H. Nissen, K. Klein, & R. Hirschheim (Eds.), *Information systems research: Contemporary approaches and emergent traditions* (pp. 397–403). Amsterdam: Elsevier.

Chiappetta, E. E., Ganesh, T. G., Lee, Y., & Phillips, M. C. (2006). *Examination of science textbook analysis research conducted on textbooks published over the past 100 years in the United States.* Paper presented at the annual meeting of the National Association for Research in Science Teaching, San Francisco, CA.

Council of Ministers of Education, Canada (CMEC). (n.d.). *Education in Canada: An overview.* Retrieved from www.cmec.ca/299/Education-in-Canada-An-Overview/

Council of Ministers of Education, Canada (CMEC). (1997). *Common framework of science learning outcomes K to 12: Pan-Canadian protocol for collaboration on school curriculum.* Toronto, ON: Council of Ministers of Education, Canada.

Crocker, R. K. (1990). *Science achievement in Canadian schools: National and international comparisons.* Ottawa, ON: Economic Council of Canada.

Cronholm, S., & Goldkuhl, G. (2004). Conceptualising participatory action research—three different practices. *Electronic Journal of Business Research Methods, 2*(2). Retrieved from www.vits.org/publikationer/dokument/465.pdf

DiGiuseppe, M. (2014). Representing nature of science in a science textbook: Exploring author-editor-publisher interactions. *International Journal of Science Education, 36*(7), 1061–1082.

Fawcett, R. (1991). *Science education in Canada: Volume 265 of background paper*. Library of Parliament, Research Branch. Retrieved from http://publications.gc.ca/Collection-R/LoPBdP/BP/bp265-e.htm

Gardner, P. L. (1993). Textbook representations of science-technology relationships. *Research in Science Education, 23*, 85–94.

Gardner, P. L. (1999). The representation of science-technology relationships in Canadian physics textbooks. *International Journal of Science Education, 21*(3), 329–347.

Guzzetti, B. J., Hynd, C. R., Skeels, S. A., & Williams, W. O. (1995). Improving physics texts: Students speak out. *Journal of Reading, 38*, 656–663.

Kemmis, S., & Wilkinson, M. (1998). Participatory action research and the study of practice. In B. Atweh, S. Kemmis, & P. Weeks (Eds.), *Action research in practice: Partnerships for social justice in education* (pp. 21–36). LonJamie: Routledge.

Lebrun, J., Lenoir, Y., Laforest, M., Larose, F., Roy, G-R., Spallanzani, C., & Pearson, M. (2002). Past and current trends in the analysis of textbooks in the Quebec context. *Curriculum Inquiry, 32*(1), 51–83.

Lederman, N. G., Abd-El-Khalick, F., Bell, R. L., & Schwartz, R. S. (2002). Views of nature of science questionnaire: Toward valid and meaningful assessment of learners' conceptions of nature of science. *Journal of Research in Science Teaching, 39*(6), 497–521.

Luke, A. (1988). *Literacy, textbooks and ideology: Postwar literacy instruction and the mythology of Dick and Jane*. LonJamie: Falmer.

Martin, M. O., Mullis, I. V. S., Foy, P., & Stanco, G. M. (2012). *TIMSS 2011 international results in science*. Chestnut Hill, MA: TIMSS & PIRLS International Study Center, Boston College.

McComas, W. F. (2000). The principal elements of the nature of science: Dispelling the myths. In W. F. McComas (Ed.), *The nature of science in science education: Rationales and strategies* (pp. 53–72). Dordrecht, the Netherlands: Kluwer Academic Publishers.

McComas, W. F., & Olson, J. K. (2000). The nature of science in international science education standards documents. In W. F. McComas (Ed.), *The nature of science in science education: Rationales and strategies* (pp. 41–52). Dordrecht, the Netherlands: Kluwer Academic Publishers.

McKay, J., & Marshall, P. (2001). The dual imperatives of action research. *Information Technology and People, 14*(1), 46–59.

McTigue, E. M., & Slough, S. W. (2010). Student-accessible science texts: Elements of design. *Reading Psychology, 31*(3), 213–227.

Merton, R. K., Fiske, M., & Kendall, P. L. (1990). *The focused interview: A manual of problems and procedures* (2nd ed.). LonJamie: Collier MacMillan.

Mikk, J. (2000). *Textbook research and writing*. Berne, Switzerland: Peter Lang.

Miller, J. S., & Krumhansl, R. (2009). Learning from innovative instructional materials and making them your own. In J. Gess-Newsome, J. A. Luft, & R. Bell (Eds.), *Reforming secondary science instruction* (pp. 39–52). Arlington, VA: National Science Teachers Association (NSTA) Press.

Morrison, J. A., Raab, F. J., & Ingram, D. (2009). Factors influencing elementary and secondary teachers' views of the nature of science. *Journal of Research in Science Teaching, 46*(4), 384–403.

Murray, J. J. (2015). Re-visioning science education in Canada. *Education Canada, 55*(4), 18–21.

National Research Council. (2012). *A framework for K-12 science education: Practices, crosscutting concepts, and core ideas*. Washington, DC: The National Academy Press.

NGSS Lead States. (2013). *Next generation science standards: For states, by states.* Washington, DC: The National Academy Press.

Ninnes, P. (2001). Writing multicultural science textbooks: Perspectives, problems, possibilities, and power. *Australian Science Teachers' Journal*, 47(4), 18–27.

Oates, B. J. (2002). Co-operative inquiry: Reflections on practice. *Electronic Journal of Business Research Methods*, 1(1), 33–42.

Osborne, J. (2010). Arguing to learn in science: The role of collaborative, critical discourse. *Science*, 328(5977), 463–466.

Osborne, J., Erduran, S., & Simon, S. (2004). Enhancing the quality of argumentation in science classrooms. *Journal of Research in Science Teaching*, 41(10), 994–1020.

Osborne, J., Ratcliffe, M., Collins, S., Millar, R., & Duschl, R. (2003). What ideas-about-science should be taught in school science? A Delphi study of the expert community. *Journal of Research in Science Teaching*, 40(7), 692–720.

Pinto, L. E. (2007). Textbook publishing, textbooks, and democracy: A case study. *Journal of Thought, Spring–Summer*, 99–121.

Pinto, L. E., McDonough, G. P., & Bailin, S. (2011). *High school philosophy teachers' use of textbooks: Critical thinking or teaching to the text?* (May 18, 2011). OSSA Conference Archive. Paper 45. Retrieved from http://scholar.uwindsor.ca/ossaarchive/OSSA9/papersandcommentaries/45

Powell, R. A., & Single, H. M. (1996). Focus groups. *International Journal of Quality in Health Care*, 8(5), 499–504.

Sampson, V., Grooms, J., & Walker, J. (2011). Argument-driven inquiry as a way to help students learn how to participate in scientific argumentation and craft written arguments: An exploratory study. *Science Education*, 95(2), 217–257.

Science Council of Canada. (1984). *Science for every student: Educating Canadians for tomorrows world*. Science Council of Canada. Retrieved from http://artsites.uottawa.ca/sca/doc/Report-no.-36-Science-for-Every-Student-Educating-Canadians-for-Tomorrows-World.pdf

Stansfield, W. D. (2006). Textbooks: Expectations vs. reality: The DNA story. *American Biology Teacher*, 68(8), 464–469.

van Eijck, M. W., & Roth, W-M. (2008). Representations of scientists in Canadian high school and college textbooks. *Journal of Research in Science Teaching*, 45, 1059–1082.

Westbury, I. (1990). Textbooks, textbook publishers, and the quality of schooling. In A. Woodward & D. L. Elliott (Eds.), *NSSE yearbook 1990: Part I. Textbooks and schooling in the United States* (pp. 1–22). Chicago: NSSE.

9 An Analysis of the Representation of Nature of Science in a Chemistry Textbook in the International Baccalaureate Diploma Program

Nizar El-Mehtar and Sahar Alameh

Nature of Science (NOS) involves the basic values and beliefs that make up the scientific worldview, the epistemological and ontological foundations of science, how the scientific community goes about their work, and how society influences and reacts to scientific endeavors (Abd-El-Khalick & Lederman, 2000; Clough, 2006; Lederman, 1992). Findings of relevant research suggest that a pedagogical approach emphasizing NOS improves instructional delivery in a way that promotes students' interest and deeper understanding of science (McComas, Almazroa, & Clough, 1998). According to Driver, Leach, Millar, and Scott (1996), NOS must be integrated in science curriculum to support learners' ability to make sense of science concepts and socio-scientific issues, manage technological objects and processes, appreciate science as a main component of modern culture, and comprehend the norms of scientific community embodying moral commitment. It is also argued that NOS understanding could influence learners' scientific literacy, lifelong learning, and dispositions (NRC, 2007).

Unfortunately, common trends in school science education are not commensurate with the recognized learning gains ascribed to NOS instruction. Various studies reveal that science pedagogy reflects a poor and confusing model of science as a way of knowing (e.g., Burbules & Linn, 1991; Hewson & Hewson, 1988). Researchers claim that such pedagogy exacerbates students' naïve views about the construction and characteristics of scientific knowledge (NRC, 2007). This state of affairs has been attributed to a number of factors, including the inadequacy of science teachers' fundamental NOS understanding, the challenge of translating NOS understanding into relevant effective instructional practices, and the need for successful pedagogical approaches that guide and sustain NOS teaching endeavors (Abd-El-Khalick, Waters, & Le, 2008).

Noticeably, the role of commercial textbooks in NOS teaching and learning has been recently highlighted in some studies (e.g., Abd-El-Khalick et al., 2008, 2016; Vesterinen, Aksela, & Lavonen, 2013). The rising attention to textbooks is rationalized in terms of the considerable place these resources occupy in instructional and learning experiences. Different lines of evidence have continuously shown that K–12 teachers substantially rely on textbooks, which practically constitute the curriculum and predominantly channel science pedagogy in the majority of science classrooms (Chiappetta, Ganesh, Lee, & Phillips, 2006). Admittedly, science textbooks play a pivotal role in science instruction and have a great impact on its quality (Lemmer, Edwards, & Rapule, 2008). As far as NOS is concerned, Abd-El-Khalick (2002) maintains that students' naïve NOS views could be principally attributed to the way science is represented in science textbooks. In other words, "the lack of attention to, and naive messages about NOS, are enacted and encoded in the textbooks" (Abd-El-Khalick et al., 2008, p. 851).

Indubitably, Abd-El-Khalick's argument is well grounded in findings coming from a number of recent research studies conducted in different countries. A brief review of a recent sample of these studies is presented below. It is worth emphasizing that this review is not meant to be rigorously comprehensive and balanced, but it is certainly intended to epitomize science textbooks dominant (not unique) trends of portraying NOS aspects.

Studies focusing on science textbooks published in the United States uncovered noticeable inadequacies in NOS representation. Abd-El-Khalick et al. (2008) analyzed 14 chemistry textbooks in terms of their representation of 10 NOS aspects, namely *Empirical, Tentative, Inferential, Creative, Theory-driven, Myth of the Scientific Method, Scientific theories, Scientific laws, Social dimensions of science* and *Social and cultural embeddedness of science*. Results from this study revealed an obvious deficiency in providing a well-rounded and coherent representation of key NOS aspects. Abd-El-Khalick and his colleagues noticed that the books under study seldom addressed cultural embeddedness of science and social aspects of the scientific enterprise, kept a firm hold on the *Myth of the Scientific Method*, and transmitted a predominantly naïve view of the nature of laws, as well as the creative and tentative NOS.

The essence of the aforementioned studies was largely mirrored in the findings of a study conducted by Niaz and Maza (2011). Based on aspects that were quite similar to those adopted by Abd-El-Khalick et al. (2008), the two researchers evaluated NOS representation in 75 general chemistry textbooks and found that this representation was inconsistent and poor. In the majority of the evaluated books, there was no, or invalid, mention of issues related to NOS aspects associated with: scientific theories and laws, myth of scientific method, theory-ladenness of observations, argumentation, data interpretation, and social and historical aspects of science.

The inadequacy in U.S. textbooks' NOS representation has been recently substantiated by Abd-El-Khalick et al. in a study that assessed (among other factors) the manner and extent of treatment of NOS in 34 (16 biology and 18 physics) high school textbooks. The authors, who based their assessment on the framework and rubric developed by Abd-El-Khalick et al. (2008), found that less than 2.5percent of the analyzed textbook pages were devoted to addressing NOS aspects, while the textbooks' NOS treatment did not differ by content area and was less than favorable.

In a quantitative analysis of NOS representation in Finnish and Swedish chemistry textbooks, Vesterinen et al. (2013) found that all textbooks had a slight emphasis on *science as a way of thinking*. While the researchers identified certain examples illustrating the tentative and empirical NOS, they were also concerned about the lack of explicit discussion regarding the creative and social aspects of scientific practice. According to Vesterinen and colleagues, the absence of such discussion may cause naïve NOS views to develop, especially if learners are inclined to regard science as highly systematic, asocial, and uncreative activity of applying *the Scientific Method*.

Unsatisfactory NOS representation has been also identified in some Chinese and Thai textbooks. Wei, Li, and Chen (2013) examined the manner NOS was addressed in history of science sections chosen from three series of integrated science textbooks used in Chinese junior high schools. Based on Abd-El-Khalick et al.'s (2008) analytical framework, the authors recognized that NOS was not well treated in the resources. Although the empirical and inferential aspects were addressed relatively better than other aspects, discrepancies in NOS treatment among the book series were considered concerning. Similarly, Chaisri and Thathong (2014) assessed NOS representation in *Evolution* themes within Thai Biology textbooks (secondary level), and noticed a significant weakness in the emphasis on NOS and the explicit-reflective NOS instructional method.

Purpose and Scope of the Study

The purpose of this study was to assess NOS representation in an International Baccalaureate (IB) chemistry textbook. While the focus on chemistry originated from the authors' disciplinary expertise, an IB resource was chosen based on a number of IB program's attributes. IB is an international educational system in which students from different nationalities, backgrounds, and cultures are enrolled and educated; so addressing a system with such a global learning impact should have valuable implications for research, policymaking, and professional practice. Additionally, the IB sciences' curricula explicitly feature NOS as an overarching theme that informs science pedagogy. NOS in IBDP is particularly presented through a general framework founded on broad NOS aspects that are explicitly linked to the syllabi topics (refer to IBDP, 2014, for more information).

This study focused on a global edition of a single chemistry book, namely *Pearson Baccalaureate: Chemistry Higher Level for the IB Diploma* (hereafter referred to as *HL Chemistry Textbook*), published by Pearson Education Limited (Brown & Ford, 2014). The study did not seek to conduct a wide-ranging analysis of all IBDP chemistry textbooks available on the market. Rather, the authors aimed to address a *representative* textbook that embodies the syllabus of a reputable international educational system, while hoping that interesting outcomes may inspire comprehensive versions of similar research. It follows that exploring the *ways* and *extent* other textbooks portray the NOS-related IBDP essentials can engender valuable implications for research and practice.

The research question guiding this study was: In what *ways* and to what *extent* is NOS represented in a chemistry book that embodies the chemistry curriculum of the International Baccalaureate Diploma Program? Notably, the *ways* here refer to sophistication (i.e., informed versus naïve) and explicitness of NOS aspects representation as well as the distribution (e.g., main text versus margins) of NOS *occurrences* in the analyzed textbook chapters. Moreover, the *extent* refers to thoroughness and consistency of NOS representation throughout the textbook.

Important Facets of the International Baccalaureate

The International Baccalaureate (IB) is an international educational foundation that offers four programs for students aged 3 to 19: Primary Years Program, Middle Years Program Diploma Program, and Career-related Program (IBO, 2005–2016a). According to IB, all programs are meant to develop internationally minded people with a broad range of human capacities and responsibilities that go beyond academic success (IBDP, 2014). The International Baccalaureate Diploma Program (IBDP) is a two-year educational program aimed at students aged 16 to 19 who wish to pursue a degree in higher education. IBDP courses are offered at Higher Level (HL) and Standard Level (SL), with HL courses more demanding than SL courses in terms of knowledge, understanding, and skills (IBO, 2005–2016b).

In the following sections, we present an overview of IBDP chemistry as well as a concise description of NOS in IBDP chemistry. In addition, we provide an overview of *Theory of Knowledge* (TOK) and *International Mindedness*, which are particularly emphasized in IBDP chemistry guide as essential curricular components that support students' NOS understanding (IBDP, 2014).

Chemistry in the International Baccalaureate Diploma Program

Chemistry is an IBDP course that is designed to provide students with a broad and comprehensive experience in theoretical and experimental chemistry. Like all IBDP courses, chemistry is available at both SL and HL, hence accommodating students who wish to major in a scientific field in higher education and those who are solely seeking scientific literacy. The content and format of the chemistry syllabus are briefly described in the following sections based on the information in the chemistry curriculum guide (IBDP, 2014).

Syllabus Content

The course syllabus is divided into three parts, namely the *Core* (obligatory for SL and HL), the *Additional Higher Level—AHL* (obligatory for HL only) and the *Options* (core topics for SL and HL; *AHL* topics for HL only). The *Core* and *AHL* topics address different branches of chemistry (i.e., analytical, physical, inorganic, and organic). *Options* are more of *Applied Chemistry* topics, which fundamentally emphasize the image of chemistry as a central science, whose principles influence and explain different aspects of modern lives.

Syllabus Format

The format of the syllabus is presented in an integrated tabular form that maps topics and subtopics to (a) NOS sections providing specific, germane, and contextual examples illustrating NOS aspects, (b) lists of *Understandings* representing the main ideas to be taught, (c) *Applications and Skills* sections outlining specific applications and skills to be developed from the *Understandings*, (d) *International Mindedness* sections offering examples about the importance of chemistry in international contexts with emphasis on environmental, political, and socioeconomic considerations, (e) TOK sections presenting examples of Theory of Knowledge questions, (f) *Utilization* sections including syllabus and cross curricular links, and (g) *Aims* sections linking subtopics to general DP aims.

Nature of Science in IBDP Science Curricula

Based on the intention and philosophy designed into the structure of IBDP science curricula, NOS is explicitly featured in the chemistry syllabus as an overarching theme that informs chemistry teaching and learning. Nevertheless, IB clearly emphasizes that IBDP chemistry remains a science subject course focusing on knowledge and understanding of scientific content (Chemistry Teacher Support Material, n.d.). NOS is introduced into the curriculum of IBDP chemistry through a framework founded on five main aspects summarized below (IBDP, 2014):

1) *What is Science, and What is the Scientific Endeavor?*—assumptions about the universe; variety of methodologies; creativity, imagination, and intuition; claims and arguments.
2) *The Understanding of Science*—theories, laws, and hypotheses; testability of scientific ideas; correlation and cause.
3) *The Objectivity of Science*—qualitative and quantitative data; reliability of data collection; errors, uncertainties, accuracy, and precision; technological advancement and data collection.
4) *The Human Face of Science*—collaboration, teamwork, and exchange of results and expertise; peer review; open-mindedness; ethical, political, social, and economical factors; problem solving and improving human life.

5)   *Scientific Literacy and the Public Understanding of Science*—public scientific literacy; faulty reasoning, biases and fallacies; scientific language versus common language.

In addition to the five aspects of NOS, *Theory of Knowledge* (TOK) and *International Mindedness* are explicitly discussed in the chemistry curriculum to support NOS understanding.

Theory of Knowledge

TOK, a mandatory course for all IBDP students, is a study in epistemology designed to encourage learners' critical thinking about knowledge. Importantly, TOK is centered on questions associated with the nature, development, limitations, value, and implications of knowledge. The overarching aim of TOK is provide an epistemological framework through which IB learners' interdisciplinary and epistemological understanding is expected to prosper. Further, TOK education intends to enhance students' understanding of knowledge as a human construction and deepening their comprehension of the personal and shared aspects of knowledge (IBDP, 2006, 2013; Marshman, 2010).

TOK and NOS are intrinsically interconnected. NOS is concerned with students' epistemological values, beliefs, and understandings regarding knowledge and its development in science (Abd-El-Khalick et al., 2008). Accordingly, NOS may be regarded as a science sub-component of epistemology. Moreover, the discursive and reflective spirit of TOK reinforces students' NOS learning (IBDP, 2014).

International Mindedness

From an IB perspective (IBDP, 2014), *International Mindedness* is a stance of openness to, and inquisitiveness about, the world and different cultures. It is concerned with acquiring a deep understanding of the complexity, diversity, and drives of human actions and interactions. Science itself is an international endeavor and NOS understanding cannot occur in isolation from the essentials of *International Mindedness*. The exchange of knowledge across national boundaries has always accompanied the progress of science. Further, the processes of science, which emphasize peer review, open-mindedness, and freedom of thought, transcends politics, religion, gender, and nationality. Additionally, scientific knowledge has the potential to generate great universal benefits, or to reinforce inequalities to people and cause harm to the environment. It is the scientists' moral responsibility to ensure that scientific knowledge is equally available to all nations and that these nations have the necessary scientific capacity for developing sustainable societies.

The Research Methodology

In this study, we conducted a content analysis to assess the representation of 17 NOS aspects in an IBDP chemistry textbook (Brown & Ford, 2014). The adopted analytical scheme was built on two substantial pillars, namely an analytical NOS framework and a compatible scoring rubric. In what follows, we discuss the IB NOS framework as well as the adopted scoring rubric. We start with a justification for the choice of the textbook (Brown & Ford, 2014), and provide a brief description of its chapter format for the purpose of this study.

Higher Level Chemistry Textbook

This textbook was chosen for two reasons. First, it was written by two highly experienced IB chemistry authors to provide complete coverage of the latest two-year syllabus requirements for SL and HL curricular tracks. Accordingly, the textbook material was judged as sufficiently diverse and intricate to make its content analysis for NOS representation a worthwhile and insightful endeavor. Second, one of the authors (a former IB chemistry teacher), was familiar with the textbook, and this was considered helpful for the authors' collaborative inspection of textbook chapters.

HL Chemistry Textbook is composed of 15 chapters covering the three parts of the IB syllabus: i.e., *Core, Additional Higher Level*, and *Options*. The textbook chapters are structured to mirror the syllabus format in the IB chemistry guide. The main text of each chapter covers the topic content in accordance with the *Understandings* and *Applications and Skills*. Other substantial components of the IB syllabus (i.e., NOS, TOK, and *International Mindedness*) are featured through *colored boxes* that are interspersed through each chapter. *Colored boxes* are also used to display supportive ideas and directions (e.g., lab work suggestions, background information, and key text ideas).

The IB Analytical NOS Framework

According to IBDP (2014), the IB NOS framework in science curriculum guides is intended to promote teachers' NOS understanding, and support their ability to translate this NOS understanding into effective instructional practices. This framework is established to provide a comprehensive account of NOS in the twenty-first century through five broad NOS aspects, namely *What is Science and What is the Scientific Endeavor, The Understanding of Science, The Objectivity of Science, The Human Face of Science, and Scientific Literacy and the Public Understanding of Science*. Each of these aspects is explicated in terms of *NOS statements* that elaborate on a variety of pertinent ideas, meanings, and illustrations to enhance the comprehensibility of the target aspect, and its significance.

The authors intended to examine the IB textbook in terms of the IB NOS framework presented in the science curriculum guides. This intention was based on the assumption that using a framework that the textbook authors are knowledgeable about, and committed to follow, is more reasonable than employing any other framework. However, the original *profile* of the IB NOS framework was deemed inconvenient as an analytical instrument for

NOS representation in the IB textbook. Two factors impeded accurate analytical classification and assessment of NOS-related content in the book. The first factor was the noticeable overlap among the *NOS statements* belonging to the different aspects, while the second factor related to the relatively large number of NOS items per aspect. To mitigate the influence of the aforementioned factors on the analytical process, the authors developed an analytical NOS framework with a wider spectrum of NOS aspects. More specifically, the five aspects in the original IB NOS framework were replaced by 17 aspects that were purposefully chosen based on two important considerations. The first consideration was seeking conformity with NOS constructs as presented and classified in relevant science education literature (AAAS, 1993; AAAS & NSTA, 2007; NRC, 1996), and research-based frameworks employed in previous studies (e.g. Abd-El-Khalick et al., 2008). The second consideration was ensuring complete alignment with the ideas and explications emphasized in the original IB NOS framework. Accordingly, the authors did not make any changes to the *NOS statements*, but simply reallocated them within the developed analytical NOS framework. Notably, the second consideration was particularly important to maintain the authors' intention of analyzing the book based on the IB NOS framework without sacrificing analytical accuracy.

The IB analytical NOS framework is outlined below. The title of each aspect is indicated along with the essential ideas of the *NOS statements* as they occur in the IBDP chemistry guide (IBDP, 2014, pp. 6–12):

1) *Scope of Science*—assumptions of science about the natural world; role of pure versus roles of technology and applied science.
2) *The Process of Science*—variety of methodologies and scientific validity; errors and uncertainties; accuracy and precision; statistical treatment of data.
3) *Empirical Nature of Science*—claims, evidences, and arguments; use of evidence to develop theories and hypotheses and test models; data collection, presentation, and reliability; impact of improved instrumentation and computing power on data collection.
4) *Creativity, Discrepancy, and Intuition in Science*—creativity, imagination, exacting thinking in science; intuition and speculation in science discoveries; science achievements and unanswered questions.
5) *Language, Ideas, and Reasoning*—scientists' common terminology and reasoning process; uses of mathematics as a powerful science language; difference between scientific and everyday meaning of scientific concepts and terms.
6) *Tentative Nature of Science*—theories interdependence and liability to change; levels of confidence in scientific outcomes.
7) *Modeling and Computing Power in Science*—developmental nature and explanatory uses of models; power of computer mathematical models for making testable predictions.

8) *Scientific Theories*—theories as integrated comprehensive models and sources of testable predictions; principle of Occam's razor for theory development.

9) *Scientific Laws*—mathematical form, evidence-based testability, and predictive nature of laws.

10) *Scientific Hypotheses*—hypotheses as explanatory statements that are testable and suggestive of causal relationships or correlations.

11) *Correlation and Causation*—correlation and causation and their dependence on experimental or statistical evidence and plausible scientific mechanisms.

12) *Theory Ladenness, Biases, and Fallacies*—cognitive biases and their impact on scientific designs and interpretations; accounting for biases in scientific methodologies; pseudoscience resulting from failure of bias and fallacy management.

13) *The Human Face of Science:*

   (a) *Communal Aspects of Science*—communities of inquiry with common principles, methods, and understandings.

   (b) *Sharing and Collaboration in Science*—interdisciplinary nature of scientific enterprise; analysis, storage, publishing, and sharing of data; controversies around scientists' work.

   (c) *Science Culture and Interplay with other Fields*—open-mindedness in science; ethical and political implications of scientific work; sources of and factors influencing science funding; science contribution to improve man's lot versus its creation of problems; vitality of public understanding of science.

   (d) *Academic Embeddedness*—scientists' engagement in reading, publishing, and peer reviewing research; academic integrity in scientific research.

14) *Science and Technology*—science and technology interaction for mutual development.

The Adapted Scoring Rubric

The IB NOS framework is designed for pedagogical, not analytical purposes, so it is not accompanied by an assessment guide for the pedagogical treatment of its NOS aspects. For this reason, we opted to use an adaptation of Abd-El-Khalick et al.'s (2008) rubric to complement our developed analytical framework. Abd-El-Khalick et al.'s rubric was particularly chosen for a number of reasons. On the one hand, the rubric was viewed as compatible with the IB NOS analytical framework since it is not aspect-specific. On the other hand, the rubric is founded on three assertions that were of special interest to our study: 1) it builds on research findings that address the distinction between explicit and implicit instructional treatment of NOS, and show that implicit approaches are less effective than explicit ones (Abd-El-Khalick & Lederman, 2000), 2) the rubric's scoring is primarily based on the quality of NOS representation in textbooks particularly associated with informed NOS understandings, and 3) the rubric's scoring allow for examining the extent of overall consistency in the NOS representation in the analyzed textbook (Abd-El-Khalick et al., 2008).

Structure of the Adapted Scoring Rubric

Scores were oriented on a 7-point scale (ranging from -3 to +3) with a 0-midpoint score indicating that a particular NOS aspect is not addressed at all. A score of +3 indicates an explicit and informed representation of a NOS aspect, a score of +2 indicates an explicit and partially informed representation, a score of +1 indicates an implicit and informed representation, a score of -1 indicates an implicit and misinformed representation, a score of -2 indicates a mixed explicit and/or implicit messages about the target NOS aspect, and finally a score of -3 indicates an explicit and misinformed representation of the target NOS aspect.

Employment of the Adapted Scoring Rubric

A total of 15 chapters (over 900 pages) were reviewed. The review involved all sections within each chapter (content, margins, boxes, etc.); the NOS-related content was examined in terms of the NOS aspects in the developed IB analytical framework, and scored using the adapted scoring rubric. A distinction was deliberately made in the scoring sheets between 1) *Core* and *Additional Higher Level Material* and 2) *Content* and *Others* parts of the book. *Others* include the textbook's *colored boxes* that feature substantial components of the IB syllabus like NOS, TOK, *International Mindedness*, and *Utilization* (refer to the section of Higher Level Chemistry Textbook). The distinction between the different parts was essential for examining the distribution of *NOS occurrences* in the textbook (part of the research question). As emphasized previously, the analyzed textbook embodies the two-year chemistry syllabus by completely covering its content (i.e., *Core, AHL,* and *Options* topics) and reflecting its integrated format (i.e., mapping substantial components of IB). Accordingly, scrutinizing the NOS aspects distribution in the chapters was deemed necessary and significant. Consequently, each NOS aspect corresponding to one chapter was awarded a unified representative score based on the individual scores of pertinent *NOS occurrences*, i.e., terms, expressions, statements, or paragraphs that were thought to represent any of target NOS aspects.

Before the scoring rubric was formally implemented, inter-rater reliability was assessed. Both authors scored one of the book chapters together, and then they separately reviewed another chapter with a 90 percent inter-rater reliability. The reviewers met to ensure 100 percent agreement and settled their differences. Qualitative judgments were used to code the book chapters and scores were then assigned to each target NOS aspect based on the scoring rubric used.

Results and Discussion

In general, the analyzed chapters did not fare well in their representation of the target NOS aspects. It should be noted that with 17 NOS aspects being examined in the analysis, the possible cumulative score for a chapter could range from -102 to +102 points for an entire chapter (including *Content* and *Others* sections). An examination of the total score per chapter for *Core* and *AHL* indicates that cumulative scores for all chapters ranged from 11 to 42 for the *Core* and from 19 to 57 for the *AHL*. However, unlike previous research findings (e.g., Abd-El-Khalick et al., 2008; Niaz & Maza, 2011; Vesterinen et al., 2013), the analyzed book accorded some promising attention to NOS; specifically, there are no negative or zero total scores across all chapters, which reveals that, by and large, all NOS aspects were at least addressed in the book. A more detailed analysis of the *extent* and *ways* of NOS aspects representation in the examined IB textbook is presented in the following section.

Extent and Ways of NOS Representation in HL Chemistry Textbook

Core Versus Additional Higher Level Topics

The data presented in Table 9.1 shows the highest score for the *Core* was below 50 percent of the maximum possible score (that is, 51 points out of 102), and the highest score for the *AHL* was only a few points above 50 percent of the maximum possible score (i.e., 102 points). Looking more closely at these total scores, it is noticed that the total scores of NOS aspects are higher for *AHL* than they are for *Core* in all 15 chapters with differences ranging from 3 to 17 (highest possible difference is 102). Chapter 2 exhibits the highest total score difference between *Core* and *AHL*: in cases where some NOS aspects are implicitly addressed in the *Core*, they are explicit and informed in the *AHL* sections. For example, the *Tentative Nature of Science* seems to be conveyed in mixed implicit and explicit ways in the *Core*, while it is consistently addressed explicitly and is informed in the *AHL* sections. Notably, Chapter 11 has the highest total scores with respect to *Core* (42 points) and *AHL* (57 points). This chapter—entitled "Measurement and Data Processing and Analysis"—is particularly akin to NOS, as it emphasizes ideas pertinent to the limitations of measurements, progression of science, and the human face of science.

Content versus Other Sections

An overall examination of Table 9.1 reveals that NOS aspects are predominantly located in the *Other* sections of the textbook. Results show that the total

Table 9.1 Pearson Standard/Core Level and Additional Higher Level* Scores on the Target Aspects of NOS Sorted by Content (C) and Other (O)

All cell values are given as C/O.

Textbook chapter	Scope of science	Process of science	Creativity & intuition	Language discrepancy ideas & reasoning	Empirical nature	Tentative nature	Modeling & computing power	Scientific theories	Scientific laws	Scientific hypotheses	Correlation & causation	Theory ladenness aspect	Communal Sharing & collaboration	Culture & Academic interactions	embeddedness	Science & technology	Total score/chapter
1*	0/0	0/1	0/3	0/0	2/3	0/1	0/3	0/0	0/0	0/0	0/0	0/1	0/1	0/3	0/1	0/0	2/17
2	0/-2	0/3	3/6	0/3	1/6	2/1	2/1	0/5	0/0	0/2	0/0	0/1	1/2	0/2	1/3	0/6	10/39
3	0/3	0/0	0/3	0/3	0/0	0/2	0/3	1/2	0/3	0/0	0/0	0/0	0/-2	0/3	0/3	0/3	1/26
4	0/3	0/0	0/3	0/1	0/2	0/0	0/3	0/6	0/0	0/0	0/0	0/0	0/3	0/0	0/4	0/0	0/25
5	0/0	0/0	0/0	0/6	1/3	0/3	0/3	0/0	0/3	0/0	0/0	0/6	0/0	0/0	0/3	0/6	1/36
6	0/0	0/0	0/0	0/6	0/6	0/3	0/3	0/0	0/0	0/0	0/0	0/1	0/0	0/3	0/2	0/0	0/21
7	0/0	0/0	0/4	0/3	0/3	0/4	0/0	1/1	0/1	0/0	0/0	0/1	0/3	0/3	0/6	2/0	3/29
8	0/0	0/0	0/0	0/6	0/3	-2/6	0/0	0/0	0/0	0/0	0/0	3/3	0/0	0/3	3/6	2/0	6/25
9	0/0	0/-1	0/0	0/6	0/1	0/2	0/4	0/3	0/0	0/0	0/0	3/6	0/2	0/6	0/6	0/5	3/30
10	0/0	0/0	0/6	0/3	3/3	0/2	0/0	0/0	0/0	0/0	0/0	0/4	0/1	0/0	0/0	2/0	5/24
11	0/6	3/3	0/0	0/3	0/3	2/3	0/3	0/0	0/0	0/0	0/6	3/0	0/6	0/6	3/3	3/6	14/43
12	1/0	0/0	0/4	0/0	0/4	0/3	0/3	0/0	0/0	0/0	0/0	0/0	1/6	0/0	1/4	1/1	4/25
13	0/1	0/0	0/3	0/3	0/3	0/1	0/3	0/3	0/0	0/0	0/3	0/0	0/3	0/0	4/6	0/3	4/32
14	0/0	0/2	0/6	-2/3	0/0	0/0	0/0	0/0	0/0	0/0	1/2	0/1	0/4	0/0	2/2	1/1	2/22
15	0/3	0/2	0/6	-2/0	0/3	0/0	0/0	0/0	0/0	0/0	1/1	0/1	0/4	1/0	4/2	4/1	8/23
Total score/aspect	1/11	3/9	3/38	-2/43	7/37	2/32	2/26	2/20	0/7	0/2	1/11	9/24	2/29	0/23	14/49	11/28	

*Chapter 1 includes no additional higher-level material [AHL].

score per aspect across all chapters in the *Other* sections is considerably higher than those of the *Content* sections, with differences ranging from 2 to 45 (highest possible difference is 87). Similarly, total scores per chapter across all NOS aspects in the *Other* sections are also significantly higher than those in the *Content* sections, with differences ranging from 0 to 24 (highest possible difference is 51). This shows that not only are NOS aspects addressed in the *Other* sections more frequently than in the *Content* sections, but also that there appears to be a significant difference in the *way* and *extent* of this representation.

A closer examination of the *way* by which NOS aspects are represented in *Content* versus *Other* sections leads to the following conclusions. First, *Creativity, Discrepancy, and Intuition* is the only aspect that is more or less consistently addressed in an explicit and informed manner throughout the entire book. However, while it is addressed only once in the *Content* section of the core material, it appears considerably more often in the *Other* sections of *Core* and *AHL*. Second, the general aspect of the *Human Face of Science* that includes various communal, collaborative, cultural, and academic sub-aspects frequently, though at many times inconsistently, appears in the *Other* sections of the textbook. For example, *Science Culture and Interplay with Other Fields* is addressed implicitly as well as explicitly (mixed) throughout the entire book. In the *Content* sections of the textbook chapters, it is either 1) not addressed (19 such occurrences in both *Core* and *AHL*), followed by 2) implicitly informed (six such occurrences in both *Core* and *AHL*), and 3) explicitly informed (four such occurrences in both *Core* and *AHL*). On the other hand, in the *Other* sections of the chapters, this aspect is 1) not addressed (six such occurrences in both *Core* and *AHL*), 2) implicitly informed (nine such occurrences in both *Core* and *AHL*), and explicitly informed (14 such occurrences in both *Core* and *AHL*).

Third, *Language, Ideas, and Reasoning* is inconsistently represented (with mixed explicit and implicit representations) in the *Content* sections across the entire textbook, whereas it appears to be more explicitly informed in the *Other* sections of the book (with only a couple occurrences where it is implicitly informed). Fourth, both *Modeling and Computing Power* and *Correlation and Causation* are inconsistently represented across all chapters. A closer examination of *Modeling and Computing Power* shows that while this aspect is only represented in the *Content* section of SL Chapter 2 and is partially informed; it is addressed, implicitly as well as explicitly, in the *Others* sections across *Core* and *AHL*. On the other hand, *Correlation and Causation* is not addressed anywhere in the chapters until later in the textbook (Chapters 11, 14, and 15). Similarly, Chapters 14 and 15 are applied chemistry topics, which are fundamentally designed to emphasize the image of chemistry as a central science, whose principles influence and explain different aspects of modern lives. Nevertheless, although this aspect is addressed in three chapters, it is addressed in a mixed way, revealing no consistency of its representation.

A fifth conclusion that is worthy of attention pertains to the poor representation of four NOS aspects, namely *Scientific Laws, Scientific Hypotheses, Theory*

Ladenness, Biases, and Fallacies, and *Academic Embeddedness*. These aspects are represented—with various levels- only in the *Other* sections of the book. For example, *Scientific Laws* is represented in mixed explicit and implicit ways throughout the chapters, *Scientific Hypotheses* is represented only in one chapter in the entire book (specifically in a NOS box in *AHL*), with it being partially informed. In the *Other* sections of several chapters in this book *Theory Ladenness of Science* is almost always implicitly addressed. Moreover, although *Academic Embeddedness of Science* is not addressed, neither explicitly nor implicitly, in the entire *Content* sections (main text) of the book, it is well represented (explicit and informed) in all the *Other* sections.

Conclusion and Implications

As emphasized earlier in the chapter, IBDP established an overarching framework for NOS representation in the chemistry curriculum. In addition, a detailed curricular scheme was constructed to guide—through specific statements, elaborations, suggestions, and illustrations—appropriate associations between each topic in the syllabus and the NOS aspects. Importantly, TOK and *International Mindedness*—two flagship elements in IBDP education—were embedded in the curricular configuration in a way that may be expected to promote informed views of NOS. From an optimistic stance, it may be argued that the NOS manifestation in IBDP chemistry promises to inform teaching and learning in the classroom, and facilitate an adequate NOS representation in commercial IB chemistry textbooks. However, findings from this study highlight a number of inadequacies in the consistency of the treatment of NOS aspects (e.g., mixed representation in terms of explicitness and quality of treatment) and distribution of NOS occurrences in the chapters (e.g., *Core* versus *AHL*; *Content* versus *Others*).

Several explanations may be proposed for the inadequate NOS representation in the analyzed textbook. Some explanations may focus on possible gaps in the original curricular framework, while others might focus on the weakness in materializing the NOS-related curricular components in the textbook. Admittedly, the study was not designed to support or challenge any explanations pertaining to the NOS representation in the IB curriculum. However, the study results may be interpreted to suggest plausible implications associated with the representation of curricular essentials in the textbook. The textbook portrayal of NOS was deemed *below expectations*, and this performance level needs to, and can be, improved. Improvement measures may well be predicated on considerations simultaneously related to the yields of educational research and the particulars of IBDP chemistry curriculum.

Importance of Educational Research

Researchers propose a plethora of strategies, methods, and learning experiences for promoting desirable NOS teaching and learning. Common propositions are centered on explicit instruction and reflection (Abd-El-Khalick & Lederman, 2000; Khishfe & Abd-El-Khalick, 2002; Schwartz, Lederman, & Crawford, 2004), significant scaffolding between contextualized and decontextualized NOS experiences (Abd-El-Khalick, 2001; Brickhouse, Dagher, Letts, & Shipman, 2000; Clough, 2006), and inquiry-based and authentic science learning contexts (Bell, Blair, Crawford, & Lederman, 2003; Schwartz et al., 2004).

As far as the textbook industry is concerned, it is imperative that developers of textbooks take note of research findings in science education (Forawi, 2010). Authors of science textbooks who wish to address NOS effectively must deliberately develop an informed understanding of NOS-related science education literature. It is important to recognize that textbook authors are neither expected to be NOS experts, nor required to assume full responsibility for achieving a global and sustainable enhancement in NOS instruction. Educational experts, curriculum developers, faculties of education, professional development providers, and other parties should have their share in this responsibility. However, textbook authors and publishers need to be aware of research findings to ensure they are in a better position to produce textbooks in which NOS is adequately represented. Additionally, authors who are knowledgeable about research-based strategies for NOS instruction are more prepared to translate their knowledge in the content and design of their textbooks, thus providing textbooks users (i.e., teachers and students) with a helpful resource for desirable NOS teaching and learning (e.g., designing learning activities or exercises that facilitate the implementation of the research-based strategies).

Harnessing the Curricular Elements

Undeniably, the chapters in the analyzed book in this study were designed to align with the format of IBDP chemistry syllabus. Particularly, NOS, TOK, and *International Mindedness* were explicitly and clearly featured in each chapter along with *Understandings*, and *Applications and Skills*. Nevertheless, it was evident that the NOS, TOK, and *International Mindedness* sections were displayed through distinct colored boxes that were erratically spread on the pages' margins or between main text paragraphs. Seemingly, these sections were presented in a way that neither reflected any kind of purposeful systematic pattern, nor respected the sections intrinsic interrelatedness that was particularly highlighted in the chemistry curriculum guide.

In this study the textbook alignment with the mandated syllabus format was explicit, yet largely mechanical, favoring a compartmentalized view of the supposedly interconnected curricular components. Arguably, such a view does not promote a desirable NOS representation in textbooks and is unlikely to reinforce learners' NOS understanding. Alternatively, adopting an integrative perspective towards IB curricular components should result in more desirable NOS-related educational gains. A *concept-based* curricular model is suggested as an appropriate platform for such a perspective.

Erickson (2012) identifies IBDP as a three dimensional concept-based model in which facts and skills are assembled with disciplinary concepts, generalizations, and principles. This model is distinguished from traditional two-dimensional models commonly focusing on factual content, and skills with tacit rather than purposeful consideration for conceptual understanding and knowledge transfer. Erickson intimates that in concept-based approaches, facts are used in concert with concepts and generalizations to engender higher order synergistic thinking. This form of thinking, which capitalizes on cognitive interaction between the factual and conceptual levels of mental processing, is essential for intellectual development.

NOS integration in IBDP chemistry is a manifestation of a three-dimensional concept-based approach for two complementary reasons. On the one hand, subject-specific knowledge and skills are taught through an overarching conceptual NOS framework founded on the paradigmatic NOS views in the twenty-first century (IBDP, 2014). On the other hand, NOS understanding may be perceived as a corollary benefit of synergistic thinking associated with the cognitive interplay between ideas of, and about, science. In fact, integrating NOS in science education is more of an intellectual endeavor for all concerned, including students, teachers, and textbook authors. As far as IBDP textbook authors are concerned, their success depends to a large extent on their ability to develop a robust understanding of the underpinnings of IBDP and the rationales of its curricular constructions. For instance, authors need to comprehend the significance and implications of a concept-based curriculum, appreciate the distinctive roles of TOK and *International Mindedness* in IBDP education, and recognize that these components are intrinsically linked to NOS, and can play a supportive role in NOS instruction. As expected, authors' understanding of IBDP would allow them to harness its pertinent components for an adequate NOS representation. Plausible forms of harnessing include the orchestration between TOK, NOS, and *International Mindedness* sections to enhance synergistic thinking and NOS understanding, the creation of learning exercises that purposefully address NOS aspects, and the integration of NOS-related material in the main text of chapters.

In conclusion, NOS integration in science education is an intellectual challenge at the levels of learning, instructional practice, and curricular design. Accordingly, the success of this integration is a shared and collaborative responsibility among concerned professionals and scholars in the field of science education. Indeed, textbooks authors possess a significant share in this responsibility because their product (i.e., the textbook) constitutes the main resource that guides teaching and learning in many science classrooms. For these reasons, authors who are willing to portray NOS aspects adequately in their textbooks should be well versed in NOS-related educational literature. In particular, authors of IBDP chemistry books need to increase their efforts as they empower themselves through developing a comprehensive understanding of the Diploma Program's underpinnings and curricular constituents. This understanding is crucial to facilitate explicit, informed, and conceptual NOS representation in textbooks that support favorable NOS teaching and learning.

References

Abd-El-Khalick, F. (2001). Embedding nature of science instruction in preservice elementary science courses: Abandoning scientism, but . . . *Journal of Science Teacher Education, 12*(3), 215–233.

Abd-El-Khalick, F. (2002). *The development of conceptions of the nature of scientific knowledge and knowing in the middle and high school years: A cross-sectional study.* Paper presented at the annual meeting of the National Association for Research in Science Teaching, New Orleans, LA.

Abd-El-Khalick, F., & Lederman, N. G. (2000). Improving science teachers' conceptions of nature of science: A critical review of the literature. *International Journal of Science Education, 22*, 665–701.

Abd-El-Khalick, F., Bell, R. L., & Lederman, N. G. (1998). The nature of science and instructional practice: Making the unnatural natural. *Science Education, 82*(4), 417–436.

Abd-El-Khalick, F., Myers, J. Y., Summers, R., Brunner, J., Waight, N., Wahbeh, N., . . . Belarmino, J. (2017). A longitudinal analysis of the extent and manner of representations of nature of science in U.S. high school biology and physics textbooks. *Journal of Research in Science Teaching, 54*(1), 82–120.

Abd-El-Khalick, F., Waters, M., & Le, A. P. (2008). Representations of nature of science in high school chemistry textbooks over the past four decades. *Journal of Research in Science Teaching, 45*(7), 835–855.

American Association for the Advancement of Science [AAAS]. (1993). *Benchmarks for science literacy.* New York: Oxford University Press.

American Association for the Advancement of Science [AAAS] & National Science Teachers Association [NSTA]. (2007). *Atlas of science literacy: Project 2061.* Washington, DC: AAAS.

Bell, R. L., Blair, L. M., Crawford, B. A., & Lederman, N. G. (2003). Just do it? Impact of a science apprenticeship program on high school students' understandings of the nature of science and scientific inquiry. *Journal of Research in Science Teaching, 40*, 487–509.

Brickhouse, N. W., Dagher, Z. R., Letts, W. J., & Shipman, H. L. (2000). Diversity of students' views about evidence, theory, and the interface between science and religion in an astronomy course. *Journal of Research in Science Teaching, 37*(4), 340–362.

Brown, C., & Ford, M. (2014). *Pearson baccalaureate: Chemistry higher level for the IB diploma* (2nd ed.). Nitra, Slovakia: Pearson.

Burbules, N. C., & Linn, M. C. (1991). Science education and the philosophy of science: Congruence or contradiction? *International Journal of Science Education, 3*(3), 227–241.

Chaisri, A., & Thathong, K. (2014). The nature of science represented in Thai biology textbooks under the topic of evolution. *Procedia-Social and Behavioral Sciences, 116*, 621–626.

Chemistry Teacher Support Material. (n.d.). *Nature of science.* Retrieved from https://ibpublishing.ibo.org/server2/rest/app/tsm.xql?doc=d_4_chemi_tsm_1408_1_e&part=1&chapter=2

Chiappetta, E. L., Ganesh, T. G., Lee, Y. H., & Phillips, M. C. (2006). *Examination of science textbook analysis research conducted on textbooks published over the past 100 years in the United States.* Annual meeting of the National Association for Research in Science Teaching, San Francisco, CA.

Clough, M. P. (2006). Learners' responses to the demands of conceptual change: Considerations for effective nature of science instruction. *Science & Education, 15*(5), 463–494.

Driver, R., Leach, J., Millar, R., & Scott, P. (1996). *Young people's images of science.* Buckingham: Open University Press.

Erickson, H. L. (2012). *Concept-based teaching and learning.* Retrieved from www.ibmidatlantic.org/Concept_Based_Teaching_Learning.pdf

Forawi, S. (2010). Impact of teachers' conceptions of the nature of science and use of textbooks on students. *International Journal of Learning, 17*(5), 281–293.

Hewson, P., & Hewson, M. (1988). On appropriate conception of teaching science: A view from studies of science learning. *Science Education, 72*(5), 529–540.

International Baccalaureate Diploma Program, IBDP. (2006). *Theory of knowledge guide, first assessment 2008.* Cardiff: International Baccalaureate Organization.

International Baccalaureate Diploma Program, IBDP. (2013). *Theory of knowledge guide, first assessment 2015.* Cardiff: International Baccalaureate Organization.

International Baccalaureate Diploma Program, IBDP. (2014). *Chemistry guide, first assessment 2016.* Cardiff: International Baccalaureate Organization.

International Baccalaureate Organization, IBO. (2005–2016a). *Programmes.* Retrieved from www.ibo.org/en/programmes/

International Baccalaureate Organization, IBO. (2005–2016b). *Diploma Programme.* Retrieved from www.ibo.org/programmes/diploma-programme/

Khishfe, R., & Abd-El-Khalick, F. (2002). Influence of explicit and reflective versus implicit inquiry-oriented instruction on 6th-graders' views of nature of science. *Journal of Research in Science Teaching, 39,* 551–578.

Lederman, N. G. (1992). Students and teachers' conceptions of the nature of science: A Review of the research. *Journal of Research in Science Teaching, 29,* 331–359.

Lemmer, M., Edwards, J. A., & Rapule, S. (2008). Educators' selection and evaluation of natural sciences textbooks. *South African Journal of Education, 28*(2), 175–187.

Marshman, R. (2010). *Concurrency of learning in the IB Diploma Programme and Middle Years Programme.* Retrieved from https://blogs.ibo.org/positionpapers/files/2010/09/Concurrency-of-learning_Roger-Marshman2.pdf

McComas, W. F., Almazroa, H., & Clough, M. P. (1998). The nature of science in science education: An introduction. *Science & Education, 7,* 511–532.

National Research Council [NRC]. (1996). *National science education standards.* Washington, DC: The National Academies Press.

National Research Council [NRC]. (2007). *Taking science to school: Learning and teaching science in grades K-8.* Washington, DC: The National Academies Press.

Niaz, M., & Maza, A. (2011). *Nature of science in general chemistry textbooks.* Dordrecht, the Netherlands: Springer.

Schwartz, R. S., Lederman, N. G., & Crawford, B. A. (2004). Developing views of nature of science in an authentic context: An explicit approach to bridging the gap between nature of science and scientific inquiry. *Science Education, 88,* 610–645.

Vesterinen, V. M., Aksela, M., & Lavonen, J. (2013). Quantitative analysis of representations of nature of science in Nordic upper secondary school textbooks using framework of analysis based on philosophy of chemistry. *Science & Education, 22*(7), 1839–1855.

Wei, B., Li, Y., & Chen, B. (2013). Representations of nature of science in selected histories of science in the integrated science textbooks in China. *School Science and Mathematics, 113*(4), 170–179.

10 An Analysis of South African School Science Textbooks for Representations of Nature of Science

Umesh Ramnarain

South Africa's reformed school science curriculum places a strong emphasis on the goal of learners acquiring an understanding of nature of science (NOS), and textbooks are regarded as a key resource by teachers in advancing these curriculum goals. This chapter is a synthesis of research conducted in South Africa on the analysis of school science textbooks used in the middle school and high school phases on their portrayal of NOS. Following a discussion on the place of NOS in current curriculum documents, the chapter goes on to present research findings on the analysis of high school textbooks used in Grade 10 Life Sciences and Physical Science, and Grade 9 Natural Science. From a methodological perspective, the chapter explicates on the procedure and frameworks that guided the analysis. Finally, the chapter concludes with some thoughts on the implications of the findings, and recommendations thereof.

Curriculum Reform, NOS, and the Role of Textbooks

The launch of an outcomes-based curriculum on March 24, 1997 was the most significant curriculum reform in the history of South Africa. This marked not only a dramatic departure from the Apartheid curriculum, but also a paradigm shift in terms of pedagogy and the manner in which learners experience a particular discipline. Since 1997, there have been waves of reforms, resulting in the publication of the National Curriculum Statement (NCS) (Department of Basic Education, 2003), and ultimately the Curriculum and Assessment Performance Statement (CAPS) (Department of Basic Education, 2011a).

The previous curriculum depicted to the learner and teacher a view of science which was not compatible with NOS. The learners were exposed only to the products of the scientific enterprise in the form of facts, concepts, principles, and laws of the physical world. This knowledge is referred to as the substantive aspects of science. This static view of science has in no small part contributed to the rote learning of science that is common in South Africa. Science teaching has emphasized the factual recall of science content to the exclusion of the knowledge generation process, referred to as the syntactic dimension of science (McComas, Clough, & Almazroa, 1998). Research has shown that this view of science portrayed to learners is, to a large extent, due to the teachers' own notions of NOS (Dekkers & Mnisi, 2003; Linneman, Lynch, Kurup, & Bantwini, 2003). Science schooling in South Africa is heavily content-based and characterized by teacher-centeredness and learner passivity. In a typical classroom, learners sit in straight rows of desks facing the front of the class, and have few opportunities to interact or work in cooperative learning groups. Experimental tasks, if utilized, often embody a cookbook approach, where learners followed 'recipes' for the execution of procedures handed down by teachers. Many of the activities carried out by learners merely confirm or illustrate what has been taught in class (Ramnarain, 2014). This apparent disregard for NOS in school science is not a phenomenon confined to South Africa. Although NOS is fundamental to science, it has assumed less importance in science classrooms worldwide (Duschl, 1985; Osborne, 2010; Schwartz, Lederman, & Crawford, 2004). In designing the new South African curriculum, planners were faced with the demand of producing a curriculum which was more representative of NOS.

There are many disagreements among philosophers, historians, sociologists, and science educators on the exact meaning of NOS. According to Hodson (2014) these disagreements stem from the significant differences among the sub-disciplines of science in terms of the types of research questions framed, the methods used, and the criteria to establish the validity and reliability of evidence collected. Despite these disagreements, key proponents of NOS in science education research (Abd-El-Khalick, 2012a; Lederman, 2007; McComas, Clough, & Almazroa, 1998) describe a 'consensus view' of NOS. According to this view, scientific knowledge is tentative and subject to change; scientific knowledge is subjective; people from all cultures contribute to science; and scientific ideas are affected by their social and cultural milieu.

Research findings (Driver, Leach, Millar, & Scott, 1996; Songer & Linn, 1991) have revealed that knowledge of NOS assists learners in their conceptual understanding of science. Incorporating NOS in teaching also conveys to learners a view of science as a human activity steered by our sense of curiosity in trying to understand the physical world. This view of science can enhance interest in the subject (Matthews, 2000). An understanding of NOS has also been presented as essential for informed decision-making, especially in evaluating the effect of technological innovations on society (Driver et al., 1996). An adequate understanding of NOS is therefore a central element of students' scientific literacy (National Research Council [NRC], 1996).

A key imperative in the reformed school science curriculum in South Africa is now for learners to acquire an understanding of NOS. In the CAPS Physical Sciences (Physics and Chemistry) document for the Further Education and Training (FET) phase (Grades 10–12) there is a clear intent for learners to be initiated into NOS. This intention is reflected in the Specific Aims of the curriculum; for example, Specific Aim 3 states that the subject should promote "an understanding of the nature of science and its relationships to technology, society and environment" (Department of Basic Education, 2011c, p. 8). This intent is also underlined in the FET Life Sciences (Biology) CAPS document where it is stated that by studying science, learners will develop "scientific skills and ways of thinking scientifically that enable them to see the flaws in pseudo-science in popular media" (Department of Basic Education, 2011b, p. 8). The senior phase (Grades 7–9) CAPS document for Natural Sciences (General Science), does not specify a focus on NOS366; however, the importance of addressing NOS in the classroom is underlined through Specific Aim 1 where it is stated that "Learners should be able to complete investigations, analyse problems and use practical processes and skills in evaluating solution" (Department of Basic Education, 2011b, p. 10).

An analysis of the CAPS documents for science subjects including Life Sciences (Biology), Physical Sciences (Chemistry and Physics) and Natural Sciences (General Science), also reveals excerpts that adhere very closely with the tenets of NOS as articulated by Lederman (2007). For example, the tenet that "science is empirically-based" is reflected in the statement that "To be accepted as science, certain methods of inquiry are generally used. These methods include formulating hypotheses, and designing and carrying out experiments to test the hypothesis" (Department of Basic Education, 2011a, p. 11). The statement from CAPS that "scientific knowledge changes over time as scientists acquire new information and people change their ways of viewing the world" (Department of Basic Education, 2011a, p. 11) resonates with the tenet that "scientific knowledge is tentative, yet durable" (Lederman, 2007). Furthermore, the NOS tenet on "social and cultural embeddedness of science" is affirmed in CAPS through the statement that "In all cultures and in all times people have wanted to understand how the world works. Sometimes their lives depend on understanding it and, sometimes, people want to make sense of the physical world and they need explanations that satisfy them" (Department of Basic Education, 2011a, p. 11).

In South Africa, teachers at public schools are mandated to use textbooks from a list compiled by the Department of Basic Education. New textbooks proposed by publishers are first screened by a panel chosen by the Department of Basic Education before being included in a list of books from which schools can order. In the screening process, a panel of reviewers evaluates the books against criteria drawn up by the department. Textbook studies in post-Apartheid South Africa have largely centered on how textbooks address challenges posed by integration as well as constitutional imperatives for the recognition of diversity. For example, in a large-scale study by the Human Sciences Research Council (2005), 61 textbooks in use in South African primary schools were analyzed. The analysis of Grade 1 readers revealed inequity in gender representation and significant under-representation of rural, poor, and working-class communities. However, racial diversity was better represented. Representation in relation to gender, race, social class, and rural/urban location (but not disability) was generally better in the Natural Sciences texts than in Language texts, though still needed improvement. A study by Green and Naidoo (2008) showed Grade 10 Physical Sciences textbooks that were written for the revised curriculum to be less mono-cultural, Eurocentric, and male-centered than older textbooks. Their study also showed there were attempts to incorporate indigenous knowledge in the newer books.

Despite the new curriculum focus on NOS, teachers have received little support on how to develop materials that would facilitate this shift. The lack of guidance on how to design curriculum materials opened the door for a plethora of textbooks on the market. Textbooks are a crucial resource in ensuring that the goals of the South African national school science curriculum are met. Research conducted in South Africa has revealed that there is a heavy reliance on textbooks by science teachers (Malcolm & Alant, 2004; Ramnarain & Padayachee, 2015). Textbooks traditionally offer teachers the comfort and convenience of having some lessons planned out in advance and worksheets easily available on demand (Swanepoel, 2010). Given this state of affairs, it becomes necessary to analyze South African school science textbooks to establish how well textbooks affirm a key intent of the curriculum, namely representations of NOS. Previous international studies on the analysis of science textbooks for NOS shows that aspects of NOS are not sufficiently addressed (Abd-El-Khalick, Waters & Le, 2008; Chiappetta & Fillman, 2007; Lumpe & Beck, 1996; McComas, 2003). For example, Abd-El-Khalick et al. (2008) in their analysis of high school chemistry books used over four decades in the United States, rated them poorly in their representations of NOS. In other work, McComas (2003) found in his analysis of U.S. biology textbooks that the distinction between laws and theories was not evident. He recommended that authors take more care to provide accurate and complete definitions, coupled with useful examples.

Analysis of School Science Textbooks in South Africa

In South Africa, each wave of curriculum reform has been accompanied by a renewal of textbooks to advance new curriculum imperatives. As discussed earlier, a key imperative in the reformed curriculum has been the emphasis placed on learners' understandings of NOS, and the three studies on text-book analysis for NOS representation that are reviewed in this section constitute research that has been conducted in South Africa thus far.

Padayachee's (2012) study compared representations of NOS in three Grade 10 high school Life Sciences textbooks written for the reformed curriculum, and three Grade 10 Biology textbooks written for the previous curriculum. The investigation targeted four broad NOS constructs: science as a body of knowledge, science as a way of investigating, science as a way of thinking, and the interaction between science, technology and society. Books that were extensively used in classrooms throughout South Africa were targeted for analysis. This research used a framework developed by Chiappetta, Sethna, and Fillman (1991). This framework addresses four themes. The theme 'Science as a body of knowledge' reflects science as a body of knowledge such as the facts, concepts, principles, laws, theories and models. The theme 'The investigative nature of science' addresses the enactment of inquiry-based learning and here the student is involved in the methods and processes of science such as observing, measuring, classifying, inferring, recording data, and making calculations. Thinking, reasoning and reflection aspects of science are revealed in the theme 'Science as a way of thinking,' and provides students with insight into the operation of the scientific enterprise. The fourth theme, 'Interaction of science, technology and society' pertains to the application of science and how technology helps or hinders humankind.

In adopting the Chiappetta, Sethna, and Fillman (1991) framework, a deductive content analysis process was followed when coding the text. The units of analysis included complete paragraphs, activities, worked examples, figures with captions, tables with captions, charts with captions, and marginal comments. The findings of the study revealed that Life Sciences textbooks still overwhelmingly represent the theme 'Science as a body of knowledge.' Despite significant curriculum reform that underlines a more balanced perspective of science encompassing the acquisition of knowledge through inquiry, limited coverage was given to the themes 'The investigative nature of science,' 'Science as a way of thinking,' and 'The interaction of science, technology and society.' The investigative approach to the teaching and learning of science is portrayed moderately by all three Life Sciences textbooks as evidenced by the 28 percent coding of units to the theme 'The investigative nature of science.' This coverage is even more limited in the three Biology textbooks, where only 12 percent of units were devoted to this theme. The theme 'Science as a way of thinking' is poorly represented in all six textbooks. For the Life Sciences textbooks, an average of 7 percent of units was coded to this theme. This theme was not addressed in any of the three Biology textbooks. The average percentage coverage of units for all three Life Sciences books given to the theme 'The interaction of science, technology and society' was only 12 percent. The average coverage of this theme in the Biology textbooks was 4 percent. Despite significant curriculum reform that underlines a more balanced perspective of science encompassing the acquisition of knowledge through inquiry, the limited coverage given to the themes 'The investigative nature of science,' 'Science as a way of thinking,' and 'The interaction of science, technology and society' in the new books does not reflect this reform. Furthermore, a comparison of the Biology textbooks of the previous curriculum and the Life Sciences textbooks of the reformed curriculum revealed only minimal shifts towards addressing these themes in NOS (Ramnarain & Padayachee, 2015).

A recent study by Ramnarain and Chanetsa (2016) analyzed three Grade 9 middle school CAPS Natural Sciences textbooks for NOS representations. The textbooks are compliant with the South African school science curriculum and widely used in schools throughout South Africa. The analysis was framed by an analytical tool developed and validated by Abd-El-Khalick and a team of researchers in a large-scale study on high school textbooks in the United States (Abd-El-Khalick et al., 2008). The framework describes 11 key aspects in NOS that are intricately related to the basic tenets explicated by Abd-El-Khalick, Bell and Lederman (1998). The aspects are: Empirical; Inferential; Creative; Theory-driven; Tentative; Myth of The Scientific Method; Scientific theories; Scientific laws; Social dimensions of science; Social and cultural embeddedness of science; and Science versus pseudoscience. The tenet 'Empirical' underlines the need for observational or experimental evidence to support knowledge claims on natural phenomena. 'Inferential' refers to the crucial distinction between observations and inferences. Observations are based on sensory experiences about which observers can reach consensus. Inferences, on the other hand, are statements about phenomena that are not directly accessible to the senses. The 'creative' NOS tenet implies that science is not an entirely rational or systematic activity, but also involves human imagination and creativity. The 'theory driven' NOS aspect reflects that scientists' beliefs, their disciplinary commitment, prior knowledge, and training influence their work. The 'tentative' NOS aspect means that while scientific knowledge is reliable and durable, it is always subject to revision and change whenever new evidence appears. The 'Myth of the Scientific Method' is often manifested in the belief that there is a recipe-like step-wise procedure that typifies all scientific practice. The framework also makes provision for the distinction between 'scientific theories' and 'scientific laws.' Laws are descriptive statements of relationships among observable phenomena, while theories, by contrast, are inferred explanations for observable phenomena or regularities in those phenomena. The 'Social dimension of science' is socially negotiated by being subjected to well-established venues for communication and criticism within the scientific enterprise. 'Social and cultural embeddedness of science' emphasizes that science is a human enterprise that is practiced in the context of a larger cultural milieu, and hence is affected by various cultural elements and spheres, including social fabric, worldview, power structures, philosophy, religion, and political and economic factors. 'Science versus pseudoscience' distinguishes science from other disciplines of inquiry (e.g., religion, philosophy).

In adopting this framework, the study of the Grade 9 Natural Sciences textbooks followed a more fine-grained analysis for NOS tenets compared to the framework by Chiappetta et al. (1991) on scientific literacy themes, which was utilized in Padayachee's study. However, similarly, the analysis adopted a predominantly qualitative approach and, more specifically, a deductive content analysis design in which a predetermined instrument was used to capture information. In applying the NOS framework, pre-formulated categories were brought into connection with the text by analyzing textural material and identifying the category into which they can be placed. In this case, the categories comprised each of the aspects of NOS listed above.

A score ranging from +3 to -3 was assigned to a unit of analysis, depending on the extent to which that unit represented a targeted aspect. The rubric draws a distinction between an explicit versus an implicit representation of the targeted NOS aspect. Research by Abd-El-Khalick, Bell, and Lederman (1998) on implicit versus explicit instructional approaches revealed that implicit strategies, such as engaging in scientific activities, do not translate into an understanding of NOS, whereas an explicit approach is more effective in ensuring comprehension of NOS. An explicit approach would, for example, entail teachers differentiating between observation and inference during activities as opposed to the learners having to infer this crucial distinction from their activities. The units of analysis comprising of all texts and information on each page of the three Grade 9 Natural Sciences textbooks were therefore scored on the targeted NOS aspects on a scale of -3 to +3, which reflected the explicitness with which these aspects were addressed. As individual scores for NOS tenets range from -3 to +3, for the 11 aspects of the NOS, the cumulative score can range from -33 to +33. The higher the cumulative score, the more explicit, informed, and consistent is the representation of NOS in the textbook.

The results on the scoring of the 11 NOS tenets for the three textbooks (referred to as textbooks A, B, and C here) revealed cumulative scores that ranged from +4 to +7 out of a possible score of +33. This indicates that all three textbooks poorly portrayed the examined aspects of NOS. Only three of the NOS aspects were addressed by all three textbooks, and these were 'empirical,' 'tentative,' and 'social and cultural embeddedness.' All three textbooks were scored +1 for 'empirical,' indicating an implicit, informed, and consistent representation of this NOS aspect. A representative quote for this aspect from textbook B was: "The more you observe the world around you, the more you realise that nothing works on its own." The textbooks for this aspect did not explicitly reflect the use of theories to interpret such empirical evidence, and hence the NOS representation for this aspect was considered implicit. The books were also scored +1 for 'tentative.' For example, the quote "The microscope was improved by . . ." from textbook C conveys an implicit and informed perspective on the tentative nature of scientific knowledge, yet does not explicitly underscore that scientific claims change as new evidence is brought to bear. The implicit and informed representation for 'social and cultural embeddedness' is underlined in the quote from textbook B: "I would like to adopt a child but my husband wants us to try in vitro fertilization, but that's so expensive and there is only a 30% chance of success." This quote shows the influence of social and economic factors on decision-making on a scientific application, but does not explicitly address how the scientific enterprise is being influenced. The aspects 'myth of scientific method,' 'scientific theories,' and 'science versus pseudo-science' were completed disregarded by all analyzed textbooks. For the other five NOS aspects (inferential; creative; theory-driven; scientific laws; social dimension) there was no consistent trend on explicitness/implicitness across the three books, with some books showing implicit representation for an aspect, while others did not address the aspect.

In a research study by Ramnarain (submitted), three commonly used high school Grade 10 Physical Sciences textbooks written for the reformed CAPS curriculum were analyzed using the framework by Abd-El-Khalick et al. (2008). As with the analysis of the Grade 9 Natural Science textbooks, the research followed a deductive content analysis approach, in relating the units of analysis (complete paragraphs, activities, worked examples, figures with captions, tables with captions, charts with captions, and marginal comments) with the aspects of NOS already described. The selection of these books was based on information about school book orders provided by the Department of Basic Education.

As was the case with the Natural Sciences textbooks, the Physical Sciences books (referred to as Textbooks D, E, and F here) weakly depicted the NOS. Out of a possible score of +33, the books D, E, and F scored +5, +7, and +9, respectively. This is only marginally higher than the NOS representation for the Natural Sciences textbooks. The three books scored similarly on the implicitness/explicitness of the NOS aspects. Textbook D reflected implicit representations (+1) for empirical, inferential, creative, theory-driven, scientific theories, social dimensions, and social and cultural embeddedness aspects, but had a stronger explicit representation (+2) for the tentative aspect of NOS. Textbook E depicted implicit representations (+1) of empirical, creative, scientific theories, and social and cultural embeddedness, and was explicit (+2) on inferential, theory-driven, and tentative aspects. Textbook E was the only book that was explicit on the inferential aspect and is represented through the quote "At the microscope level you cannot see the atoms or molecules under a microscope, but you can imagine what the atoms and molecules look like by referring to the diagrams in Chapter 1." Textbook F was implicit (+1) on inferential and theory-driven aspects, and explicit on empirical, tentative, scientific theories, and scientific laws aspects. In particular textbook F was the only book representing explicitly the scientific theories and scientific laws aspects of NOS. The quote "The purpose of a scientific theory is to explain and help us understand the physical world. To do this it needs to: . . . agree with experimental observations; predict what will happen if circumstances change." This underscores the role of scientific theory in explaining observations, and in enabling scientists to make predictions. The explicitness of scientific laws in textbook F is reflected in the quote "In the beginning of the 19th century, Proust saw that no matter how you prepared a chemical compound, it always contains the same elements. They were always joined in the same proportion by mass. He stated these findings in the Law of

Constant Composition." This quote clearly shows that laws are based on observation and measurement.

It is interesting to note that all three Physical Sciences textbooks were explicit on the tentative aspect of NOS. However, the evidence for this emanated solely from the section on the development of the atomic model. For example, textbook D explicitly referred to this as follows: "Many other scientists have contributed to our present-day model of the atom and many scientists are researching and defining new refinements to the model." It is a concern that both textbooks E and F showed explicit, naïve representations of the myth of the 'scientific method.' This is evident in the following quotes: "All sciences use the scientific method, which is a scientific approach to research. We use this method for all our research and experiments" (Textbook D) and "Scientific method—scientists ask questions and want to be sure of the answers they obtain. To do this they follow the scientific method" (Textbook F).

Overall, textbook E had a slightly stronger NOS representation than textbook D and F with explicit representations for inferential, theory-driven, and tentative aspects. Both books D and E depicted an implicit naïve representation for 'scientific laws' due to evidence on the notion that laws can be proven.

A comparison of NOS representation for the middle school Natural Sciences and high school Physical Sciences textbooks reported here shows both sets of textbooks had a similar emphasis on NOS, with the three middle school Natural Sciences textbooks cumulatively having a score of +17 and the high science Physical Sciences textbooks with a score of +21 out of a possible score of +99. From this it is inferred that science textbooks at different phases have a similarly low representation of NOS. A closer analysis also shows that both sets of textbooks had a strong emphasis on the presentation of scientific knowledge rather than the nature of scientific knowledge, or the processes in the development of such knowledge. Further to this, there was consistency in the degree of explicitness/implicitness with which the textbooks from the different publishers depicted NOS with only slight variation in the manner in which the NOS aspects were represented.

Discussion

The findings of these three studies are incommensurate with the strong emphasis in a reformed school science curriculum that underlies the need for learners to understand the scientific enterprise, and how scientific knowledge develops. To a large extent the review of studies on South African science textbooks has shown that these books are inadequate in advancing an informed and accurate conception of NOS. It has already been pointed out that an understanding of NOS is indispensable in promoting the development of scientifically literate citizens who are empowered to make informed decisions on issues related to science and technology. The findings of this study therefore highlight a serious deficit in the science schooling of learners. Textbooks are considered to play a pivotal role in driving curriculum reform in South Africa, especially in a climate where teachers reportedly have a limited capacity to design curriculum material. Furthermore, Abd-El-Khalick (2012b) posits that NOS cannot be learned implicitly through engagement in doing science but "should rather be planned for instead of being anticipated as a side effect or secondary product" (Akindehin, 1988, p. 73). A textbook that depicts a balanced and informed perspective on NOS can be employed as a resource that teachers can use in consciously addressing the goal of enhancing learners' conceptions of NOS. Science textbooks have often been faulted for focusing on the 'products' of science, namely the concepts, theories, principles, and laws of nature, instead of the activities that give rise to these products (Phillips & Chiappetta, 2007). As a result learners are provided with a skewed perception of the scientific enterprise. The review of research on textbook analysis for NOS reported in this chapter certainly confirms this assertion for South African school science textbooks.

While many science teachers and teacher educators assume that learners will acquire an understanding of NOS implicitly by means of inquiry-based learning (DiGiuseppe, 2014), studies suggest, however, that this is not the case (Abd-El-Khalick, Bell, & Lederman, 1998; Osborne, 2010) and that NOS must be addressed explicitly and reflectively (Schwartz et al., 2004). Given the textbook dependency of South African science teachers, having textbooks that afford attention to NOS will enable explicit attention to be given to NOS themes. A concern from the findings on the comparison of the Grade 10 Biology textbooks from the previous curriculum, and the current Grade 10 Life Sciences textbooks is that NOS representation has changed very little. It is therefore not surprising that teacher pedagogy in South Africa is still directed at content coverage, with minimal attention being on the provision of learning opportunities that give learners an insight into the scientific enterprise (Ramnarain, 2014).

The findings of the studies reported in this chapter reinforce the need for a review on the mandate by the Department of Basic Education given to textbook publishers and writers so that a stronger focus be placed on the development of materials that better represent the tenets of NOS. As alluded to earlier, new books are evaluated against criteria drawn up by the department. To improve the chances of approval, publishers instruct writers to ensure that books adhere to these criteria. Given this scenario, it is likely that a change in the textbooks being produced can be effected should the department reflect in these selection criteria a more balanced perspective of NOS. According to DiGiuseppe (2014) publishers should also include NOS experts in their development teams who may provide guidance on how NOS may be represented in the writing of the textbooks.

Teachers often teach, and authors often write, to cover the material that appears in examinations (Wilkinson, 1999). In the South Africa education system, there is a strong focus on high-stakes summative assessment in the form of tests and examinations. A possible solution could be a stronger emphasis on the development of assessment activities focused on NOS, which may result in a corresponding increase in emphasis given to these areas by teachers and textbook authors. While this chapter does not maintain that textbooks should be the sole curriculum resource used to develop knowledge, in a developing country such as South Africa where teacher preparedness is sometimes lacking, the textbook remains indispensable to science teaching. It is therefore imperative that more attention be given to addressing how textbooks better represent a critical educational outcome, namely NOS.

References

Abd-El-Khalick, F. (2012a). Examining the sources for our understandings about science: Enduring conflations and critical issues in research on nature of science in science education. *International Journal of Science Education, 34*(3), 353–374.

Abd-El-Khalick, F. (2012b). Nature of science in science education: Toward a coherent framework for synergistic research and development. In B. J. Fraser, K. G. Tobin, & C. J. McRobbie (Eds.), *Second international handbook of science education* (pp. 1041–1060). Dordrecht, the Netherlands: Springer.

Abd-El-Khalick, F., Bell, R., & Lederman, N. (1998). The nature of science and instructional practice: Making the unnatural natural. *Science Education, 82,* 417–437.

Abd-El-Khalick, F., Waters, M., & Le, A. (2008). Representations of nature of science in high school chemistry textbooks over the past four decades. *Journal of Research in Science Teaching, 45*(7), 835–855.

Akindehin, F. (1988). Effect of an instructional package on preservice science teachers' understanding of the nature of science and acquisition of science-related attitudes. *Science Education, 72*(1), 73–82.

Chiappetta, E. L., & Fillman, D. A. (2007). Analysis of five high school biology textbooks used in the United States for inclusion of the nature of science. *International Journal of Science Education, 29*(15), 1847–1868.

Chiappetta, E. L., Sethna, G. H., & Fillman, D. A. (1991). A qualitative analysis of high school chemistry textbooks for scientific literacy themes and expository learning aids. *Journal of Research in Science Teaching, 28,* 939–951.

Dekkers, P., & Mnisi, E. (2003). The nature of science: Do teachers have the understandings they are expected to teach? *African Journal of Research in Mathematics, Science and Technology Education, 7,* 21–34.

Department of Basic Education. (2011a). *Curriculum and assessment policy statement: National curriculum statement grades 7–9 natural sciences.* Pretoria: Government Printer.

Department of Basic Education. (2011b). *Curriculum and assessment policy statement: National curriculum statement grades 10–12 life sciences.* Pretoria: Government Printer.

Department of Basic Education. (2011c). *Curriculum and assessment policy statement: National curriculum statement grades 10–12 physical sciences.* Pretoria: Government Printer.

Department of Education. (2003). *National curriculum statement grades 10–12: Life sciences.* Pretoria: Government Printer.

DiGiuseppe, M. (2014). Representing nature of science in a science textbook: Exploring author—editor—publisher interactions. *International Journal of Science Education, 36*(7), 1061–1082.

Driver, R., Leach, J., Miller, R., & Scott, P. (1996). *Young people's images of science*. Buckingham: Open University Press.

Duschl, R. A. (1985). Science education and philosophy of science: Twenty-five years of mutually exclusive development. *School Science and Mathematics, 87*(7), 541–555.

Green, W., & Naidoo, D. R. (2008). Science textbooks in the context of political reform in South Africa: Implications for access to science. *Science Education International, 19*(2), 235–250.

Hodson, D. (2014). Nature of science in the science curriculum: Origin, development, implications and shifting emphases. In M. R. Matthews (Ed.), *International handbook of research in history, philosophy and science teaching* (pp. 911–970). Dordrecht, the Netherlands: Springer.

Human Sciences Research Council. (2005). *Textbooks for diverse learners: A critical analysis of learning materials used in South African schools*. Cape Town: HSRC Press.

Lederman, N. G. (2007). Nature of science: Past, present, and future. In S. K. Abell & N. G. Lederman (Eds.), *Handbook of research on science education* (pp. 831–879). Mahwah, NJ: Lawrence Erlbaum.

Linneman, S. R., Lynch, P., Kurup, R., & Bantwini, B. (2003). South African science teachers' conceptions of the nature of science. *African Journal of Research in Mathematics, Science and Technology Education, 7*, 35–50.

Lumpe, A. T., & Beck, J. (1996). A profile of high school biology textbooks using scientific literacy recommendations. *The American Biology Teacher, 58*(3), 147–153.

Malcolm, C., & Alant, B. (2004). Finding direction when the ground is moving: Science education research in South Africa. *Studies in Science Education, 40*, 49–104.

Matthews, M. R. (2000). *Time for science education: How teaching the history and philosophy of pendulum motion can contribute to science literacy*. New York: Kluwer Academic Publishers.

McComas, W. F. (2003). A textbook case: Laws and theories and biology instruction. *International Journal of Science and Mathematics Education, 1*(2), 1–15.

McComas, W. F., Clough, M. P., & Almazroa, H. (1998). The role and character of the nature of science in science education. *Science & Education, 7*(6), 511–532.

National Research Council. (1996). *National science education standards*. Washington, DC: National Academy Press.

Osborne, J. (2010). Arguing to learn in science: The role of collaborative, critical discourse. *Science, 328*(5977), 463–466.

Padayachee, K. (2012). *A study of the analysis and use of life sciences textbooks for the nature of science*. Unpublished masters' dissertation, University of Johannesburg, Johannesburg.

Phillips, M. C., & Chiappetta, E. L. (2007). *Do middle school science textbooks present a balanced view of the nature of science?* Paper presented at the annual meeting of National Association for Research in Science Teaching, New Orleans, LA.

Ramnarain, U. (submitted). A comparative analysis between South African physical sciences textbooks used in a traditional curriculum and a reformed curriculum. *Educational Studies*.

Ramnarain, U. (2014). Teachers' perceptions of inquiry-based learning in urban, suburban, township and rural high schools: The context-specificity of science curriculum implementation in South Africa. *Teaching and Teacher Education, 38*, 65–75.

Ramnarain, U., & Chanetsa, T. (2016). An analysis of South African grade 9 natural sciences textbooks for their representation of nature of science. *International Journal of Science Education, 38*(6), 922–933.

Ramnarain, U., & Padayachee, K. (2015). A comparative analysis of South African life sciences and biology textbooks for the inclusion of the nature of science. *South African Journal of Education, 35*(1), 1–8.

Schwartz, R. S., Lederman, N. G., & Crawford, B. (2004). Developing views of nature of science in an authentic context: An explicit approach to bridging the gap between nature of science and scientific inquiry. *Science Education, 88*(4), 610–645.

Songer, N. B., & Linn, M. C. (1991). How do students' views of science influence knowledge integration. *Journal of Research in Science Teaching, 28*(9), 761–784.

Swanepoel, S. (2010). *The assessment of the quality of science education textbooks: Conceptual frameworks and instruments for analysis.* Unpublished doctoral dissertation, University of South Africa, Pretoria.

Wilkinson, J. (1999). A quantitative analysis of physics textbooks for scientific literacy themes. *Research in Science Education, 29*(3), 385–399.

11 Representations of Nature of Science in German School Chemistry Textbooks

Karl Marniok and Christiane S. Reiners

For many years, international research in science education has continually highlighted the importance of an informed understanding of nature of science (NOS), which is also reflected in many national educational standards (AAAS, 1993; NGSS, 2013; Schecker & Parchmann, 2007). In a modern society based on scientific progress, it is essential that students should not only be taught scientific subject matter, but also how the scientific enterprise works, including a consideration of which problems can be answered through science and which ones cannot. An important goal of this process is the development of students' scientific literacy:

> When people know how scientists go about their work and reach scientific conclusions, and what the limitations of such conclusions are, they are more likely to react thoughtfully to scientific claims and less likely to reject them out of hand or accept them uncritically.
>
> (AAAS, 1993, p. 3)

Knowledge of NOS can enable students to participate in chemistry-related debates affecting their daily lives, such as discussions on the use of food additives, environmental issues, or pharmaceuticals. Since textbooks generally play a vital role in science teaching, it is worthwhile to examine the views of NOS conveyed by them. A lack of history and philosophy-related content in science textbooks has been pointed out as a main obstacle for the adequate inclusion of NOS (Höttecke & Silva, 2011). Likewise, an informed understanding of NOS cannot be taken for granted, even among teachers. Textbooks may therefore offer some guidance to teachers on how to incorporate NOS into chemistry lessons.

The German School System

The German education system is marked by its federal character. As 16 federal states are responsible for their own educational policies, there are effectively 16 different school systems and curricula in Germany, albeit with certain similarities and numerous recent attempts at harmonization.

Generally, children attend a primary school (*Grundschule*) from the age of six to 10, although this may be longer, depending on the state (e.g., *Grundschulen* in Berlin comprise six grades). After primary school, there are three basic types of secondary schools: *Hauptschule*, *Realschule* and *Gymnasium*, the latter being the highest level, enabling students to qualify for university with the *Abitur* exam. *Hauptschulen* provide a basic level of education, while *Realschulen* are middle schools providing extended education targeted towards vocational training. *Realschulen* were originally created in the nineteenth century as institutions for teaching subjects that were considered more work-oriented, such as modern languages, in contrast to the classical education including Latin and Greek. Additionally, there are comprehensive schools (*Gesamtschulen*) that combine all kinds of qualification levels in one institution. Since the educational reforms of the 1960s and 1970s, more and more *Gesamtschulen* have started to emerge. While historically only a few students were privileged to go to the *Gymnasium* and take the *Abitur* exam, it became the most popular kind of secondary school in Germany over the second half of the twentieth century. When students leave the *Gymnasium* after their *Abitur*, they are usually about 18 years old, although it is still subject to change from state to state whether this occurs after the twelfth or thirteenth grade.

Since the 1990s, but especially fueled by the relatively poor results for Germany in the first PISA (*Program for International Student Assessment*) study in 2001, there has been a shift in curriculum from a content orientation towards an output orientation, manifested in *competences* established by the *Standing Conference* of the Ministers of Education in all German states (*Kultusministerkonferenz*). These competences describe "capabilities, skills, and readiness" (Risch, 2010, p. 270) and are part of the "criteria for educational quality and instruments to assess student achievements" (Schecker & Parchmann, 2007, p. 148) called *Bildungsstandards* (national educational standards), published by the board of the ministers for the whole of Germany. These standards "describe the abilities that students are expected to have attained at the end of lower secondary education" (p. 149) and are based on certain competences specified for every subject.

Chemistry as a Subject in German Schools

At the primary level, chemistry is taught as part of an integrated science curriculum, alongside the other science disciplines. As a separate subject, chemistry is introduced in secondary school, usually starting in the seventh grade; however, it is not always continuously taught in the secondary school grades. In general, chemistry is a mandatory subject until the tenth or eleventh grade, and is usually taught in two or three lessons (45 minutes each) every week. *Gymnasium* (or *Gesamtschule*) students may take chemistry as one of their *Abitur* exam subjects with additional weekly classes.

The national educational standards (*Bildungsstandards*) prescribe scientific literacy as a goal of school chemistry, calling for students to "understand the language and history of the science" and "deal with its specific methods of gaining knowledge and their limits" (Sekretariat der Ständigen Konferenz der Kultusminister der Länder in der Bundesrepublik Deutschland [KMK], 2005, p. 6, translation by Schumacher (2015), p. 29). They define four competences for the subject of chemistry: 1) subject matter knowledge (*Fachwissen*), 2) methodology/epistemology (*Erkenntnisgewinnung*, literally 'ways of gaining knowledge'), 3) communication (*Kommunikation*), and 4) judgment (*Bewertung*). Although the term nature of science (NOS) is not explicitly mentioned in German educational directives, aspects of NOS can be found as part of the methodology/epistemology competence, which is summarized as "using experimental and other methods of inquiry, as well as models" (p. 9). The standards list several abilities students are expected to acquire by the ninth or tenth grade (depending on the state). These include using empirical methodology, but also being able to point out "links between social developments and chemical discoveries" (p. 12).

Since the federal states bear the responsibility for implementing the standards, some states, such as North Rhine-Westphalia (NRW), have developed core curricula (*Kernlehrpläne*) as guidelines for schools. Recently, another core curriculum for the higher level of secondary education (leading to the Abitur exam) has been released (Ministerium für Schule und Weiterbildung des Landes Nordrhein-Westfalen [MSW NRW], 2014), establishing advanced expectancies. According to this document, the methodology/ epistemology field includes reflections on "the peculiar character of sciences with their specific ways of working and reasoning" (p. 18). The aim of the judgment competence area implies the linkage of chemical knowledge and skills to other disciplines as well as to everyday life, and discussing and judging on social-relevant statements. The learning outcomes for the epistemology (E) and judgment (B) fields to be acquired until the tenth grade include abilities such as (pp. 60–63; all translations by the authors):

1) formulating hypotheses and ways of testing them in order to solve a chemical problem (E3),
2) choosing models on a rational basis and using them to describe, explain, and predict chemical processes (E6),
3) describing the importance, but also the tentative nature of scientific rules, laws, and theories (E7),
4) specifying criteria for evaluating scientific and technical issues (B1),
5) weighing up the pros and cons and taking a well-reasoned position (B2),
6) showing up ethical conflicts and possible solutions in chemical topics (B3),
7) depicting possibilities and limits of chemistry-related problems and views with regard to goals of science (B4).

These standards are further carried on with the extended requirements for competencies to be acquired until the twelfth grade, including abilities such as:

1) generating hypotheses deductively, relating to theories, concepts and laws, as well as means of testing them (E3),
2) analyzing data qualitatively and quantitatively with regard to relationships, rules, or laws, and generalizing the results (E5),
3) developing models as well as using theoretical or mathematical models, thought experiments, or simulations to explain or predict chemical processes (E6),
4) reflecting on scientific principles and reasoning as well as their changes throughout history and their cultural development (E7),
5) using examples of chemistry-related conflicts to show up controversial interests and their consequences, including an ethical evaluation (B3).

This demonstrates that several NOS-related topics are already present in German curricula, although there is no specific term such as *nature of science* to encapsulate its broad scope.

German School Textbooks

In most cases, German school textbooks have to be approved by state authorities (Stöber, 2010) and are reviewed for curricular and political aspects (i.e., whether they are in accordance with the German constitution). Because of the diversity of educational policies in Germany, requirements for teaching materials differ between the 16 states, thus publishers of school textbooks need to produce several distinct editions, each designed for certain regions of Germany or even individual states.

The market for school textbooks in Germany is divided between a few specialized publishers, the biggest being Cornelsen (including the Oldenbourg imprint), Klett, and the Westermann publishing group (with imprints such as Schroedel, Diesterweg, Diercke, Schöningh, and Winklers), with a total market share of 90 percent (Bode, 2004, p. 14); in addition to a few smaller independent publishers, such as C. C. Buchner. Since each school conference can decide on the books they prefer, all publishers compete for market shares in every state. German schools usually buy class sets of books which are then lent to the students for a school year, because learning material is traditionally expected to be free, although this has recently been subject to change (Brandenberg, 2006). It is difficult to obtain detailed sales figures, market shares, and statistics on textbook usage in German schools. The expenses for school textbooks (or more precisely, any printed teaching material) in the year 2008 were estimated at approximately 434 million euros, with an average retail price of about 15 euros for one book (Baer, 2010). School textbooks make up approximately

8 percent of the entire book production industry in Germany (Brandenberg, 2006).

For decades, textbooks have been an under-represented research topic in science education (Merzyn, 1994); hence, empirical studies on the actual usage of chemistry textbooks in German schools are rare. One study has shown that most teachers use chemistry textbooks once a month or less frequently, mostly for repetitive reasons (Beerenwinkel & Gräsel, 2005). Only 25 of 221 teachers (11.4 percent) stated that they use textbooks in class every week. The teachers generally found the chemistry textbooks to be only faintly interesting for the students, while also being difficult to understand at first glance. Teachers often found the textbooks' language to be scientifically precise but incomprehensible to students, while also suggesting more focus on real-life applications. The authors observed that these findings are in accordance with studies on German physics textbooks.

Little research has focused on textual analysis of German science textbooks, with the few published works focusing on terminology and comprehensibility (Merzyn, 1998), subject matter aspects (Sauer & Sommer, 2013), or the design of exercises in order to comply with competence orientation (Kizil, 2010; Mikelskis-Seifert, Freisfeld, & Knittel, 2013).

However, there have been several international NOS-related studies focused on representations in chemistry (Abd-El-Khalick, Waters, & Le, 2008; Niaz & Maza, 2011), physics (de Pagliarini & Silva, 2007; Leite, 2002), and biology (Chiappetta & Fillman, 2007; Irez, 2009) textbooks. Hence the following study is the first published analysis of NOS representations in German textbooks. It focuses on chemistry textbooks for *Gymnasium* schools, being the most popular kind of secondary school in Germany. Because of regional distinctions in the federal school system leading to various textbook editions, the study is also focused on Germany's most populous state, North Rhine-Westphalia (NRW), with a total population of about 17.5 million. According to official figures of the Federal Statistical Office, in 2014 there were 625 *Gymnasien* with 538,862 students in NRW.

Method

This textbook analysis includes chemistry textbook series produced by all major German publishers, the most common for *Gymnasium* schools being Chemie heute (Schroedel), Elemente Chemie (Klett), Chemie 2000+ (C. C. Buchner), Fokus Chemie and Chemie im Kontext (Cornelsen). All series consist of two or more volumes adapted for certain age groups. The selected textbooks were published between 2006 and 2010, therefore after the German educational standards were formulated. For a comparison, a pre-standards edition of Elemente Chemie from 2000/02 was included, as well as a chemistry textbook from 1972 (Lehrbuch der Chemie) to explore the historical development. Furthermore, a popular book on chemistry teaching (Chemiedidaktik heute) targeted at pre-service and in-service teachers was included in the analysis in order to assess what relevance is given to NOS-related knowledge in German science education books.

The method is based on an analytical framework developed by Abd-El-Khalick et al. (2008), in regard to both the compilation of relevant NOS aspects, and the scoring rubric. Accordingly, the following 10 NOS aspects were assessed: 1) The *empirical* nature of science states that all science is based on natural phenomena and highlights the importance of observation; 2) the *inferential* nature of science, emphasizing the difference between observation and inference. While, for instance, phenomena on a macroscopic scale can be observed directly, science also relies on theoretical entities such as electrons, whose existence has been inferred based on their effects; 3) the *creative* nature of science emphasizes how science is not solely a procedural activity, but often involves scientists' creativity in order to come up with experimental setups or explanations. An historical example for the use of creativity in chemistry is the emergence of structural theory in the nineteenth century: Creative thinking led to the idea of using the arrangement of atoms in order to explain the properties of chemical compounds; 4) the *theory-driven* nature of science means that any observation is influenced by the theories that scientists have in mind. As a result, scientists can never be entirely neutral and objective. This even concerns the choice of methods for a particular investigation; 5) the *tentative* nature of science states how scientific knowledge has always been subject to change and will always be subject to change as new results or ideas arise. Consequently, scientific knowledge is never absolute; (6) the myth of 'the Scientific Method' is the popular notion that there is one single sequence of steps consisting of hypotheses, observation, and measurement that lead every scientific investigation to success. In reality, scientists may use any elements of scientific methodology in any order, as long as the procedure is appropriate to solve the problem. Hence, there is no single 'Scientific Method' but several scientific methods; 7) the nature of *scientific theories* is different from the colloquial meaning of the word *theory*. Contrary to popular belief, a scientific theory is not an assumption or a mere guess, hence the phrase 'just a theory' demonstrates a faulty understanding. Scientific theories are systems of explanations that have been inferred from a large number of observations and often postulate non-observable entities such as electrons in order to explain natural phenomena. As an example, chemists were largely collecting and classifying substances and describing chemical reactions, but only scientific theories on the structure of particles and on chemical bonding explanations on why and how substances formed and behaved in a certain manner; 8) The nature of *scientific laws* has a similar semantic difference between the word's colloquial and scientific meanings. In everyday usage, the term law conveys a normative and an absolute meaning. In science, laws are "descriptive statements of relationships among observable phenomena" (Abd-El-Khalick et al., 2008), often expressed as a formula. Thus, laws are a different category of knowledge than theories and both kinds of knowledge are neither convertible into each other nor hierarchically related. As an example, the gas *laws* have been discovered since the seventeenth century and can be used to describe how gases behave under specified conditions. But only the kinetic *theory* of gases can provide an explanation for this behavior by postulating the (non-observable) motion of particles; 9) the *social dimensions* of science include the influence of the scientific community or the peer-review process, but also how a scientist's authority and reputation among peers may influence scientific research and the adoption of new ideas; 10) the *social/cultural embeddedness* of science implies that science is influenced by factors like culture, politics, religion, or economy. As an example, funding may affect the direction of scientific research and the interpretation of its results just like politics (e. g., research for military purposes) or social factors (e. g., the influence of feminism on the interpretation of biological topics since the twentieth century) (Schumacher, 2015).

Textbooks were analyzed for evidence of representation in any of these 10 categories, with relevant excerpts collated and assigned a score by two raters. Few differences between the raters emerged and consensus was reached after discussion and further consultation. Scores for each aspect were based on how informed each of the NOS representations were. Differing from Abd-El-Khalick et al.'s study, the scoring scale was simplified to a scale between-2 and +2 points. This was done after a pilot phase produced problems among raters on how to differentiate between 'informed' and 'partially informed' representations, as the German books didn't provide enough information to adequately differentiate for this complexity. Correct and explicit representations of a NOS aspect were awarded +2 points, implicit representations +1 points, no mention 0 points, implicit misrepresentations -1 points, and explicit misrepresentations -2 points. The following examples illustrate the difference between implicit and explicit statements: "used his imagination to come up with the benzene formula" would count an implicit statement on the creative NOS with a corresponding score of +1, while "Creativity and imagination are often important factors for the development of chemical ideas" would be an explicit statement leading to a score of +2. If several statements varied between +1 and +2 in one book, the higher score was awarded; with the same procedure applying to negative statements, while contradictive statements were assigned a score of 1.

If a textbook series consisted of multiple volumes, those were treated as one single work for the scoring. The selection of chapters for analysis was more difficult than expected because of a lack of any specific NOS-focused chapters, or any explicit elaborations on chemistry "as a science." As such, we chose to review the complete textbooks in order to find NOS aspects included within the individual chapters. In particular, we focused on the "side notes," which were predominantly located in chapter introductions, historical anecdotes, comments on the structure of atoms, statements about gas laws, and explanations about reaction mechanisms and their rationales.

It is noteworthy that in German textbooks, the term 'theory' is largely avoided. It may be a regional idiosyncrasy for German textbooks to call all chemical theories 'models,' reflecting the term's frequent use in national science education. Consequently, both terms were treated as synonyms in this analysis to preserve the comparability.

Results and Discussion

The results of the study indicated that all books achieved a positive total score (refer to Table 11.1). Compared to results obtained in the United States (Abd-El-Khalick et al., 2008), one could get the impression that German textbooks were actually better at representing NOS. However, in general, the German textbooks largely avoid explicit statements on NOS-related aspects, which also explain the accumulation of scores of +1 and 0 across the examined aspects. German textbooks appear to focus on 'school chemistry,' and avoid references to scientific methodology, whereas the excerpts in Abd-El-Khalick et al.'s study show more evidence of explicit NOS-related statements across the examined textbooks. Despite these identifiable tendencies, one should bear in mind that the results are not directly comparable to Abd-El-Khalick et al.'s study due to the scoring rubric.

The representation of NOS in German textbooks was very selective, and often implicit. For example, the series Chemie heute shows a scanning tunneling microscope (STM) image of a surface, along with the caption:

> The images obtained in that way are indeed not real photographs of atoms. In this imaging method, a metal wire with an extremely fine tip is led across the crystal, and a computer processes the scanning signals. The picture of a hilly landscape made of atoms is thus not a photograph in the normal sense, but rather a computer-generated image.
>
> (Asselborn, Jäckel, & Risch, 2010; all translations by the authors)

Although this is an accurate depiction of inference in science, the textbook never explicitly mentions it as an essential part of chemistry, or science in general. Similarly, the creative nature of science is not addressed in any book, except for implicit statements on the significance of experimental practice in chemistry. As an example, Chemie 2000+ states that Alfred Werner developed his inorganic structural theory merely based on other chemists' works without performing an experiment himself, implying that creativity was needed to interpret their findings. On the other hand, Elemente Chemie (2000/02 edition) claims that all knowledge on atomic theories came solely from experimental data, falsely implying that creativity played no part in their development.

Since explicit statements on NOS aspects are rare in German textbooks, it is concerning that the only book that scored -2 points in three categories was the textbook designed for teachers (Chemiedidaktik heute,

Table 11.1 Results of the Analysis, Sorted by Total Score

Textbook	Empirical	Inferential	Creative	Theory-driven	Tentative	Scientific method	Theories	Laws	Social aspects	Social, cultural	Σ
Chemie im Kontext	1	2	0	1	2	0	2	1	1	0	10
Chemie heute	2	1	0	1	1	0	1	1	1	1	9
Fokus Chemie	2	2	0	0	1	0	2	-1	1	1	8
Chemie 2000+	1	1	1	1	0	-1	2	1	1	0	7
Elemente Chemie (2000/02)	1	1	-1	1	2	0	-1	0	0	0	3
Elemente Chemie (2009)	1	1	0	0	1	-2	-1	1	0	1	2
Lehrbuch der Chemie (1972)	1	1	0	0	1	0	-1	-1	0	1	2
Chemiedidaktik heute	2	1	1	2	2	-2	-2	-2	0	1	3
Σ categories across all books	11	10	1	6	10	-5	2	0	4	5	

Barke & Harsch, 2001). This textbook included a scheme on 'the empirical scientific method' with several consecutive steps hierarchically linked to each other with arrows. This 'method' starts with observations and experiments and goes from formulating a hypothesis through verification or falsification to theories, which then turn into laws. This is not only a 'textbook example' of the myth of 'the Scientific Method,' but also misrepresents the nature of both theories and laws. Apart from this example, only two textbooks mentioned scientific methodology. One (Elemente Chemie, 2009 edition, p. 8) explicitly claims that any presumption may become a scientific law through "the always same" procedure, presenting a similar fixed sequence of steps from observation to "developing a theory." The other textbook (Chemie 2000+, p. 280) implies that a specific "pathway of research" can be applied to any scientific research. These results indicate that it still appears to be a tenaciously held myth that there is a general scientific method every chemist has to follow (McComas, 1998). This NOS aspect was the lowest-scored category at -5 across all analyzed books, showing that scientific methodology is either misrepresented or not mentioned at all.

Three textbooks (Chemie im Kontext, Chemie 2000+ and Fokus Chemie) included adequate representations of chemical theories (when treating the term *model* as a synonym), which appear to comply with the requirements for school books for some German states. For example, the state of Bavaria, stipulates that textbooks are obliged to deal with the necessity of models and theories in chemistry, including their development and limitations (Bayerisches Staatsministerium für Unterricht und Kultus, 2009). As an example, Fokus Chemie offers an effective representation:

> How do we actually know about the structures of particles that are submicroscopically small and therefore invisible? Just like in many cases in sciences, we rely on physical means that give us indirect answers to our questions to nature. However, we must stay aware that our interpretations of those answers are actually models, i.e., conceptions created by human beings, which only keep their validity as long as they are consistent and lead to correct predictions about the behavior of substances.
> (Demuth, Parchmann, & Ralle, 2006)

Another book included a sophisticated depiction of scientific paradigms and the structure of scientific revolutions according to Thomas S. Kuhn (Asselborn, Jäckel, & Risch, 2009), but this kind of philosophical depth was unique among all textbooks. Social and cultural aspects of science were often reduced to superficial, historical anecdotes and contributed to a stereotypical view of scientists as lonely geniuses. In several books (Chemie heute, Chemie im Kontext, Chemie 2000+, Fokus Chemie), the social dimension of research was implicitly addressed by including statements such as "Ernest Rutherford also had a *team* with him for his scattering experiments." None of the analyzed textbooks included an extensive description of chemical laws, and the typical notion of laws as absolute knowledge, and theories as speculations was sometimes evident. For example, in the oldest examined textbook, Lehrbuch der Chemie (Lüthje & Hefele, 1972), the authors suggest that any claim remaining un-refuted for long enough may be called a law. It is notable that the oldest textbook had the lowest overall score for the examined NOS aspects, which suggests a recent improvement in German textbooks.

In conclusion, the textbook analysis indicates that school chemistry textbooks in this study fall short of the requirements included in the national educational standards, and that the awareness of NOS as an integral component of chemistry teaching is not being fully recognized in Germany. None of the analyzed textbooks included references to all 10 NOS aspects, even the highest-rated textbook Chemie im Kontext had some deficiencies. This is even more disillusioning considering that book series were treated as a whole, with some NOS categories scattered across four volumes of one series, making some results appear more favorable. The textbook authors paid the least attention to the creative NOS and scientific methodology, with five books completely ignoring these aspects. Social aspects of science were also unlikely to be found, while the nature of theories/models and the empirical and inferential aspects of science were covered to some degree by all textbooks. Although the focus on scientific models in German standards may explain their extended coverage, half of all textbooks performed poorly. However, when only counting the current school textbooks, four of five had a positive score. It can be assumed that the inclusion of further NOS aspects into national standards would improve their coverage in future textbooks.

Implications and Recommendations

The findings of this study are similar to other textbook analyses (Abd-El-Khalick et al., 2008; Niaz & Maza, 2011), in that chemistry textbooks generally poorly represent NOS. Most authors only effectively addressed NOS aspects when they were required to address the nature of scientific models. Apart from this aspect, the authors did not appear to ascribe importance to NOS, instead focusing on subject matter content. Thus, there are several approaches for improving NOS representations in German chemistry textbooks.

To begin, the administrative prerequisites for the inclusion of NOS have already been accomplished, with science literacy as a major goal in German educational standards. The required competences, however, are limited to very basic NOS understandings, and fail to treat NOS as an important curricular outcome. The standards convey the impression that NOS aspects can be taught implicitly by engaging in scientific activity, although research has shown that an explicit and reflective approach is much more promising for effectively improving NOS understandings among both students and teachers (Abd-El-Khalick, 2013; Abd-El-Khalick, Bell, & Lederman, 1998). A possible step towards improvement would be to extend the national educational standards and core curricula to incorporate NOS as a cognitive target, and a vital aspect of chemistry education and science literacy. If NOS is treated as a distinct topic in chemistry education that requires explicit attention, authors and publishers will automatically put more effort into its representation in textbooks.

Another aspect is the lack of attention to NOS in science teacher education. NOS is rarely a component of university courses in which pre-service teachers are trained, since it is not compulsory in either chemistry or science education programs. If pre-service teachers are never exposed to instruction about NOS, it is hardly surprising that in-service teachers have low awareness of its importance, inaccurate NOS conceptions, and no foundation for teaching NOS to their students. Irez (2009) notes that teachers often tend to trust the authority of textbooks if they are not knowledgeable enough about NOS. However, even if there are a few well-written NOS-related paragraphs in German textbooks, a teacher with little understanding of NOS would not be able to use them effectively without further guidance (Höttecke & Silva, 2011).

Unfortunately, since the results of our analysis have been released in German (Marniok & Reiners, 2016), there has been virtually no resonance from publishers or authors. Abd-El-Khalick et al. (2008) have pointed to an 'author effect' rather than a 'publisher effect' related to NOS aspects; thus, it could be worthwhile to approach German textbook authors directly. For this reason, we are currently developing improved instructional material that connects NOS with subject matter as well as offering a simple introduction to all major NOS aspects. This material may be used as a template or guidance for authors in order to bring NOS into future editions of their textbooks. As stated earlier, it has been found that textbooks in Germany have been used rarely and mostly for repetition in chemistry classes (Beerenwinkel & Gräsel, 2005). Teachers often conceived their textbooks as overstuffed with content and a desire for more relevance to the 'real world.' Improved material with references to 'real' science and scientists could make these materials more appealing.

Although extended research has been focused on the contexts and approaches that are best suited for enabling science teachers and students to develop an adequate understanding of NOS (e.g., Abd-El-Khalick, 2013; Abd-El-Khalick, Bell, & Lederman, 1998), frameworks that enable teachers to match various contexts with NOS instructional outcomes and pedagogical approaches are still needed. The gap between chemistry education research and chemistry teaching still has to be bridged and could hopefully be improved by material developed by science education researchers and practitioners.

References

Abd-El-Khalick, F. (2013). Teaching *with* and *about* nature of science, and science teacher knowledge domains. *Science & Education, 22*(9), 2087–2107.

Abd-El-Khalick, F., Bell, R. L., & Lederman, N. G. (1998). The nature of science and instructional practice: Making the unnatural natural. *Science Education, 82*(4), 417–436.

Abd-El-Khalick, F., Waters, M., & Le, A-P. (2008). Representations of nature of science in high school chemistry textbooks over the past four decades. *Journal of Research in Science Teaching, 45*(7), 835–855.

American Association for the Advancement of Science [AAAS]. (1993). *Benchmarks for science literacy.* New York: Oxford University Press.

Asselborn, W., Jäckel, M., & Risch, K. T. (Eds.). (2009). *Chemie heute (Sekundarstufe II)* (1st ed.). Braunschweig: Schroedel.

Asselborn, W., Jäckel, M., & Risch, K. T. (Eds.). (2010). *Chemie heute (Sekundarstufe I)* (2nd ed.). Braunschweig: Schroedel.

Baer, A. (2010). Der Schulbuchmarkt. In E. Fuchs, J. Kahlert, & U. Sandfuchs (Eds.), *Schulbuch konkret: Kontexte, Produktion, Unterricht* (pp. 68–82). Bad Heilbrunn: Klinkhardt.

Barke, H.-D., & Harsch, G. (2001). *Chemiedidaktik heute: Lernprozesse in Theorie und Praxis.* Berlin: Springer.

Bayerisches Staatsministerium für Unterricht und Kultus. (2009). *Kriterienkataloge zur Beurteilung von Lernmitteln—Gymnasium.* Retrieved from www.km.bayern.de/down load/1591_kriterienkatalog_lernmittelbeurteilung_gymnasium.pdf

Beerenwinkel, A., & Gräsel, C. (2005). Texte im Chemieunterricht: Ergebnisse einer Befragung von Lehrkräften. *Zeitschrift für Didaktik der Naturwissenschaften, 11,* 21–39.

Bode, V. (2004). Kampf um Anteile. *Börsenblatt, 38,* 12–15.

Brandenberg, V. (2006). *Rechtliche und wirtschaftliche Aspekte des Verlegens von Schulbüchern: Mit einer Fallstudie zum bayerischen Zulassungsverfahren.* Retrieved from www.alles-buch. uni-erlangen.de/Brandenberg.pdf

Chiappetta, E. L., & Fillman, D. A. (2007). Analysis of five high school biology textbooks used in the United States for inclusion of the nature of science. *International Journal of Science Education, 29*(15), 1847–1868.

Demuth, R., Parchmann, I., & Ralle, B. (Eds.). (2006). *Chemie im Kontext (Sekundarstufe II)* (1st ed.). Berlin: Cornelsen.

de Pagliarini, C. R., & Silva, C. C. (2007). *History and nature of science in Brazilian physics textbooks: Some findings and perspectives.* Retrieved from www.ucalgary.ca/ihpst07/pro ceedings/IHPST07%20papers/2122%20Silva.pdf

Höttecke, D., & Silva, C. C. (2011). Why implementing history and philosophy in school science education is a challenge: An analysis of obstacles. *Science & Education, 20*(3), 293–316.

Irez, S. (2009). Nature of science as depicted in Turkish biology textbooks. *Science Education, 93*(3), 422–447.

Kizil, A. (2010). *Eine Analyse von Chemie-Schulbüchern zum Kompetenzbereich Kommunikation.* Master thesis, Carl-von-Ossietzky-Universität Oldenburg, Oldenburg. Retrieved from http://oops.uni-oldenburg.de/1090/

Leite, L. (2002). History of science in science education: Development and validation of a checklist for analyzing the historical content of science textbooks. *Science & Education, 11,* 333–359.

Lüthje, H., & Hefele, G. (Eds.). (1972). *Lehrbuch der Chemie für die Sekundarstufe I* (1st ed.). Frankfurt am Main: Diesterweg-Salle.

Marniok, K., & Reiners, C. S. (2016). Die Repräsentation der Natur der Naturwissenschaften in Schulbüchern. *CHEMKON, 23*(2), 65–70.

McComas, W. F. (1998). The principal elements of the nature of science: Dispelling the myths. In W. F. McComas (Ed.), *The nature of science in science education: Rationales and strategies* (pp. 53–70). Dordrecht, the Netherlands: Kluwer Academic Publishers.

Merzyn, G. (1994). *Physikschulbücher, Physiklehrer und Physikunterricht.* Kiel: IPN.

Merzyn, G. (1998). Sprache und naturwissenschaftlicher Unterricht. *Physik in der Schule, 36*(6), 203–206.

Mikelskis-Seifert, S., Freisfeld, A., & Knittel, C. (2013). Bewertungskompetenz—eine Schulbuchanalyse. In S. Bernholt (Ed.), *Inquiry-based learning—Forschendes Lernen* (pp. 137–139). Kiel: IPN.

Ministerium für Schule und Weiterbildung des Landes Nordrhein-Westfalen (Ed.). (2014). *Kernlehrplan für die Sekundarstufe II Gymnasium/Gesamtschule in Nordrhein-Westfalen: Chemie* (1st ed.). Retrieved from www.schulentwicklung.nrw.de/lehrplaene/upload/klp_SII/ch/KLP_GOSt_Chemie.pdf

NGSS Lead States. (2013). *Next generation science standards: For states, by states.* Washington, DC: The National Academies Press.

Niaz, M., & Maza, A. (2011). *Nature of science in general chemistry textbooks.* Dordrecht, the Netherlands: Springer.

Risch, B. (2010). Germany. In B. Risch (Ed.), *Teaching chemistry around the world* (pp. 267–279). Münster: Waxmann.

Sauer, A., & Sommer, K. (2014). Analyse von Chemieschulbüchern auf materialwissenschaftliche Inhalte. In S. Bernholt (Ed.), *Naturwissenschaftliche Bildung zwischen Science- und Fachunterricht: Gesellschaft für Didaktik der Chemie und Physik, Jahrestagung in München 2013* (pp. 642–644). Kiel: IPN.

Schecker, H., & Parchmann, I. (2007). Standards and competence models: The German situation. In D. Waddington, P. Nentwig, & S. Schanze (Eds.), *Standards in science education: Making it comparable* (pp. 147–164). Münster: Waxmann.

Schumacher, A. (2015). *Paving the way towards authentic chemistry teaching: A contribution to teachers' professional development.* Berlin: Logos.

Sekretariat der Ständigen Konferenz der Kultusminister der Länder in der Bundesrepublik Deutschland (Ed.). (2005). *Bildungsstandards im Fach Chemie für den Mittleren Schulabschluss (Jahrgangsstufe 10).* München: Luchterhand.

Stöber, G. (2010). Schulbuchzulassung in Deutschland: Grundlagen, Verfahrensweisen und Diskussionen. *Eckert.Beiträge, 2010/3.* Retrieved from www.edumeres.net/urn/urn:nbn:de:0220–2010–00146

12 Where to From Here? Implications and Future Directions for Research on Representations of Nature of Science in School Science Textbooks

Christine V. McDonald and Fouad Abd-El-Khalick

A key goal of many national science education reform documents worldwide (e.g., American Association for the Advancement of Science [AAAS], 1993; Australian Curriculum and Reporting Authority [ACARA], 2015; National Research Council [NRC], 2012; Next Generation Science Standards [NGSS], NGSS Lead States, 2013) is the development of students' views of nature of science (NOS). However, a large body of research has indicated students hold deep-seated, uninformed views about NOS that require deliberate and explicit NOS instruction to facilitate positive change (e.g., Abd-El-Khalick & Lederman, 2000). Research also highlights the central role of textbooks in school science education in both developing (Irez, 2009; Kahveci, 2010; Ogan-Bekiroglu, 2007) and developed countries (Chambliss & Calfee, 1998; Roseman, Stern, & Koppal, 2010), often determining what is taught and learned about science. Importantly, very few commercially available science textbooks have been designed specifically to help K-12 students develop informed conceptions of NOS. Thus, it is imperative to investigate how NOS is represented in these dominant curricula resources.

To date, a small set of studies have investigated how NOS is represented in school science textbooks (e.g., Abd-El-Khalick, Waters, & Le, 2008; Irez, 2009; Vesterinen, Akesla, & Lavonen, 2013). This book substantially adds to this body of empirical work, as well as synthesizes prior results with findings from current studies that examined this topic across the globe. Table 12.1 presents a comprehensive summary of empirical studies conducted in the field over the past 25 years. This book has two major contributions. The first speaks to the overwhelming consistency of findings highlighting the poor representation of NOS in science textbooks across school levels, as well as nations in virtually every continent. Second, the book shows that irrespective of *their* conceptualization of, or perspective on, NOS, scholars from around the world agree that NOS representations in science textbooks are mostly limited and naïve and merit concerted efforts to address them.

Table 12.1 Summary of Empirical Studies[1] Exploring Representations of Nature of Science (NOS) in School Science Textbooks

Study[2]	Country	Level of schooling	Science discipline	Sample	Major NOS findings
Chiappetta, Sethna, and Fillman (1991)	United States	High school	Chemistry	N=7	De-emphasized NOS
Chiappetta, Sethna, and Fillman (1993)	United States	Middle school	Life science	N=5	De-emphasized NOS, naïve view of scientific method
Lumpe and Beck (1996)	United States	High school	Biology	N=7	Little attention to NOS
Wilkinson (1999)	Australia	High school	Physics	N=20	Little attention to NOS
Knain (2001)	Norway	Lower secondary	General science	N=4	Naïve NOS views
Abd-El-Khalick (2002)	United States	Middle level trade books	Science	N=4	No explicit NOS addressed
Leite (2002)	Portugal	High school	Physics	N=5	Naïve NOS views
Ford (2006)	United States	Elementary trade books	Science	N=44	Naïve NOS views
Chiappetta and Fillman (2007)	United States	High school	Biology	N=5	Increased emphasis on NOS (cf. 1991,1993)
Abd-El-Khalick, Waters, and Le (2008)	United States	High school	Chemistry	N=14	Poor representations of NOS
Irez (2009)	Turkey	Secondary	Biology	N=5	Little attention to NOS, poor representations of NOS
Gericke and Hagberg (2010)	Sweden, Australia, Canada, United Kingdom and United States	Upper secondary	Biology and chemistry	N=20	Little attention to NOS
Niaz and Maza (2011)	United States	College	General chemistry	N=75	Explicit NOS not addressed, numerous implicit NOS opportunities
Vesterinen, Aksela, and Lavonen (2013)	Finland and Sweden	Upper secondary	Chemistry	N=5 series	Little attention to NOS, poor representations of NOS

Study	Country	Level	Subject	N	Findings
Wei, Li, and Chen (2013)	China	Junior secondary	General science	N=3 series	Poor representations of NOS
Campanile, Lederman, and Kampourakis (2015)	United States	High school	Biology (genetics)	N=7	No explicit NOS representations, numerous implicit NOS opportunities
Ramnarain and Chanetsa (2016)	South Africa	Middle school	General science	N=3	Poor representations of NOS
Ramnarain (submitted)	South Africa	High school	Physical sciences	N=3	Poor representations of NOS
Abd-El-Khalick et al. (2017)	United States	High school	Biology and physics	N=34	Little attention to NOS, poor representations of NOS
Boujaoude, Dagher, and Refai (2017/this volume)	Lebanon	Middle school	Chemistry, Life & Earth science, Physics	N=3	Little attention to NOS, predominantly implicit NOS representation
Brunner and Abd-El-Khalick (2017/this volume)	United States	Elementary trade books	Science	N=50	Poor representations of NOS
El-Mehtar and Alameh (2017/this volume)	N/A	International Baccalaureate Diploma Program	Chemistry	N=1	Some attention to NOS, poor representations of NOS
Kampourakis (2017/this volume)	Greece	Middle and high school	Biology	N=5	Poor representations of NOS, numerous implicit NOS opportunities
Marniok and Reiners (2017/this volume)	Germany	Secondary	Chemistry	N=8	Poor representations of NOS
McDonald (2017/this volume)	Australia	Junior secondary	General science (genetics)	N=4	Explicit NOS not addressed, numerous implicit NOS opportunities

[1] Discipline-specific history and philosophy of science (HPS) topic studies are not included.

[2] Chronological order.

Synthesis of Findings

Stemming from a consideration of previous research, this book sought to answer a number of questions regarding representations of NOS in school science textbooks, including: Do these representations vary across countries with diverse education systems? Are there differences across the years and/ or levels of schooling? Are there differences between science textbook disciplines (biology, chemistry, physics)? A synthesis of findings in relation to these questions is presented in the following subsections.

Representations of NOS Across Countries

Studies exploring representations of NOS in school science textbooks have now been conducted in 14 countries (refer to Table 12.1) across a wide span of Asian (China, Lebanon, Turkey), African (South Africa), North American (Canada, United States), European (Finland, Germany, Greece, Norway, Portugal, Sweden, United Kingdom), and Australasian (Australia) continents of the world. Similar, discouraging findings have been reported in the large majority of these studies. To account for these findings, researchers have invoked contextual constraints in some countries, such as the presence of an examination culture, a lack of teacher preparation, and the dominance of government-mandated textbooks, as hampering goals for improving NOS representations in these countries.

For example, the influence of exam-centered educational systems in many countries (e.g., Greece, South Africa, Turkey) significantly affects how much attention is attributed to NOS in the mandated curriculum, and ultimately in science textbooks. Although most countries promote the achievement of scientific literacy as a key curricula goal for their students—with NOS viewed as an integral component—there are variations in how this goal is manifested in the mandated curriculum. More importantly, even when NOS is specified in the curriculum, there are wide discrepancies in the relative attention attributed to NOS, which does not automatically translate into an explicit emphasis on NOS in curricula resources, such as textbooks.

In countries with education systems dominated by high-stakes examinations, content memorization is privileged, as high achievement in examinations is deemed very important. Teachers often do not have the freedom to select the content they wish to teach due to the presence of a national curriculum, with educational authorities commonly assigning the mandated textbook in each subject (Irez, 2009; Kampourakis, this volume). Only content included in important examinations is required to be covered by teachers, thus textbook authors are less likely to include content related to NOS in school science textbooks, which are heavily utilized by teachers. Kampourakis (this volume) outlines the situation in Greece, noting that although Greek biology curriculum documents make explicit links to NOS, and textbooks include explicit NOS references in their introductory chapters (albeit, largely naïve representations), these chapters are not included in the list of content required for examinations.

Ramnarain (this volume) highlights the context in South Africa, stating that although a key imperative is for students to develop understandings of NOS—an imperative that is explicitly reflected in specific aims in the South African curriculum—textbooks pay limited attention to NOS. In addition, science teachers depend on textbooks as they have a limited capacity to appropriately select curriculum and design pedagogy due to a lack of adequate teacher training. The situation is even more precarious in Greece, where Kampourakis (this volume) reports that there is no compulsory pre-service science teacher training. As such, it is hardly surprising that teachers do not privilege the teaching of NOS, when they have had little or no opportunities to develop their NOS pedagogical content knowledge.

Representations of NOS Across the Years of Schooling

Studies of NOS representations in science textbooks across the full span of schooling years have been conducted, with similar findings reported at the elementary, middle, secondary, and college level (refer to Table 12.1). Two studies have examined elementary trade books for their representations of NOS, both conducted in the United States (Brunner & Abd-El-Khalick this volume; Ford, 2006). Although utilizing different NOS frameworks and conducted over a decade apart, it is disconcerting to recognize that little improvement is evident in elementary trade books' NOS representations.

Eight studies have examined representations of NOS in middle school/junior secondary textbooks. Early studies reported little attention was attributed to NOS, and naïve views were presented in examined textbooks (Abd-El-Khalick, 2002; Chiappetta, Sethna, & Fillman, 1993; Knain, 2001). More recent studies, all of which have been conducted outside of the United States, reported similar findings with poor representations of NOS identified, and a lack of explicit NOS references (BouJaoude, Dagher, & Refai, this volume; Kampourakis, this volume; McDonald, this volume; Ramnarain & Chanetsa, 2016; Wei, Li, & Chen, 2013), regardless of the NOS framework utilized in the study.

The majority of studies examining representations of NOS in school science textbooks have been conducted at the high school/secondary level of schooling, with a total of 15 studies identified. Five studies were conducted prior to 2008 and predominantly utilized a broad NOS framework, for which 'science as a way of knowing' was used as proxy. Findings generally indicated little attention was attributed to NOS (Chiappetta & Fillman, 2007; Chiappetta, Sethna, & Fillman, 1991; Leite, 2002; Lumpe & Beck, 1996; Wilkinson, 1999). Since the publication of Abd-El-Khalick et al.'s study in 2008, a number of empirical studies have been conducted at the high school/secondary level. Ten studies conducted across nine countries were identified, with half of these studies reported in the past year

(Abd-El-Khalick et al., 2008, 2017; Campanile, Lederman, & Kampourakis, 2015; El-Mehtar & Alameh, this volume; Gericke & Hagberg, 2010; Irez, 2009; Kampourakis, this volume; Marniok & Reiners, this volume; Ramnarain, submitted; Vesterinen et al., 2013). Importantly, regardless of the NOS framework utilized, findings from these more recent studies mirror previous results, with the majority of studies reporting poor representations of NOS, little attention to NOS, and a lack of explicit NOS representations in school science textbooks.

Finally, many studies have been conducted at the college level, predominantly by Mansoor Niaz and his colleagues. The majority of these studies utilized a history and philosophy of science framework, and focused on discipline-specific topics drawn from the chemical and physical sciences, with results generally showing the textbooks poorly represented many aspects of NOS. One recent study (Niaz & Maza, 2011) focused on the introductory chapters of general chemistry textbooks, with findings indicating the majority of textbooks did not adequately address NOS.

In summary, findings from this body of research indicate that students are exposed to inadequate representations of NOS from the commencement of their schooling, with no appreciable change evident in the extent, manner, and quality of representation of NOS as they progress through elementary school into high school and beyond. This conclusion is further substantiated by the findings of two recent sets of studies reported in this book that examined representations of NOS across different phases of schooling. Kampourakis (this volume) examined representations of NOS in two middle school textbooks and three high school textbooks in Greece, with findings indicating there were no substantial differences in the quality of NOS representations across the examined levels of schooling. Similar findings were reported by Ramnarain (this volume) who examined representations of NOS in three middle school textbooks (Ramnarain & Chanetsa, 2016) and three high school textbooks (Ramnarain, submitted), and reported that science textbooks at different phases of schooling portrayed NOS in a similar manner. Indeed, Abd-El-Khalick and colleagues have demonstrated that NOS representations in science textbooks have improved very little over the course of the past four or five decades.

Representations of NOS Across Science Textbook Disciplines

Representations of NOS have been examined in a variety of science textbook disciplines (refer to Table 12.1) including studies that have examined biology textbooks (e.g., Abd-El-Khalick et al., 2017; BouJaoude et al., this volume; Campanile et al., 2015; Chiappetta et al., 1993; Chiappetta & Fillman, 2007; Gericke & Hagberg, 2010; Irez, 2009; Kampourakis, this volume; Lumpe & Beck, 1996), chemistry textbooks (e.g., Abd-El-Khalick et al., 2008; BouJaoude et al., this volume; Chiappetta et al., 1991; El-Mehtar & Alameh, this volume; Gericke & Hagberg, 2010; Marniok & Reiners, this volume; Niaz & Maza, 2011;Vesterinen et al., 2013), and physics textbooks (e.g.,Abd-El-Khalick et al., 2017; BouJaoude et al., this volume; Leite, 2002; Wilkinson, 1999). In general, findings from this body of research indicate the poor representation of NOS in school science textbooks across the science disciplines.

Importantly, recent scholarship in science education has drawn attention to domain-specific conceptualizations of NOS that assert that different science disciplines have their own distinct natures of science (Kampourakis, 2016). Some recent studies sought to explore the nature of the relationship between science textbook discipline and representations of NOS. In a comprehensive review of two longitudinal studies that examined the manner and extent of representations of NOS in 14 high school chemistry (Abd-El-Khalick et al., 2008), 16 high school biology, and 18 high school physics textbooks (Abd-El-Khalick et al., 2017) in the United States (Abd-El-Khalick et al., this volume), the authors also sought to specifically examine whether representations of NOS were dependent on textbook discipline (biology, chemistry, physics). Using the analytical framework developed in earlier studies (Abd-El-Khalick et al., 2008), results indicated the overall scores for the individual textbook disciplines were similar, with no change in scores evident over several decades. However, although overall textbook scores were found to be similar across the disciplines, subtle differences were noted in the scores for the individual NOS aspects across disciplines, with biology textbooks scoring higher for the sociocultural embeddedness of science, physics textbooks scoring higher for the creative and tentative NOS, and chemistry textbooks scoring higher for the inferential NOS.

BouJaoude et al. (this volume) explored representations of NOS in three middle school textbooks in Lebanon, across chemistry, life and earth sciences, and physics textbooks, using an analytical framework developed from the Expanded Family Resemblance Approach (FRA) (Erduran & Dagher, 2014). Their findings indicated that none of the textbooks systematically or adequately addressed NOS; however, the coverage of individual NOS categories was found to vary across the textbook disciplines. The physics textbook failed to address any of the examined NOS categories, whereas the life and earth sciences textbook (which only focused on life science) addressed five NOS categories, and the chemistry textbook addressed four NOS categories. The cognitive-epistemic aspects were more frequently addressed in the life and earth sciences textbook (16 instances), than the chemistry textbook (5 instances), whereas social-institutional aspects were addressed in a similar manner in both textbooks, with social values highlighted in both texts, and five other aspects not addressed at all by either text. The authors concluded that the application of the Expanded FRA framework provided a tool for not only examining NOS representations, but also enabled them to identify areas where NOS content could be strengthened and expanded.

Key Themes and Recommendations for Practice

A central goal of this book was to provide a set of empirically justified recommendations for future research and practice with the broad aim of improving representations of NOS in school science textbooks. A critical analysis of the findings of studies reported in this book, alongside previous studies in the field, has identified a number of recommendations for future research and practice. A consistent recommendation put forward by many chapter authors in this book focused on targeting textbook authors as a means of improving how NOS is represented in school science textbooks. As discussed in Chapter 1, textbook development and production are highly influential processes impacting the content and structure of textbooks, and there are strong incentives to maintain a conservative tone in textbooks due to the various policy and societal discourses in both science and education (Sharma & Buxton, 2015). This is particularly the case in countries where teachers are mandated to use an 'official' textbook (e.g., Greece, Lebanon, Turkey). Although textbook publishers have been found to influence how NOS is represented in textbooks (DiGiuseppe, 2014), many chapter authors focused on textbook authors as key drivers for change.

One study sought to specifically investigate the 'author' versus 'publisher' effect (Abd-El-Khalick et al., 2017), based on the findings of an earlier study that suggested the effect of textbook authors outweighed that of textbook publishers (Abd-El-Khalick et al., 2008). After a comprehensive, longitudinal analysis of 34 high school textbooks, the evidence showed that, as substantial as the impact of a publisher may be, this impact is outweighed by the impact of the textbook authors. Abd-El-Khalick and colleagues (this volume) recommended:

> Science education organizations could develop evidence-based papers, which are then communicated to textbook authors, and coupled with making available to those authors resources—including material and personnel, to provide feedback on a textbook's treatment of NOS themes, as well as ways in which such treatment could be broadened and deepened, and then anchored to the textbook's scientific content and associated science processes and practices.

Other chapter authors highlighted issues with the NOS expertise of science textbook writers. For example, El-Mehtar and Alameh (this volume) noted that although textbook authors should endeavor to develop informed understandings of NOS, it is unrealistic to expect them to be NOS experts, nor have the sole responsibility for ensuring NOS is effectively presented for classroom instruction. They stated that whilst textbook authors play a critical role, other parties including faculties of education, curriculum development teams, professional development providers, and other educational authorities all contribute to decisions regarding how NOS is presented in curriculum materials.

This view was supported by Ramnarain (this volume) who suggested the need to include NOS experts on textbook development teams. The role of textbook development teams was explored by DiGiuseppe (this volume) who reported on the use of action research to examine the discourses and decision-making of a textbook development team in Canada. The author of the textbook was keen to improve NOS, and the action research activities were found to strengthen the development team members' incentive to prioritize NOS as a key focus.

Once NOS is prioritized by a textbook development team, decisions need to be made regarding how NOS will be represented in textbooks. Considerations such as how much emphasis is attributed to NOS (extent of representation in textbook pages), and the manner of NOS representation (explicit versus implicit, consistency, informed) are paramount; however, a critical analysis of the findings reported in this book drew attention to the location of NOS representation as another important factor. For example, in their analysis of middle school textbooks in Lebanon, BouJaoude et al. (this volume) found that NOS representations were spread throughout the main chapters, with no introductory chapters dedicated to NOS. The opposite situation was reported by Kampourakis (this volume) who found that NOS was only explicitly addressed in the introductory chapters of Greek biology textbooks, with numerous implicit NOS opportunities presented in the other chapters. Abd-El-Khalick et al. (this volume) quantified the extent to which NOS representations are highlighted in introductory chapters versus content chapter, and reported that emphasis placed on NOS in content chapters is, at best, dismal.

Other chapter authors focused on the location of NOS representation within individual chapters. El-Mehtar and Alameh (this volume) examined representations of NOS in an International Baccalaureate Diploma Program chemistry textbook. Determining the distribution of NOS occurrences throughout the textbook was a specific aim of the study, and the authors examined the 'Core' (main narrative) and 'Other' (colored boxes) sections of the textbook for evidence of NOS representation. Utilizing an analytical framework adapted from Abd-El-Khalick et al. (2008), findings indicated that NOS aspects were more frequently included in the 'Other' sections of the textbook, and these sections also included references to all examined NOS aspects, and a higher proportion of explicit, informed NOS representations. Conversely, in her study of Australian junior secondary textbooks, McDonald (this volume) sought to specifically examine the location of NOS representation in chapters focused on the topic of genetics. Using an analytical framework developed from the Expanded Family Resemblance Approach (FRA) (Erduran & Dagher, 2014), an analysis of NOS representations in the main narrative, science inquiry activities, historical vignettes, contemporary issues vignettes, and question sets was undertaken. Results indicated that the majority of implicit NOS representations were located in the main narrative, with two of the three explicit NOS representations also located in these sections. Many opportunities to consider other examined

NOS categories were implicitly presented in the other textbook locations, with the author concluding that textbooks are not capitalizing on opportunities to explicitly highlight relevant NOS aspects within these sections.

Importantly, many chapter authors reported the presence of multiple, implicit opportunities to consider NOS in school science textbooks. Thus, there is a need to turn these implicit NOS opportunities into explicit NOS representations. An effective suggestion in the elementary trade book context was proposed by Brunner and Abd-El-Khalick (this volume), who recommended the development of educative teacher's guides to assist teachers in developing more informed conceptions of NOS, and guide their pedagogical decision-making. These guides incorporate a reflective component in the form of questions in the sidebars of the text that encourage connections between book content, relevant NOS concepts, and the readers' own experiences. The authors note that these guides could be developed for use with existing books, thus allowing teachers to work with resources they are already familiar with. It is encouraging to note that Brunner and Abd-El-Khalick have produced such materials to support elementary teachers and their students, and collected evidence that speaks to the effectiveness of this approach (Brunner, 2016).

Importantly, educative guides based on these ideas could also be developed to accompany existing middle and high school science textbooks, providing classroom teachers and schools with a cost effective manner of improving NOS instructional materials that do not rely on purchasing new sets of science textbooks, nor implementing NOS professional development programs. Some promising work is taking place in Germany, where Marniok and Reiners (this volume) are currently developing educative materials for secondary chemistry that introduce teachers and students to important NOS aspects, and connect these NOS aspects to subject matter. Marniok and Reiners suggest these materials may also be useful to textbook authors who wish to incorporate NOS more effectively in future textbooks.

Another suggestion for improving NOS in school science textbooks is utilizing existing exemplar textbooks as a basis for future textbook development. Stemming from a consideration of the findings of studies reported in this book, a handful of textbooks have been identified that present informed views of NOS, supported by numerous explicit representations. These textbooks may be recommended for use by schools to support both science teachers and students in developing their understandings of NOS. Brunner and Abd-El-Khalick (this volume) also identified two elementary trade books that were effective in explicitly addressing several aspects of NOS.

At the high school level, Abd-El-Khalick et al. (this volume) identified two standout series of textbooks in their large-scale, longitudinal study—the *Giancoli* physics textbooks and *The Biological Sciences Curriculum Study [BSCS]* biology textbooks, with no chemistry textbooks identified by the authors. The Giancoli textbooks presented articulate-explicit or implicit informed treatments of several NOS themes, and although earlier editions concentrated most of the NOS content in a few pages of the introductory chapter, later editions integrated NOS in both the introductory chapter, and revisited and discussed NOS ideas within concepts, theories, practices, and/ or historical vignettes throughout the textbook chapters. The BSCS textbooks featured explicit and partially informed, or implicit informed treatments of the empirical, inferential, and tentative NOS, the nature of theories, and the social-cultural embeddedness of science. In addition, many editions dedicated between 3–3.5 percent of their pages to NOS, which placed them on the higher end of the analyzed textbooks. Importantly, these textbooks could also be provided to textbook authors as examples of best practice to guide future school science textbook development.

In summary, targeting textbook authors, developing educative teacher guides, and using exemplar textbooks to guide future textbook development are some practical recommendations emerging from a critical analysis of the findings of studies reported in this book. Other themes emerging from this analysis highlight the importance of considering the location of NOS representation within textbooks as a whole, and their individual chapters, with further studies needed to ascertain the optimal placement of NOS ideas to facilitate student understanding. Additional recommendations for future research are discussed in the following section.

Recommendations for Research

Over the past two decades, school science textbooks have changed in format, layout, and mode, and are no longer stand-alone commodities, with an extensive range of supplementary materials produced to support the student textbook, including teacher guides, laboratory manuals, videos, worksheets, sample tests, and various forms of online material. These online materials, which were previously considered to be supplementary to the traditional, paper-based textbooks, are now playing an important role in school science classrooms in many countries across the globe. For example, a recent study in Australia highlighted the dominant role of electronic technologies, including electronic textbooks, in the science classroom, with over 50 percent of schools utilizing these curricular resources in addition to traditional, paper-based science textbooks (McDonald, 2016).

A revolution has occurred in these classrooms with the emergence of digital learning environments, facilitated through the use of personal laptop computers and tablet devices. Interestingly, all 25 studies reported in the field that have explored representations of NOS in school science textbooks (refer to Table 12.1) examined traditional, paper-based textbooks, not electronic textbooks. Kloser (2013, p. 1250) notes that these new technologies have the potential to alter students' exposure to the scientific discipline, and may make NOS more explicit to students by incorporating:

> embedded videos of actual experiments, interactive charts and figures that allow students to manipulate how evidence is represented, or embedded hyperlinks that, through a simple click, can provide more

web-based sources that detail the historical background and methodology of an experiment in question.

However, Khine (2013) reports mixed results from the handful of studies conducted to assess the effectiveness of utilizing electronic resources, over traditional, paper-based textbooks. Thus, there is a crucial need to explore how NOS is represented in these resources, and how students negotiate the content presented in these modalities.

There is also a need for future studies to explore new NOS frameworks for analyzing school science textbooks. The majority of studies reported in this book have utilized Abd-El-Khalick et al.'s (2008) analytical framework to examine NOS representations across a variety of countries, science textbook disciplines, and levels of schooling, with similar findings reported in the various contexts. Abd-El-Khalick et al.'s analytical framework, informed from a consideration of NOS aspects highlighted in international reform documents, has enabled researchers to examine the manner (naïve versus informed, implicit versus explicit, and consistent versus inconsistent) and extent (number of textbook pages) of NOS representation in school science textbooks, and, importantly, provide compatible results that could be meaningfully compared across educational contexts and national boundaries. Due to the volume of studies reported in the field which have utilized this framework, it has substantial empirical support and provides a systematic and highly reliable method for assessing the quality of these representations.

Two studies reported in this book utilized a new NOS framework that draws on domain-general and domain-specific NOS aspects, recently reconceptualized by Erduran and Dagher (2014), and referred to as the Expanded Family Resemblance Approach (FRA). BouJaoude et al. (this volume) used the framework to explore representations of NOS in middle school textbooks in Lebanon, and McDonald (this volume) used the framework to explore representations of NOS in junior secondary textbooks in Australia. Similar to other studies conducted in the field, both studies reported a lack of explicit NOS representations in examined texts; however, some other trends were identified which were not noted by other studies. For example, BouJaoude et al. reported that the application of the framework enabled them to evaluate the depth of treatment of NOS ideas and use the knowledge gained to improve weak NOS connections, and incorporate neglected aspects. McDonald stated that the application of the framework enabled her to determine how the NOS aspects were represented in the topic of genetics, and the framework did not require that all NOS aspects be included in the chosen context. This framework may be particularly useful in studies seeking to further examine subtle differences in individual NOS aspects in the science disciplines (biology, chemistry, physics) highlighted earlier in this chapter. However, given the paucity of studies conducted utilizing the framework, further research is needed to ascertain the effectiveness of the framework for assessing NOS representations.

Importantly, the aim of additional research in this area is not to privilege one NOS framework over another. According to Niaz (this volume), who presented a rich array of examples of aspects of NOS (domain-general) along with historical episodes (domain-specific) embedded within college-level textbooks, it is more fruitful to explore how domain-general and domain-specific aspects interact than to engage in debates about the relative efficacy of one approach over the other. As stated in Chapter 1 of this book, we believe that domain-general and domain-specific NOS approaches can be synergistic (Abd-El-Khalick, 2012).

Conclusion

School science textbooks continue to have a major influence on teaching and learning in K–12 classrooms in the twenty-first century. In order to develop scientific literacy, students must be able to not only engage in scientific inquiry, but also acquire the ability to negotiate and critically evaluate written text, with expository texts (textbooks) being the dominant textual genre utilized in the school science classroom. This is no easy task, requiring students to be able to:

> not only . . . attend to the substantive scientific content of the texts (the focus of traditional science instruction), but also that they read the texts so as to determine such meanings as degree of certainty expressed, the scientific status of statements, and the roles of statements in the reasoning that ties together the elements of substantive content.
>
> (Norris & Phillips, 2003, p. 235)

The ability to achieve this level of epistemic understanding is greatly facilitated through the inclusion of explicit and informed representations of NOS embedded throughout science textbooks which are coupled with varied and structured prompts to engage students with reflection about these NOS aspects, as research continues to show that students and teachers are unable to develop informed understandings of NOS through implicit representations (Abd-El-Khalick & Lederman, 2000).

This book has provided a holistic analysis and synthesis of empirical work exploring representations of NOS in school science textbooks across the globe. Evidence from the studies reported in this book, considered together with previous work in the field, has shown that NOS is poorly represented in school science textbooks, regardless of geographical location, schooling level, or science textbook discipline. Practical recommendations for improving representations of NOS in school science textbooks stemming from a consideration of the evidence presented include targeting textbook authors, developing educative guides, and utilizing exemplar texts. Future research is needed to ascertain the optimal placement of NOS ideas in textbooks to facilitate student understanding, and unpack the nature of subtle differences in individual NOS aspects in the science disciplines (biology, chemistry, physics). Exploring new NOS frameworks, such as the Expanded Family Resemblance Approach (FRA) may help inform these future studies. Importantly, there is an urgent need to examine representations of NOS in electronic textbooks, as these resources are rapidly encroaching on science classrooms across the globe. Will these new resources present improved ways for representing NOS content to students? How is NOS included in these resources? Do all students have access to these resources? These are some of the questions requiring answers in future studies.

Critically, as highlighted earlier in this chapter, these future directions need to be considered in light of the contextual constraints present in some countries, such as high-stakes exams, lack of teacher preparation, and mandated textbooks, which have been shown to impede efforts for improving representations of NOS in school science textbooks. Making change at a national level is a complex endeavor and can only be facilitated through a shared understanding of the importance of developing students' understandings of NOS by educational authorities, science educators, curriculum developers, textbook development teams, pre-service science teacher educators, professional development providers, school administrators, and school science teachers. As key stakeholders in this process, we all have a role to play in ensuring all students have the opportunity to develop informed understandings of NOS. The provision of high quality school science textbooks containing explicit, informed representations of NOS is one important step in the right direction.

References

Abd-El-Khalick, F. (2002). Images of nature of science in middle grade science trade books. *New Advocate, 15*(2), 121–127.

Abd-El-Khalick, F. (2012). Examining the sources for our understandings about science: Enduring conflations and critical issues in research on nature of science in science education. *International Journal of Science Education, 34*(3), 353–374.

Abd-El-Khalick, F., Belarmino, J., Brunner, J. L., Le, A.-P., Myers, J. Y., Summers, R., . . . Zeineddin, A. A. (2017/this volume). A longitudinal analysis of the extent and manner of representations of nature of science in U.S. high school chemistry, biology, and physics textbooks. In C. V. McDonald & F. Abd-El-Khalick (Eds.), *Representations of nature of science in school science textbooks: A global perspective* (pp. 20–60). New York: Routledge.

Abd-El-Khalick, F., & Lederman, N. G. (2000). The influence of history of science courses on students' views of nature of science. *Journal of Research in Science Teaching, 37*(10), 1057–1095.

Abd-El-Khalick, F., Myers, J. Y., Summers, R., Brunner, J., Waight, N., Wahbeh, N., . . . Belarmino, J. (2017). A longitudinal analysis of the extent and manner of representations of nature of science in U.S. high school biology and physics textbooks. *Journal of Research in Science Teaching, 54*(1), 82–120.

Abd-El-Khalick, F., Waters, M., & Le, A-P. (2008). Representations of nature of science in high school chemistry textbooks over the past four decades. *Journal of Research in Science Teaching, 45*(7), 835–855.

American Association for the Advancement of Science [AAAS]. (1993). *Benchmarks for scientific literacy: A project 2061 report*. New York: Oxford University Press.

Australian Curriculum and Reporting Authority [ACARA]. (2015). *Australian curriculum: Science F-10*. Sydney: Commonwealth of Australia.

BouJaoude, S., Dagher, Z. R., & Refai, S. (2017/this volume). The portrayal of nature of science in Lebanese 9th grade science textbooks. In C. V. McDonald & F. Abd-El-Khalick (Eds.), *Representations of nature of science in school science textbooks: A global perspective* (pp. 79–97). New York: Routledge.

Brunner, J. L. (2016). *Enriching science trade books with explicit-reflective nature of science instruction: Impacting elementary teachers' practice and improving students' learning*. Unpublished doctoral dissertation, University of Illinois at Urbana-Champaign, Champaign, IL.

Brunner, J. L., & Abd-El-Khalick, F. (2017/this volume). Representations of nature of science in U.S. elementary science trade books. In C. V. McDonald & F. Abd-El-Khalick (Eds.), *Representations of nature of science in school science textbooks: A global perspective* (pp. 135–151). New York: Routledge.

Campanile, M. F., Lederman, N. G., & Kampourakis, K. (2015). Mendelian genetics as a platform for teaching about nature of science and scientific inquiry. *Science and Education, 24*, 205–225.

Chambliss, M. J., & Calfee, R. C. (1998). *Textbooks for learning: Nurturing children's minds*. Malden, MA: Wiley.

Chiappetta, E. L., & Fillman, D. A. (2007). Analysis of five high school biology textbooks used in the United States for inclusion of the nature of science. *International Journal of Science Education, 29*(15), 1847–1868.

Chiappetta, E. L., Sethna, G. H., & Fillman, D. A. (1991). A quantitative analysis of high school chemistry textbooks for scientific literacy themes and expository learning aids. *Journal of Research in Science Teaching, 28*, 939–951.

Chiappetta, E. L., Sethna, G. H., & Fillman, D. A. (1993). Do middle school life science textbooks provide a balance of scientific literacy themes? *Journal of Research in Science Teaching, 30*, 787–797.

DiGiuseppe, M. (2014). Representing nature of science in a science textbook: Exploring author-editor-publisher interactions. *International Journal of Science Education, 36*(7), 1061–1082.

DiGiuseppe, M. (2017/this volume). Improving representation of nature of science in textbooks through action research: A Canadian perspective. In C. V. McDonald & F. Abd-El-Khalick (Eds.), *Representations of nature of science in school science textbooks: A global perspective* (pp. 152–169). New York: Routledge.

El-Mehtar, N., & Alameh, S. (2017/this volume). An analysis of the representation of nature of science in a chemistry textbook in the International Baccalaureate Diploma Program. In C. V. McDonald & F. Abd-El-Khalick (Eds.), *Representations of nature of science in school science textbooks: A global perspective* (pp. 170–187). New York: Routledge.

Erduran, S., & Dagher, Z. (2014). *Reconceptualising the nature of science in science education*. Dordrecht, the Netherlands: Springer.

Ford, D. J. (2006). Representations of science within children's trade books. *Journal of Research in Science Teaching, 43*(2), 214–235.

Gericke, N. M., & Hagberg, M. (2010). Conceptual incoherence as a result of the use of multiple historical models in school textbooks. *Research in Science Education, 40*, 605–623.

Irez, S. (2009). Nature of science as depicted in Turkish biology textbooks. *Science Education, 93*(3), 422–447.

Kahveci, A. (2010). Quantitative analysis of science and chemistry textbooks for indicators of reform: A complementary perspective. *International Journal of Science Education, 32*(11), 1495–1519.

Kampourakis, K. (2016). The "general aspects" conceptualisation as a pragmatic and effective means to introducing students to nature of science. *Journal of Research in Science Teaching, 53*(5), 667–682.

Kampourakis, K. (2017/this volume). Nature of science representations in Greek secondary school biology textbooks. In C. V. McDonald & F. Abd-El-Khalick (Eds.), *Representations of nature of science in school science textbooks: A global perspective* (pp. 118–134). New York: Routledge.

Khine, M. S. (2013). Analysis of science textbooks for instructional effectiveness. In M. S. Khine (Ed.), *Critical analysis of science textbooks: Evaluating instructional effectiveness* (pp. 303–310). Dordrecht, the Netherlands: Springer.

Kloser, M. (2013). Exploring high school biology students' engagement with more or less epistemologically considerate texts. *Journal of Research in Science Teaching, 50*(10), 1232–1257.

Knain, E. (2001). Ideologies in school science textbooks. *International Journal of Science Education, 23*(3), 319–329.

Leite, L. (2002). History of science in science education: Development and validation of a checklist for analyzing the historical content of science textbooks. *Science & Education, 11*, 333–359.

Lumpe, A. T., & Beck, J. (1996). A profile of high school biology textbooks using scientific literacy recommendations. *The American Biology Teacher, 58*(3), 147–153.

Marniok, K., & Reiners, C. S. (2017/this volume). Representations of nature of science in German school chemistry textbooks. In C. V. McDonald & F. Abd-El-Khalick (Eds.), *Representations of nature of science in school science textbooks: A global perspective* (pp. 201–214). New York: Routledge.

McDonald, C. V. (2016). Evaluating junior secondary science textbook usage in Australian schools. *Research in Science Education, 46*, 481–509.

McDonald, C. V. (2017/this volume). Exploring representations of nature of science in Australian junior secondary school science textbooks: A case study of genetics. In C. V. McDonald & F. Abd-El-Khalick (Eds.), *Representations of nature of science in school science textbooks: A global perspective* (pp. 98–117). New York: Routledge.

National Research Council. (2012). *A framework for K-12 science education: Practices, crosscutting concepts, and core ideas.* Washington, DC: The National Academies Press.

NGSS Lead States. (2013). *Next generation science standards: For states, by states.* Washington, DC: The National Academies Press.

Niaz, M. (2017/this volume). Relationship between domain-specific and domain-general aspects of nature of science in science textbooks. In C. V. McDonald & F. Abd-El-Khalick (Eds.), *Representations of nature of science in school science textbooks: A global perspective* (pp. 61–78). New York: Routledge.

Niaz, M., & Maza, A. (2011). *Nature of science in general chemistry textbooks.* Dordrecht, the Netherlands: Springer.

Norris, S., & Phillips, L. (2003). How literacy in its fundamental sense is central to scientific literacy. *Science Education, 87*, 224–240.

Ogan-Bekiroglu, F. (2007). To what degree do the currently used physics textbooks meet the expectations? *Journal of Science Teacher Education, 18*, 599–628.

Ramnarain, U. (submitted). A comparative analysis between South African physical sciences textbooks used in a traditional curriculum and a reformed curriculum. *Educational Studies.*

Ramnarain, U. (2017/this volume). An analysis of South African school science textbooks for representations of nature of science. In C.V. McDonald & F. Abd-El-Khalick (Eds.), *Representations of nature of science in school science textbooks: A global perspective* (pp. 188–200). New York: Routledge.

Ramnarain, U., & Chanetsa, T. (2016). An analysis of South African grade 9 natural sciences textbooks for their representation of nature of science. *International Journal of Science Education, 38*(6), 922–933.

Roseman, J. E., Stern, L., & Koppal, M. (2010). A method for analysing the coherence of high school biology textbooks. *Journal of Research in Science Teaching, 47*(1), 47–70.

Sharma, A., & Buxton, C. A. (2015). Human-nature relationships in school science: A critical discourse analysis of a middle-grade science textbook. *Science Education, 99,* 260–281.

Vesterinen, V.-M., Akesla, M., & Lavonen, J. (2013). Quantitative analysis of representations of nature of science in Nordic upper secondary school textbooks using framework of analysis based on philosophy of chemistry. *Science & Education, 22,* 1839–1855.

Wei, B., Li, Y., & Chen, B. (2013). Representations of nature of science in selected histories of science in the integrated science textbooks in China. *School Science and Mathematics, 113,* 170–179.

Wilkinson, J. (1999). A quantitative analysis of physics textbooks for scientific literacy themes. *Research in Science Education, 29*(3), 385–399.

Contributors

Fouad Abd-El-Khalick—*University of North Carolina at Chapel Hill*
Fouad Abd-El-Khalick is Dean and Professor of the School of Education at the University of North Carolina at Chapel Hill. Abd-El-Khalick is Co-editor of the *Journal of Research in Science Teaching* (2015–2019). His research focuses on the teaching and learning about nature of science (NOS) in precollege grades, and in pre-service and in-service science teacher education settings.

Sahar Alameh—*University of Illinois at Urbana-Champaign* Sahar Alameh is a doctoral student in Curriculum and Instruction at the University of Illinois at Urbana-Champaign. She is currently an editorial associate in the Journal of Research in Science Teaching (JRST). She has also worked on a number of projects related to document analysis examining the Nature of Science (NOS) in textbooks as well as in science standards. Her current research is on how philosophically informed models of scientific explanation can guide K-12 science instruction, learning, and assessment.

Jeremy J. Belarmino—*University of Illinois at Urbana-Champaign* Jeremy J. Belarmino is a Ph.D. Candidate in Philosophy of Education at the University of Illinois at Urbana-Champaign. Previously a Philosophy instructor at the University of Nevada, Las Vegas, he received his M.A. in Philosophy of Education from Teachers College, Columbia University and his B.A. in Philosophy from the University of Washington.

Saouma BouJaoude—*American University of Beirut* Saouma BouJaoude is a professor of science education and director of the Center for Teaching and Learning at the American University of Beirut, Beirut, Lebanon. His research interests include evolution education, curriculum, teaching methods, and the nature of science. He teaches science methods courses in the teaching diploma program and graduate courses in the science education master's program.

Jeanne L. Brunner—*University of Massachusetts Amherst* Jeanne Brunner, Ph.D. is an assistant professor in the Department of Teacher Education and Curriculum Studies at the University of Massachusetts Amherst.

Her research focuses on improving learning and instruction in science throughout the elementary grades, with a specific focus on nature of science and language use in science learning.

Zoubeida R. Dagher—*University of Delaware* Zoubeida R. Dagher is a Professor of Science Education at the School of Education and a Faculty Fellow at the Center for Science, Ethics, and Public Policy, University of Delaware. She teaches undergraduate elementary and middle school science methods courses, and graduate level courses in curriculum design and the learning sciences. She serves currently as President of the International History and Philosophy of Science Teaching (IHPST) Group.

Maurice DiGiuseppe—*University of Ontario Institute of Technology* Maurice DiGiuseppe is Associate Professor of Science Education at the University of Ontario Institute of Technology (UOIT) in Oshawa, Ontario, Canada. His areas of interest include science teacher education, science textbooks and digital resources, nature of science, and environmental education. Maurice has authored numerous science textbooks and has conducted research in professional development, science textbook development, nature of science, scientific inquiry, and digital learning resources.

Nizar El-Mehtar—*Lebanese University* Nizar El-Mehtar is currently a lecturer of Science Education at Lebanese University. Prior to this, he served as chemistry teacher and chairperson, curriculum writer, and academic programs' coordinator at an international school located in Lebanon. El- Mehtar completed his Ph.D. in Science Education at Lebanese University in 2015 and his research interest is focused on NOS.

Kostas Kampourakis—*University of Geneva* Kostas Kampourakis is a researcher in science education at the University of Geneva, where he teaches courses at the University Teacher Training Institute and the Section of Biology. He is the Editor-in-Chief of the journal *Science & Education* and the book series *Science: Philosophy, History and Education* (Springer). His main research interests include the teaching, learning, and public understanding of evolution, genetics, and nature of science.

An-Phong Le—*Florida Southern College* An-Phong Le, Ph.D. is an assistant professor of chemistry and co-coordinator of the biochemistry and molecular biology program at Florida Southern College. His research interests include the development of online tools for data analysis in the instructional laboratory, characterization of the movement of small molecules in food during preparation and cooking, and the development of inexpensive sensors for environmental analyses.

Karl Marniok—*University of Cologne* Karl Marniok graduated from the University of Cologne in Chemistry and History and obtained a Masters' degree in Teacher Education. At present he is enrolled as a Ph.D. student at the University of Cologne, supervised by Christiane S. Reiners.

Christine V. McDonald—*Griffith University* Christine V. McDonald is Senior Lecturer in Science Education at Griffith University, Australia, where she is also the Program Director of the Doctor of Education program. Her research predominantly focuses on nature of science (NOS), with particular interests in this area including NOS in school science textbooks, NOS in curriculum documents, and the development of NOS learning progressions.

John Y. Myers—*University of Illinois at Urbana-Champaign* John Y. Myers is a Ph.D. student in Curriculum and Instruction at the University of Illinois at Urbana-Champaign, and an editorial associate for the Journal of Research in Science Teaching. His research interests include the experiential realism of scientific portrayals in screen media, history and philosophy of science education, and epistemology of science.

Mansoor Niaz—*Universidad de Oriente* Mansoor Niaz is a Professor of Science Education at the Universidad de Oriente, Venezuela. He has published over 160 articles in international refereed journals and 10 books including: *Chemistry Education and Contributions from History and Philosophy of Science* (2016) and *From 'Science in the Making' to Understanding the Nature of Science* (2012).

Umesh Ramnarain—*University of Johannesburg* Umesh Ramnarain is a professor in science education at the University of Johannesburg, South Africa. His research that centers on inquiry-based science education and nature of science has been published in top-tier journals such as the *Journal of Research in Science Teaching*, *International Journal of Science Education*, and *Research in Science Education*.

Sara Refai—*American University of Beirut* Sara Refai holds a Master's degree in social psychology from the London School of Economics and is presently a graduate student at the Department of Education, American University of Beirut majoring in Educational Leadership and Policy Studies. She is also an English language middle school teacher at a local school in Beirut, Lebanon.

Christiane S. Reiners—*University of Cologne* Christiane S. Reiners is Professor of Chemistry Education at the University of Cologne where she runs the Institute of Chemistry Education. From 2003 to 2005 she was Vice-Rector of the University of Cologne. Her research includes work on the development of students' and teachers' conceptions of Nature of Science.

Ryan G. Summers—*University of North Dakota* Ryan G. Summers, Ph.D. is assistant professor of Secondary Science Education in the Department of Teaching and Learning in the College of Education and Human Development at the University of North Dakota. His research is focused on attitudes toward science, and teaching about nature of science.

Nader Wahbeh—*A.M. Qattan Foundation* Nader Wahbeh is Director of the Science Studio at the A.M. Qattan Foundation, and Lecturer in Curriculum and Instructions in the College of Education at Birzeit University, both in Ramallah, Palestine. He earned his Ph.D. in Science Education from the University of Illinois at Urbana-Champaign, United States, and his M.A. and B.Sc. in Chemistry from Birzeit University, Palestine.

Noemi Waight—*University at Buffalo* Noemi Waight, Ph.D. is associate professor of science education in the Department of Learning and Instruction in the Graduate School of Education at the University at Buffalo, SUNY. Her research examines Nature of Technology (NoT) and the design, development, implementation, adoption, and enactment of technological tools in the context of reform-based, K-12 science teaching approaches.

Mindy Waters—*St. Joseph-Ogdon High School* Mindy Waters teaches high school chemistry at St. Joseph-Ogdon High School in St. Joseph, Illinois. She earned a B.S. degree from Illinois State University, at Bloomington-Normal, and a Master's degree in education from the University of Illinois at Urbana-Champaign.

Ava A. Zeineddin—*University of Illinois at Urbana-Champaign* Ava A. Zeineddin is assistant professor of science education. She worked at Wayne State University in Detroit, Michigan. Ava earned a Ph.D. in science education from the University of Illinois at Urbana-Champaign, and Master's in science education from the American University of Beirut, Lebanon.

Index